One With The World

One With The World

A LOVE STORY

⬥

Dr. Richard Orzeck

Purrfect Love Publishing
2088 Trumansburg Road
Trumansburg, NY 14886

ISBN-13: 9781514632239
ISBN-10: 1514632233

First Edition
Library of Congress Control Number: 2015906448
CreateSpace Independent Publishing Platform
North Charleston, South Carolina

Dedication

Dedicated to the good people of Trumansburg, New York and the surrounding Finger Lakes region, whose patronage and trust and patient tolerance of my unceasing wanderlust helped make this book of travel tales possible. Also, throughout the book whenever I use the pronoun "I" for the sake of good grammar or efficient story flow, I actually mean to say "we." This is because my dear wife—without one single exception—shared every one of these adventures with me. And for this ever-faithful companionship, I consider myself a truly blessed man.

Acknowledgments

Travel does not exist without home ... If we never return to
the place we started, we would just be wandering, lost. Home
is a reflecting surface, a place to measure our growth and
enrich us after being infused with the outside world.

— JOSH GATES, *DESTINATION TRUTH: MEMOIRS OF A MONSTER HUNTER*

As long as it doesn't violate my marriage vows, or offend my—
or anyone else's—God, my goal for my life is to see and do
and experience everything that living on this planet—this
stunningly amazing and beautiful planet—has to offer!

— RICHIE ORZECK

ALL OF THE GREAT TRAVELERS have had a home base, a place they couldn't wait
to escape, but within days or weeks after their departure, longed to return.
Somerset Maugham had his villa in the south of France, Bruce Chatwin
had his farmhouse in Gloucestershire, Herman Melville had Arrowhead
Farm, and Ernest Hemingway had his homes in Key West and Sun Valley.
Although not quite in the same league as these eminent gentlemen of letters, my wife and I have our humble Finger Lakes home and our veterinary
practice to return to. But why did we end up here?

Tons have been written in the travel literature about the lives of famous travelers and their impulsive urges to give up the safety of hearth and home in exchange for the chance to experience the uncertainty of the unknown; about their obsessive desires to forgo the bonds of family and community in their quests to wander alone among the strange and the stranger; or of their seemingly single-minded willingness to ruthlessly break the hearts of kith and kin in their relentless, uncontrollable pursuit of becoming "one" with the whole world. But something no one has ever talked about is what makes a person, a couple, or a family decide to live where they do. Most people, I imagine, have probably not given this question any thought. And so, before beginning these traveling tales I'd like to share the story of how we ended up where we did.

When I started veterinary school in 1987, I was unlike any other student in my class. Besides the usual pressing needs of moving to a new area and hunkering down to face a challenging four years of medical schooling, I needed to also find (or build) a home for my wife and my small herd of cattle and sheep, our farm equipment, and the contents of another home we'd just sold. We were blessed with finding a bare, fifteen-acre corner lot with a hay and corn field just eleven miles from the university. It was here over the next four years, between studying and classes, that we built a small house and farm. After graduating in May 1991, I started my first job/internship at a large veterinary practice two hours' drive away.

What to do after my internship was over, was an ongoing discussion that we began having between my third and fourth year of vet school. Our future options at the time were infinite and most had the potential for being very advantageous for us, at least financially. There was one big problem, one that I never in a million years anticipated: It turned out that in spite of our mutual wanderlust, neither of us wanted—at least not yet—to leave our home! Our neighbors and friends seemed to have taken to us, and we to them! The final decision to explore the possibility of remaining where we were came in the summer of 1990.

"We are both antevasins, my dear."
"What is that?"

It was haying season, and I was trying to get our cantankerous old Ford haybaler repaired so I could bale up a field of timothy grass that I had cut down the day before. One of our local expert farm mechanics, Mr. D. (I'll withhold his exact name to protect the innocent) was graciously and heroically trying his best to help me fix the ancient piece of machinery. His wife sat quietly and patiently in their pickup truck, seemingly just happy to be out in the country enjoying the beauty of that day.

And it was a beautiful morning, a stunningly beautiful July morning that makes living in New York's Finger Lakes region so very special. Just a couple of weeks before, I'd finished my third year of vet school at Cornell and was now trying my best not to think about the grueling upcoming fourth and final year, which was going to begin in another month. As we were busting our knuckles trying to repair the old baler, Mr. D. and I talked about things that men involved in farming always talk about when together: the weather, the price of corn, how the beef price is always in the toilet, the soybean crop in South America and county politics.

Then Mr. D. brought up the subject of where I was going to practice after I'd graduated. I told him that we really had nothing definitely planned. I mentioned that Theresa and I were kicking around the possibility of returning to our old hometown about one hundred miles to the east. I talked about how my father had an eye on a commercial lot near his home in Florida that would be an excellent spot to set up a veterinary practice. I even told him about possibility of heading to California to work in emergency clinics, which at the time held great financial promise. However, as we were talking, we suddenly heard the door of his old Chevy pickup truck open and immediately slam shut.

A little bit surprised, we both looked up from our work, and saw Mrs. D. walking quickly toward us. She had that determined look of a woman on a mission. She stopped and stood directly in front of me, looked me squarely in the eye, pointed her finger about four inches from my nose, and then, like she'd been waiting her whole life to do so, shrieked at me, "You Cornell students are always doing this to us: You come here, you live among us, and we accept you as neighbors. You take the best our community has to offer, and then you leave! Why can't any of you, just once, ever give something back?" And that was all she had to say on the matter. Without another word, as quickly as she appeared, the sweet little lady walked away and returned to the sanctuary of the truck. Her mission was complete, and that was that.

Later that afternoon, as we sat at one of our local restaurants savoring one of Marcia and Carol's great cheeseburgers and fries, I told Theresa about what happened that morning. As we sat there enjoying the feast, we, for the first time, kicked around the idea of maybe hanging up my shingle in Trumansburg after I finished all my schooling and internship. Over the next year, we explored the idea, attempted to develop a viable business plan to convince the highly skeptical bankers, and ultimately decided to give it a try. And the rest is history.

A QUICK NOTE ON PHOTOGRAPHS

All photographs in these stories that are without attribution were taken either by Theresa or myself. Several of these that are of poorer quality are scans from old-fashion photographic prints. Others reflect our experiences with the earlier model digital cameras. Despite publisher's protests that I should use only the best quality images, I decided for the sake of authenticity to use these pictures anyway.

I'm including photographs from a few other sources as well. For several reasons: A computer hard-drive crash two years ago completely wiped out whole photo records of many of our trips; hardest hit were Tonga, Italy, India and Scotland. And so with the help of many kind and generous fellow travelers from around the world, I've been able to fill in these gaps beautifully. For this, I am in their debt. Also, in the course of doing some up-to-date research, I discovered several pictures that I wish I'd the talent, or foresight, to have taken for myself. A paid subscription source of images called Shutterstock helped fill in what blanks remained. Finally, I'm beholden to that miraculous thing out there called the worldwide web for maps and non-copy written images.

Finally, the cost of printing books with color photographs is prohibitively expensive! In the original draft of this book I had included 145 pictures that I thought were vital to the spirit of the work. The financial reality of it all set in and I ruthlessly pared the number down to forty. To make up for this, I've created a supplemental blog to share with everyone these rejected photos. Please find me at: http://richardorzeck.blogspot.com/

Thank you for reading my book. It has been a true labor of love!

A Morning On The Camino

CHAPTER 1

The Way of Saint James

—⊶⊷—

MY PILGRIMAGE

Give me my scallop-shell of quiet,

My staff of faith to walk upon,

My scrip of joy, immortal diet,

My bottle of salvation,

My gown of glory, hope's true gage;

And thus I'll take my pilgrimage!

—SIR WALTER RALEIGH

WHILE ENJOYING OUR FIRST RESTING stop on the morning of the first day of our pilgrimage along Spain's Camino de Santiago, our trail guide, Alex, shared with our small group of hikers a story. It concerned an eighty-five-year-old woman he'd once met a few years back at the very spot where we were all now sitting. We were then just five miles west of our starting point in the northern Spanish border town of Roncesvalles, and still very high up in the Pyrenees Mountains. As we sat there listening on that gloriously sunny September morning beside a freezing-cold, crystal-clear, mountain stream—the very stream where local legend says the writer Ernest Hemingway some sixty years before had chilled his favorite Rioja wine while he and his companion fished for trout—Alex began his story by telling us that this lady had actually started her long Camino journey in Switzerland, over one thousand miles away.

Amazed at this huge achievement by a person of such advanced years, and knowing that she still had over six hundred more miles to go before reaching the great cathedral in Santiago, he asked her why in the world she would take on such a daunting task. It took all of about a second for her to consider his question and to reply; and as she proceeded to tell him her story, Alex said that a loving and all-knowing smile came upon the woman's beautifully tanned and gently lined face. He said that her radiant blue eyes beamed with a pureness of joy and contentedness that's only possible from someone who has accomplished something truly monumental and whose soul now seemed at peace with the world.

She said, "Son, on a late winter morning about a year ago, I was sitting alone at my home in Switzerland, squandering away yet another precious day in front of my television set, when suddenly, I began to feel very old and utterly worthless. I'm not sure how or why, but I had the absolute certainty that at that moment I was going to die. Then, no sooner had the dark cloud of death begun to descend upon me that I heard a voice, a resplendent and glorious voice, the voice of an angel—or maybe even of Saint James himself—thunder at me and say, "Wilma, get up NOW! and walk!" And so, rather than giving in to that horrifying fate, I did just what the angel said, and I got up and I started walking. "And young man," she said, with all the seriousness of a heart attack, "I don't plan to stop."

"Ever!"

As we all stood back up from our break, I took a few minutes before beginning the walk again to kneel down upon a flat rock sticking out from the side of the stream. I cupped my hands, scooped up some of the cold—very cold—and pristine water, brought it to my lips, and drank it down. As I did so a second time and a third, I thought to myself, "Wow! I was now "one" with the Pyrenees Mountains, with old Ernest Hemingway, with the millions of pilgrims who went forth upon this journey before me, as well as with the amazing Ms. Wilma from Switzerland!" And just like Hemingway, I, too, would soon drink my fill of the region's delicious Rioja wine.

If you think about it, the 1,000-year-old pilgrim trail known as El Camino de Santiago (the Way of Saint James) has no real beginning; you can start the journey from anywhere in the world. It does, however, have a clear and definitive end point: the northwestern Spanish city of Santiago de Compostela.

For over a millennium, millions of anonymous pilgrims, pious penitents, would-be adventurers, and just plain tourists have made their way to Santiago by foot, donkeys, bicycles, and automobiles for the sole purpose of visiting the city's famous cathedral and its precious holy relics. In medieval times, the Camino was considered one of the three mandatory pilgrimages that every Christian, if able, had to participate in. (The other two were a journey to Rome and to Jerusalem.) King Ferdinand and Queen Isabella of Spain were long ago themselves pilgrims on the Way of Saint James, as were El Cid, Saint Francis of Assisi, King Louis VII of France, Dante, and most recently, the beloved Pope John Paul II.

How the apostle James (son of Zebedee and brother of John) came to have his final resting place in this Spanish city is really quite amazing. Legend says that after the death of Jesus, James was entrusted with the task of preaching the Gospel throughout the whole of the ancient Iberian Peninsula. It was said that the good saint had a special fondness for this region of his earthly appointment. In the later years of his ministry, however, he was called back to Jerusalem, and there he became the first of the twelve apostles to suffer martyrdom by decapitation at the hands of the wicked King Herod.

After his death, Saint James was miraculously transported in a stone boat under guidance of the heavenly angels to northern Spain. There he was buried in a field in what is now the city of Santiago de Compostela. The good people of Spain, in thanks for the great blessing they were granted by the angels, then built over his bones the magnificent Cathedral of Saint James.

It was into this great mass of flowing humanity that our small group of pilgrims and I found ourselves. As Catholics, Theresa and I wrote on each of our pilgrim's passport that we intended to perform the walk as bona fide pilgrims. This meant that I first needed to have an intention for the walk. [I dedicated the walk to a cousin who was suffering from liver disease, two women I knew who had breast cancer, and a lady friend who had lupus.] It also signified that during the walk, I would try my best to be as reverent as possible, pray, and attend Mass as often as I was able at one of the hundreds of small churches and cathedrals along the route, walk the last one hundred kilometers (sixty miles) of the trip continuously, and to attend the pilgrim's Mass at Saint James Cathedral when finished.

For doing so, I would then receive a Compostela, which is a certificate of accomplishment given to pilgrims upon completion of the Way of Saint James. An additional benefit of this parchment is that it will allow the bearer—providing he/she doesn't commit any mortal sins—to skip purgatory after death and proceed directly to heaven.

We would be walking the most popular of the Camino trails across the north of Spain called the French Route. Beginning high up in the Pyrenees Mountains in the village of Roncesvalles, the route would snake its way for more than six hundred miles over mountain passes through the land of the Basque peoples, across the high plains of the Navarra region, and then cross over the mountains of Cantabria and into the Province of Galicia. Our plan for the pilgrimage consisted of walking fourteen to twenty-four miles each day, depending on the terrain, and our itinerary included passing through the most scenic, historical, or just plain interesting sights along the way.

Ultimately, due to time constraints with my veterinary business, we would travel The Walk of Saint James for about 290 miles. The Way took us trekking mostly along country roads and through forests and vineyards and almond groves, and on some mornings, when you saw the golden sunlight showering down from a stark blue sky upon the boundless miles of wheat fields, it looked like God himself begat the whole world new again. The trail went past paddocks of fat, grazing sheep, and more than a dozen times our group found ourselves sharing the trail with small herds of hulking blonde and white dairy cows, who, not concerned in the least with our presence, were returning to their pastures after their morning's milking. The smell of plowed earth, damp and musky oak woodlands, freshly mowed alfalfa—not to mention the aroma of farm animal manure—all helped to consummate within me the total sensual richness of our encounter.

I don't want to give the impression, however, that the whole of the pilgrim's route was an Edenic paradise from start to finish. At the time, it seemed to me that there was an awful lot of walking up hills and then down the hills and then up a hill again and then down the hill. Also, even though the path managed to meander its way through medieval back alleys, well-groomed town squares, and bustling city streets that were, as a whole, quite pleasant, it also passed through some nasty suburban industrial zones. And more than I care to mention, large sections of the trail shared the way with heavily traveled highways jammed solely with smoke-belching, speeding diesel trucks. (Pedestrian accidents and, oddly, drowning are the major cause of death for the modern-day pilgrim.)

But that's all that I'm going to say about that. I'm not going to expound upon the day-to-day details of the walk. They were filled with long stretches of time for contemplation and personal reflection, as would befit any sacred passage, but dwelling upon them in a travelogue fashion (as many writers are wont to do) would get pretty boring. We visited churches and cathedrals and attended Mass when available, got our pilgrim's passports stamped at museums, bars, and restaurants all along the way, and stopped often to take in the breathtaking scenery.

Instead, as would be expected from a grand tradition that's been around for over a thousand years, every church, village, bridge, and mountain pass along the pilgrim trail seemed to have its own story to tell. And it is a few of these amazing tales that I would like to share.

Among the first of the interesting legends we encountered along the Camino involved a rather plain and unimposing old Roman stone bridge that we crossed over at the end of our second day of walking. The bridge, with its center pier and twin arches, crossed the Arga River in the little valley town of Zubiri. (Zubiri in the Basque language means "village of the bridge.") As a veterinarian, what caught my attention the most about the bridge was its name: El Puente de la Rabia, "the bridge of rabies."

It turns out that there was a much-venerated fifth-century Christian martyr in this border region between France and Spain and Portugal named Saint Quiteria. Not too much is officially known about this pious woman except that she was the virgin daughter of a Galician prince and that her father had her martyred because she refused to renounce her Christianity. During her short life it was said that she once held at bay two rabid dogs who were about to attack a group of children using only her saintly voice as a weapon. Because of this incident, Saint Quiteria's intercession is prayed to for help in the protection and prevention of rabies. And this is where "the bridge of rabies" and the blessed saint cross paths.

It turns out that some—or all—of Saint Quiteria's relics are embedded in the central pier of the bridge. And for over fifteen hundred years, and still to this very day, local farmers believe that if they march their animals three times over the central pier, the beasts will be immune to rabies. Also, they believe that if they walk a rabies-infected animal three times around the central pier (the river in the summer is not all that deep) that it will be cured of the disease.

O'Cebreiro smells like wood fires, manure and pilgrim B.O.

–RICK STEVES

After battling a cold and grueling fourteen-mile uphill walk—the last hour of which included a torrential downpour—we arrived soaked to the bone at the tiny Galician mountaintop village of O'Cebreiro. "A nice thing about reaching where we are now is that the trail is mostly all downhill from here," said Alex as we all stood puffing to catch our breaths on the edge of the village square. Upbeat in that way that all good guides usually are, he added, "Too bad it's so cloudy and rainy this morning; there's one heck of a view from up here!" As for me, all I could think of was, "Thank God we don't have to do that hill again." We then walked over to a small café across the square where I ordered a big mug of hot chocolate. I'm not sure if it was because I was so frozen and hungry or because the drink was made of the local fresh unpasteurized cow's milk or because the cool mountain air had so invigorated my sense of taste, but that cup of chocolate was the best I've ever tasted.

The village of O'Cebreiro's seventh-century parish church, Santa María la Real, is thought by historians to be the oldest church along the French Route branch of the Way of Saint James. Besides serving the spiritual need of her parishioners for over a millennium, this humble (very humble) little pre-Romanesque fieldstone building is famous in Camino lore for its astonishing story of the miracle of the Eucharist.

Local legend says that during a severe winter blizzard on a Sunday morning around the year 1300, a Benedictine priest, certain in his heart of hearts that no one would be foolish enough to brave the elements, was preparing to celebrate the morning's Mass alone. Just as he was about to begin, a farmer named Juan Satín faithfully walked through the front door, shook the snow and ice from his simple garments, genuflected in front of the holy altar, and then sat down. Perhaps it was just a genuine concern for the safety of his parishioner, or perhaps it involved some even greater weakness of faith on the part of the good father. Whatever the reason, as soon as Mr. Satin sat down, the priest began to admonish the old farmer severely for foolishly risking his life just so that he could receive a wafer of bread and a sip of wine. The humble parishioner just sat there and never said a word; he knew better.

When the holy Mass finally began, farmer Juan prayed more fervently than he'd ever prayed in his life. He prayed not only for his family and community but for a miracle from God that would prove to this worthy, but cynical, priest that the Eucharist was more than simply bread and wine. The farmer's prayers were soon answered, for as he approached the altar to receive Holy Communion, the Host in the hand of the incredulous priest literally changed into the flesh of the Lord, and the chalice of wine began to overflow with his blood.

Pilgrims, either visiting or attending Mass at the Church of Santa María today, can still see the chalice and paten used by the doubting priest during O'Cebreiro's miraculous Eucharist. Visitors can also venerate—and even touch—the relics of the priest and the devoted farmer. And as I stood there, still soaking wet, receiving Holy Communion in front of that simple altar, inside of that beautiful mountaintop church, I once again truly felt at "one" with the millions of believers who came before me.

There's a little-known story, a story from my youth that I haven't told too many people; a true story that someday, if I ever get around to writing my U.S. Navy memoirs, I'd like to tell. The gist of story is this: It is a fact that I walk this earth today because, on a dark and sultry old Hong Kong evening many years ago, five Australian sailors came to my rescue and literally saved my life.

When I think about it, I can't recall any serious objections that I might have with any of the many peoples I've encountered on my journeys across the face of this astonishing planet. The few unpleasant or annoying times that I did had mostly involved dealing with bureaucrats, drunken soldiers, police roadblocks, and border guards. Put simply, I just do my best to not pass too much judgment upon others and try to love and respect everybody at everyplace I've ever been to. Having said all that, I do have some favorites.

When pressed hard for actual examples from each of the following broad categories, I usually give these answers: In my humble opinion, the good people of the island of Newfoundland have got to be the friendliest and most personable on the planet, my fellow Americans the most generous, the Cambodians and Ethiopians the most beautiful, the Angolans the saddest, the Swiss and the New Zealanders the most rugged, the people of the subcontinent of India the most mysterious and alluring, and the South Africans, the most adventurous. But if pushed absolutely to name my overall favorite of the earth's peoples, it would have to be the Australians, a race of men and women descended from Christian missionaries, buccaneers, farmers, whalers, and convicts, whose most favorite of past times seems to be just smoking, drinking, and gambling. They really do seem to enjoy life.

On our journey along the Camino, every night we would settle in to a country inn, bed-and-breakfast, or a small hotel. With every evening meal, we would be fed to the point of almost bursting with the bounty of the local farms; all accompanied by endless liters of local Spanish wines, especially Rioja wines. As our pilgrimage progressed westward toward Santiago, it was noted by some in our group that any excess un-emptied bottles of wine tended to end up in front of either me or an Australian lady in our group who I'll call Ms.V.

This lovely lady, one of eight children all named after Christian saints, had just recently sold her accounting business and was walking the Way of Saint James as part of an extended world tour. Although the events of that night have since taken on the status of legend, my own recollection of the contest is that it all started out quite innocently.

After what seemed like yet another harmless comment made by Alex about how the majority of the meal's wine bottles were ending up in front of Ms.V. or me, I, without much thought to any potential consequences (as is often the case), made one of those downright stupid and braggadocios comments about my fellow Americans and our infinite capacity to consume adult drink. As I did so, by chance I happened to look over toward Ms.V. and noticed that she had a slightly mischievous smile on her face. Then, as quick as you could say "Vegemite sandwich," she (rather innocently) asked Alex if it was possible to get a couple more bottles of wine. "No problem," said Alex, "you can have as many as you like."

That was all it took. When the waiter brought them to our table, nobody seemed to want any more, having already consumed as a group a dozen or more bottles. "Richard," said Ms.V. quite innocuously, "you'll have another bottle with me, won't you?"

Completely unaware that I was falling into a trap, I said, "Sure, why not? It's pretty good wine; no sense in it going to waste!" What I didn't realize, however, was that when Ms.V. said "another bottle," what she really meant was another bottle each! And so, not wanting to seem wimpy, I let the undeclared war began. The wine was indeed delicious, the conversation cordial, and before I ever knew what hit me, the one bottle each had led to two, and then to three. A couple of the older pilgrims soon called it a day, and went to bed. The remainder watched as the bottle count in front of each of us went from three to four. It was at this point that my face began to feel a bit flushed and I was physically beginning to tire, but the wine still tasted good, each glass still going down as smooth as mother's milk. But even if it hadn't, I'd have still battled through it; as great as the Aussies are, I still had the honor of America to defend.

However, halfway through bottle number four, I came to the realization that I was in trouble. Even though I still had my wits about me, the words coming out of my mouth were starting to slur, and I felt my head starting to bob. Ms. V., all the while, still looked as cool as an Arctic sunset. As a matter of fact, she seemed to be accelerating her consumption. By the time I'd finally downed the dregs of bottle four, she was nearly done with number five!

Most of our group, including Theresa, had by then gone to bed. Alex (who, we've been told, still speaks of that evening's wine consuming contest with the same sort of reverent awe with which he spoke of Wilma from Switzerland) was still there as were the pair of Canadians in our group, John and Lois. It was at this time that Ms. V., probably wanting to get the whole thing over with so all of us could go to bed as well (or, maybe she just sensed my impending defeat), looked me square in eye, and with the calmness and confidence of a she-lion fixing to pounce upon an innocent gazelle calf, said to me, "Richard, let's see if they have any brandy or maybe something even stronger!"

Stunned as to how this tiny wafer of a woman could so thoroughly—and so seemingly effortlessly—thrash me, I conceded defeat. And as bad as I might have felt in letting my country down, I take great satisfaction in knowing I lost to a worthy adversary. For her part, Ms. V. was as gracious in victory as she was before and as she still is to this very day. As we all went our separate ways, she said, "Richard, we have to do this again sometime!"

Smiling, I gave her the universal but somewhat unsteady thumbs-up indicating my agreement. But if the truth were to be told, I remember at the time thinking to myself, "Richard, NEVER AGAIN

Santo Domingo de la Calzada/Donde cantó la gallina después
De asada.
[Santo Domingo de la Calzada/Where the
chickens sang after being roasted.]

—A SPANISH PILGRIM'S FOLK SONG

There were many, many more legends and tales we heard and read about on our pilgrimage to the tomb of Saint James, but to me, the most wondrous one of all involved the town of Santo Domingo de la Calzada, its magnificent cathedral, and the story of its miraculous chickens.

Sitting directly on the pilgrims' route in the heart of Spain's famous Rioja wine district, the town of Santo Domingo de la Calzada was founded in the year 1090 by its namesake, Saint Domingo de la Calzada. This former hermit turned engineer dedicated his life to the safety and welfare of the pilgrims of his day by building for them roads and bridges and even a hospital. He also began work on a church that ultimately would become the beautiful Cathedral of Santo Domingo de la Calzada.

One of the first things I noticed as our group walked into this church was the faint smell of chicken poop. A little bit surprised, I looked upward, and there, directly across from the Tomb of Saint Domingo, in two separate cages, were a pair of white chickens. One was obviously a rooster; the other was a plump little hen. As our group listened in reverent silence in front of the saint's tomb in the quiet of that lovely sanctuary, Alex told us the story of the Miracle of the Chickens.

Sometime in the middle of the fourteenth century, a family of great virtue and piety stopped to rest their weary bodies for a couple of days at an inn located in the then small village of Santo Domingo. This family consisted of a father and mother and their handsome sixteen-year-old son. During their short stay, it is said that the innkeeper's daughter fell passionately in love with the young son. In the words of a sixteenth-century English travel writer, Andrew Boorde, *"... she was a wenche whych wolde haue had hym to medyll with her carnally."* In other words, she wanted him for a lover. The young man, however, being of rare and exceptional moral excellence, declined outright the young women's lustful advances. He was, after all, on holy pilgrimage.

The old saying, "Hell hath no fury like a woman scorned" in this situation turned out to be somewhat of an understatement. This troubled young lady was livid! Enraged beyond words at the boy's rejection of her offering to bed him, the innkeeper's daughter plotted the ultimate revenge. During the night before the family was planning to depart, she hid a silver goblet in the boy's knapsack. Then, in the morning, just after the family had resumed their pilgrimage to Santiago, she told her father of the "theft" of the innkeeper's silver.

The local sheriff and his deputies then tracked the family down, and when they searched the hapless young man's backpack, they did indeed find the silver goblet. As the falsely accused boy screamed and pleaded his innocence, he was mercilessly brought before the magistrate for the theft. The judge found him guilty of the crime and sentenced the boy to death by hanging. All the young man's parents could do was stand by in abject horror as the wardens dragged their son to the gallows on the outskirts of town, slip a noose over his neck, and then open the trapdoor beneath his feet. It was ordered that he be left dangling for a week as a stern reminder to all who passed of the penalty for being a thief.

That evening just after the sun had gone down, the distraught parents returned to the site of their son's execution to mourn him one last time before setting out to fulfill their obligation to complete their pilgrimage. They could do nothing else; the magistrate had issued the edict that he remain where he was. As they tearfully approached what they thought was their dead son's body, they were confronted by a great surprise. Their boy was still alive!

Still hanging from the gibbet by the rope around his neck, the boy, when he saw his tearful parents, calmly spoke to them. "Fear not, my dear father and mother," he said. "Blessed Saint Domingo holds me in his arms as I now speak. Run, run with all your might and tell the honorable judge that I'm still alive. Saint Domingo will perform a miracle!"

Without a second's hesitation, the father and mother rushed back into Santo Domingo to the home of the magistrate. After frantically knocking on his door for over a minute, they were finally let in to the inner court-yard, only to be informed by the judge's servant that the justice was eating his evening meal and he absolutely did not want to be disturbed. The determined parents, however, would not be deterred. Barging into the home, they quickly found the dining room.

Prostrating themselves before the seated magistrate, they quickly told him of the miracle taking place involving their son. The judge, who was just about to begin cutting up the two roasted chickens he was about to eat as his dinner, rather than being annoyed—or even worse, downright pissed off—at this intrusion into his home, was moved by a sort of mocking compassion. Legend says that he looked the anxious parents directly in the eye and bluntly said to them as he pointed to his dinner plate, "My dear pilgrims, your boy can no more be alive than these chickens could get up right now and crow!"

The words had no sooner sprung forth from the magistrate's lips than the Good Saint Domingo performed his second miracle of the evening. Immediately, the two chickens, a rooster and a hen, came to life, squawking and scurrying across the table, and then running outside, back to their barnyard roost. Upon witnessing this miracle, the judge fell to his knees in fearful penitence, and after begging the Lord for his forgiveness, he granted clemency to the parents' beloved son.

"And it is the direct descendants of these two birds," said Alex, "that are in the glass cages that we see across from Saint Domingo's tomb. They are maintained by the Confraternity of Santo Domingo in a special place called a gallinero; they are never eaten. Finding one of their feathers lying about the cathedral guarantees a successful completion of your pilgrimage. Also it is said that if the rooster crows while a pilgrim is in the church, those people who hear it are considered to have special favor in the eyes of Saint Domingo.

"Maybe it's just me," he said jokingly before leaving us on our own to explore the beautiful cathedral, "but in the two years I've been guiding pilgrims, I've never heard the rooster crow even one time!"

And perhaps it was just me (and/or the group I was with), but as I explored the interior of that beautiful Gothic church, with its much-venerated and beloved saint, I managed to find not just one, but three white chicken feathers. I kept one and gave one to my wife. The third one, which I had intended to keep as a spare, I later gave away to one of the members of our group. But even more important than finding any of these feathers, I/we all must have truly found supreme favor in the eyes of good Saint Domingo, because as we left the good saint's holy sanctuary, the rooster not only crowed one time for our avian blessing, but FOUR times!

And there came also Nicodemus, which at the first came to Jesus
by night, and brought a mixture of myrrh and aloes, about a
hundred-weight. Then they took the body of Jesus, and wound it in
linen clothes with the spices, as the manner of the Jews is to bury.

–JOHN 19:39-40

In the city square just outside the front door of the Cathedral of Burgos sits (literally) a stark reminder to all of the modern day wayfarers who pass through the city on the Way of Saint James that there was a time in the pilgrim route's history when men and women undertook their journey strictly for spiritual and often desperate life-or-death reasons. The statue has no name, he is just referred to by tour guides as *The Pilgrim*. The young man, a leper, sits there alone on a bench, his pilgrim's staff in his left hand, and obviously beaten down by life and physically worn out; his naked pox- and carbuncle- riddled body adorned only by a scallop shell necklace. His hopeless expression beckons those with enough compassion (or at least the courage) to "please sit down beside me and give me companionship." He is for all the world to behold, every man, or at least he could potentially be: "There, but by the grace of God go all of us!"

Following the example of the famous episode from the life of Saint Francis (who actually resided at a nearby monastery in Burgos during his pilgrimage of the Camino), and even though it was a bit creepy feeling, I summoned up the humanity, as millions of pilgrims who had come before me had, to sit down beside him. Tradition says that if you are in some way sick or infirmed, that if you touch the area of his body where your malady exists, it will elicit a cure.

Looking at him closely as I sat beside him, I could see from the polished regions on his bronze skin that the most common areas touched were his head (probably to cure mental illness or something as mundane as baldness), several of his various oozing wounds, his upper leg muscles (probably for the physical strength to carry on with the journey), his groin, and his feet (probably as a method to ward off or cure the pilgrim's most common ailment, heel blisters). I chose to rub his belly just below his scallop shell to help cure my cousin's liver disease, and his chest to aid in the cure of the two women I knew with breast cancer.

But, unlike Saint Francis, I never completely had the courage to embrace the poor soul—which is probably why he, Francis, is a saint, and I'm not. The Pilgrim was just a statue, and even though it may sound a bit silly, I'm still ashamed (just a little) as I write these words and think back upon that beautiful day and at that moment when my Christian compassion completely failed me. But I've since resolved that if I ever pass his way again, I won't hesitate for a second.

The Cathedral of Burgos rates high on my list as one of the most beautiful churches I've ever seen. Dedicated to Saint Mary, the Mother of Christ, this Gothic church, in all of its sheer magnificence, and its surrounding plazas have been declared by the United Nations Educational, Scientific, and Cultural Organization (UNESCO) a World Heritage Site. Although the church's secular claim to fame is that it contains the tomb of old Spain's military hero, El Cid, one of its chapels, the Capilla del Santo Cristo de Burgo, is also renowned for containing one of the most famous of Spain's religious objects of devotion, the Black Christ.

The statue that hangs above the altar in the chapel portrays that of the crucified Christ, and as I stood there in awe looking up at Him, it was easy to see why the image is so venerated by the Spanish people: It has to be one of the most realistic likenesses of Christ I've ever seen. He actually has real hair, a real crown of thorns, and—although just a bit creepy—some sort of actual real skin. This naturalistic portrayal of the crucified Jesus was explained to our group by one of the cathedral's official guides.

He told us of the legend that says that the statue's creator was none other than Saint Nicodemus himself, a member of the Jewish Sanhedrin, and at the time, a secret follower of Jesus. On the night of the Lord's Passion it was Nicodemus (along with Joseph of Arimathea and several unnamed disciples) who helped to lower Christ's scourged and wracked body down from the Cross. His being in the physical presence the crucified Son of God gave Nicodemus a firsthand insight into that divine event that no artist in the subsequent history of the world could ever have had, which is why, said the tour guide, the Black Christ as an image of the crucified Christ seems so corporeally real.

> Lord, may this stone, a symbol of my efforts on the pilgrimage that
> I lay at the foot of the cross of the savior, one day weigh the balance
> in favor of my good deeds when the deeds of my life are judged.

–THE PRAYER OF THE CRUZ DE FERRO

I knew that what was coming up had to be quite important, because as we approached the quarter-mile-wide plateau of Mount Irago, Alex asked that everyone in the group please be silent as we approached. It was a foggy morning, very cold, and we couldn't see anything except occasional traces of the pine forest surrounding us and the road; even so, I do admit that I was still quite excited by it all. Then suddenly, just as we reached what would be the highest point that pilgrims will traverse on the Camino, the mists opened up into a cloudy sky, and we could see the famous pile of rocks with its cross sticking out of its center known as the Cruz de Ferro, the Iron Cross.

The story of this iron cross (an oak pole actually, with an iron cross embedded in its top) actually predates Christianity by at least a couple of thousand years. One theory is that, because Mount Irago is such a high place, the ancient Celts who originally inhabited the area may have used the location for some ritual function. There seems to be some evidence as well that suggests that when the Romans occupied this area just before the birth of Christ that they used a then much smaller mound of stones as an altar to Mercury, the god of travel.

Another legend says that as the apostle James himself passed through the region on one of his early evangelizing missions, he witnessed with a great repugnance how the local pagan priests were performing human sacrifices upon the large granite platform. With a raging anger directed toward the perpetrators of such senseless slaughter mixed, as well, with a loving and infinite compassion for the innocent victims of such cruelty, the saint called out to the Lord for guidance and help. He then reached into the pocket of his cloak, pulled from it a small stone that he had carried with him all the way from Jerusalem, and with the entire might of God Almighty behind him, threw the rock and smote the pagan altar, reducing it to dust. In its place he erected the original iron cross upon the spot to remind the local heathens of the one true God.

Today, every pilgrim who passes by, whether they be believers, agnostics, atheists, or pagans, leaves a stone on the pile. In the act of throwing the stone over his or her shoulder, the pilgrim symbolically leaves behind them upon this pile any physical, spiritual, or emotional burdens they may be carrying in their hectic daily lives. For many pilgrims (with the possible exception of the physical act of reaching the cathedral at Santiago itself), this ritual represents the spiritual culmination of their journey along the Camino.

Whatever the origin of the tradition might be, the millions of pilgrims who have passed over the top of this mountain in the thousand-year history of the Camino de Santiago have added considerably to the gigantic mound of stones that stands there today; the pile stretches over fifty feet across at the base and is about twenty-five feet tall. Because we were told in advance by our tour organizers to do so, my wife and I each brought a fist-sized rock with us from the cow pasture out back of our home in upstate New York. Theresa set her stone down near the top of the pile, at the base of the cross. I threw mine to land down about halfway up.

At the time, I wasn't conscious of any "burdens" I might have been leaving behind, but I did find myself thinking about a couple of things. First, and only briefly, and I have no idea why, I thought about the Vietnam War and my days in the navy; nothing specific really, but I remember contrasting how warm those days in Southeast Asia were compared to the cold, damp air I now stood in. The second issue that occupied my reflections was quite a bit more specific. It began as a vague feeling of guilt—or maybe just a regret—and grew into a vision that seemed to have been inspired by the actual pile of stones in front of which we now stood.

One of the problems of our modern, workaday world, especially if you are going to have any chance of success at all, is that you must put aside many other things in your life in order to do so; important things that end up being put aside and put aside and then put aside again for so long that they are eventually forgotten. Forgotten, sadly, for so long that you don't realize how important they were to your life until they are gone forever.

I didn't have a word(s) for it at the time, but today I call it my *stack of stuff* theory, and it works as follows. An item, say a letter or an email from an old friend, comes into your life. The gracious and considerate guy who resides inside your consciousness tells you that it would be a thoughtful gesture to reply to the person who sent it in some way other than just a cursory, half-assed manner. And so you decide to do so by either phoning him or by writing a long letter in reply; but then something comes up and so you put the notion into the stack of things to do when you have the time. Another item, say perhaps a small request from your wife then pops up, and, realizing it's important—but not that important—you put it in the stack as well. Then you see an article in a newspaper or a blurb in a college alumni journal mentioning a former mentor or colleague, and you say to yourself that it would be nice to send a card; but you're busy at the moment, and so you put that into the stack as well.

And on and on and on until the stack of stuff has gotten so big that whatever rests on the bottom of the pile now no longer has any chance of being realized: That postponed visit to the young college library aide who taught you how to use a word processor that's no longer possible because she has died from cervical cancer; that meaningless congratulation that you send two years after the fact to the professor who wrote you the letter of recommendation that was so instrumental in your early success; the put-off moments of intimacy with your spouse you can never get back; or that phone call to your parents or brother or sister-in-law—and on and on and on, until it's too late.

It was this aspect of my life, though not exactly these particular incidents, that passed through my mind as I stood upon that venerable and eternal Spanish mountaintop on that overcast, damp and chilly day. I don't remember if I made any vow or notion to change things, but I know for sure that I haven't done anything yet to improve. I still have this gigantic stack of stuff and I just keep adding more and more to it. Who knows? Maybe it's just the way it's always going to be.

I don't know; I sure hope not

As we got about forty miles from Santiago, I began to notice an unusually shaped cheese in many of the village markets; unusual because, rather than being round like a wheel or square like a brick, these cheeses were formed in the exact image of a woman's breast. The local residents call it Queso gallego de Tetilla or, as it translates loosely into English, "titty cheese." Because I'm interested in these sorts of things (that is, I'm interested in the story behind the breasts—I mean their shapes, not the breasts themselves!) I asked Alex about them. Sure enough, like everything else on the Camino, these, too, had a story. When a pilgrim walks up the grand stairway into the Cathedral of Saint James and enters into the main portico, one of the many arrays of statues decorating the walls is a group of four men representing the four Old Testament

prophets. Although they appear quite serious in their countenance, full of hellfire and damnation, one of them, the prophet Daniel, quite uncharacteristically is smiling up a storm.

Alex went on to say that in order to discover why, all you had to do is turn yourself around. There you would see a graphically depicted, bare-chested, Queen Esther in all of her feminine glory. That is, this is what a pilgrim centuries ago was able to see. You don't, however, see her boobs today because some unnamed archbishop in the fifteenth century felt (no pun intended) the breasts were a little too much for most pious pilgrims to have to bear (pun intended), so he had them ingloriously chiseled off. From that time on, the local dairy farmers, furious at what they felt was a desecration of their holy cathedral, and as a sign of solidarity with the wounded Jewish heroine, began to form their native brand of cheese in the provocative form they exist in to this very day.

Upon the completion of the long journey, pilgrims who did the Walk of Saint James for religious or spiritual purposes line up on the second floor of a nearby building, get their pilgrim passports inspected, and then receive their Compostela. Afterwards, both pilgrims and tourists alike attend the Pilgrim's Mass with its famous swinging of a 120-pound botafumeiro (incense burner) spewing the pungent odor of frankincense high above their heads; it is indeed a grand sight to behold. If the pilgrims are practicing Catholics, they receive Holy Communion. The final obligatory tradition is to climb up the stairway of the main altar built over the grave of Saint James, stand behind the statue of the good apostle, and then give him a big hug, thanking him for his protection and blessings.

Then, and with the greatest of sorrow, the pilgrimage is over. Now you have to re-enter the world.

> A journey, after all, neither begins in the instant we set out,
> nor ends when we have reached our door step once again. It
> starts much earlier and is really never over, because the film of
> memory continues running on inside of us long after we have
> come to a physical standstill. Indeed, there exists something like
> a contagion of travel, and the disease is essentially incurable.
>
> –RYSZARD KAPUSSCINNSKI

For me, this withdrawal was the hardest part of my Camino experience. After sixteen days of being intimately a part of something so alive with history and humanity, the question is always: What do you do now that the journey is over? After being embraced by the sheer spiritual transcendence of this Way of Saint James, how do you return to the temporal, often mundane—and often oppressive—dog-eat-dog demands of daily modern life? That infamous stack of stuff! Because this sudden feeling of withdrawal happens to me every single time at the end of my trips, I've often asked myself, "Richard, if you know this heartbreak happens again and again and again with each journey's end, why do you bother to put yourself through it?

Gustav Flaubert, French novelist and fellow traveler, spoke of these moments as *melancholies du voyage*, the sad realization that a journey is over. In one form or another, I believe that all but the most insensitive of wanderers suffer from this fate. At moments like these, all of the shared reflections and recollections of the more verbally gifted travelers who have roamed this earth before me re-emerge from my deepest memories in their mostly futile attempt to give me solace. I think to myself: "Travel makes one modest. You see what a tiny place you occupy in this world (Bill Bryson)." "Travel brings power and love back into your life (Rumi)." "Why do you go away? So you can come return (Terry Pratchett)." "Roam abroad in the world, and take thy fill of its enjoyments before the day shall come when thou must quit it for good (Unknown)." "It is good to have an end to journey towards; but it is the journey that matters in the end (Ernest Hemingway)."

So why is it that travelers doggedly persist in answering the beckoning call of the world, breaking the hearts as they do so of their kith and kin who so desperately long to hold them back, only to once again endure the pain of detachment that wrenches at their soul at the journey's end? As I sit here at my desk on a dreary, cold, rainy upstate New York December morning trying to place into words the answer to this most unanswerable question, I think the quote by Mr. Hemingway (a truly hard-core traveler and fellow lover of Rioja wine) comes the closest to the answer: "It is only the Journey that matters in the end." But having said this, I think the answer may be even more profound.

I say this because, if you really think about it, the same sentiment about a journey being over can be applied to any trip anyone has ever undertaken. Whether it's a day trip to Niagara Falls with a friend, an early morning climb guided only by moonlight up to the summit of Africa's Mt. Kilimanjaro, an autumn afternoon's visit to a cousin's apple farm, or—if you really want to get philosophical on the matter—whether it's a simple reflection of this most ultimate of journeys through life itself that every single one of us is embarked upon, the whole thing boils down to one fundamental and unavoidable truth: All journeys, by their very nature, must come to an end. And it's in this realization that I finally have found comfort.

Big and small, real or imagined, all journeys are versions of our lives in miniature: they are symbolic of all life's beginnings, middles, and end. We embark on a trip filled with the hopes of adventure and of an encounter with the unknown. We arrive at where we're going, we discover something new about the world and ourselves and the lives of others. We savor (or not) our common humanity, and with a little bit of luck, we ultimately become "one" with the whole experience. But when the journey comes to an end, that's it; it's all over. We must then move on.

Therein, I believe, is the answer to the question. Although it's often bone-crushingly sad at that final moment when we must say our last goodbye and let it all go, the realization that all journeys must end embodies within its essence the true traveler's greatest source of joy. We know this because with one journey's end comes the irresistible promise of yet another journey, and another, and another.

For this, I'm glad.

St. Francis's Beloved Portiuncula

Photo by Rob Harris

CHAPTER 2

St. Catherine's Monastery and Jebul Musa

⟨∞⟩

... But Mr. DJ, please
I'm beggin' on my knees
I just can't take no more of Billy Ray

Don't play that song
That "Achy Breaky" song
I think it's driving me insane
Oh, please don't play that song
That irritating song
I'd rather have a pitchfork in my brain ...

—*"Achy Breaky Song"* by Weird Al Yankovic

IF I HAD TO PUT a number on it, I'd say that at least a third of our travels around this astonishing planet are intentionally taken as pilgrimages to sacred places and holy sites. From Jerusalem's Dome of the Rock (sacred to Muslims, Jews, and Christians), to the source of the River Ganges sixteen thousand feet up in the Himalayas (sacred to Hindus), to Tibet's forbidden Potala Palace (sacred to Tibetan Buddhists), and to all of the other mystical places in between, we've been truly blessed by the power of presence that these patches of hallowed earth so radiates. My sincerest hope before

I forever depart this veil of tears and begin that most ultimate of journeys each and every one of us must someday travel is that I can experience every single holy place on earth at least once—twice, if given the time. The absolute sense of transcendence above and beyond this often ordinary mortal existence and the nearness to the Divine I feel each time I find myself within the confines of these remarkable places just fills me with elation and leaves me—for lack of a better phrase—speechless!

> See to it, my sons, that you never abandon this place. For this
> [the Portiuncula] is truly holy and is the dwelling place of God.
>
> —St. Francis of Assisi

If pressed to name the most holy spot on earth that I've visited so far, I would have to say that it is the little church of the Portiuncula located just outside of Assisi, Italy. In this austere little church, a place that was so important to the life—and death—of Saint Francis and his early Franciscan brothers, there is something, some titanic force, some great connection with God, that is greater than anything I've ever experienced anywhere else.

From this humble sanctuary, Saint Francis and his early followers set down their Rules of Order for the Franciscan mission. From this church, they set out on their travels throughout the whole of the known world at the time to spread the simple word of God's love. And it was here, as per his last earthly request, that Francis returned "to die naked on the bare earth" in the oak woods that he so very much loved.

But before I finish sharing more of my thoughts about this holy place and leave the reader with the belief that they can still travel to this place and experience for themselves the total peace and beatified bliss that so moved the good saint, I need to tell the proverbial "rest of the story." And this additional comment basically holds true for nearly every important holy site of any religious tradition that one might wish to visit: these places aren't always the simple, sanctified settings they originally started out as being!

Progress, along with the need to accommodate large numbers of pilgrims, combined with mankind's natural tendency toward entrepreneurship, often result in these places being a bit more theatrical, a lot more opulent, and a whole lot more commercial then was originally intended. Therefore, pilgrims intent on visiting these places with the hope of becoming "one" with the divine must also develop the ability to extract the sacred from all the glitz, the excess, and sadly, even the profane.

This is especially true of the Portiuncula. The original simple stone building in the oak woods that Saint Francis and his brothers found ruined and abandoned in the early thirteenth century, and which they lovingly restored with their own hands, still stands. However, today this special church is enclosed—engulfed would be a better word to use—in the giant edifice of Saint Mary of the Angels Basilica, the seventh largest Catholic building on earth! The church is like the Vatican and the Houston Astrodome all in one; quite an impressive sight to behold.

Long gone are the trees and birds, the brambles, and the mud. Today there is marble mosaic flooring worn and polished smooth by the footsteps of millions of pilgrims. I'm not sure how good Saint Francis would react today to all of the sumptuousness that his grateful and faithful followers over the centuries have bestowed upon his most precious and beloved little church, but if he was a practical man, I think he'd be pleased. The building now resides securely within the bosom of the great basilica, forever safe from the rain and snow and the relentless Tuscan sun.

Likewise, the modern design and layout of the basilica's floor plan makes the Portiuncula surprisingly accessible to the multitudes of visitors who flock to Italy each year from all over the world; millions of people who long with all of their hearts to share for just one brief moment the ecstasy and transcendent joy as did Saint Francis as he knelt and prayed upon on this hallowed ground. To one who has never been there, I guess it's easy to be cynical of the whole experience. But as I witnessed—and experienced!—firsthand, the fact remains that beyond all of the gaudiness, the intolerably obnoxious and rude tourists, the tacky souvenir stands, and pain-in-the-ass panhandlers, this little house of God that Saint Francis so, so loved still has the power to overwhelm all who are graced to have been in its humble presence.

... Their churches are to be respected. They are neither to
be prevented from repairing them nor the sacredness of
their covenants. No one of the Nation [Muslims] is to dis-
obey the covenant till the Last Day [end of the world].

–Prophet Muhammad, in an edict to the
monks of Saint Catherine, 628 A.D.

Located in the very heart of Egypt's Sinai Peninsula, about a three hours'
drive north of the southern Red Sea resort town of Sharm-al-Sheikh is
the ancient UNESCO World Heritage Site called the Sacred and Imperial
Monastery of the God-Trodden Mount of Sinai. Or, as she is more com-
monly known, Saint Catherine's Monastery. This desert fortress/monas-
tery, built around the year 527 at the request of Emperor Justinian, sits at
the foot of Jebul Musa (Mount Sinai, the mountain of Moses) and rests on
top of the traditional site of the Bible's burning bush. Considered sacred
by Jews, Christians, and Muslims alike, this ultimate holy of all holy places
is where God Almighty Himself, the God of Abraham, Isaac, and Jacob,
resided with the ancient Israelites and shared with the people of the covenant His Ten Commandments.

Named after the Christian martyr Catherine of Alexandria, the monastery today is under the ascendency of the Greek Orthodox Church of
Jerusalem. Although the actual construction of her buildings and walls
date back only to the sixth century, the monastic tradition of worship by
desert hermits and Christian pilgrims goes back in history to the 200s.
The fact that this lonely outpost survived relatively unscathed to today—
in spite of the endless religious and secular wars that have convulsed the
Near East since time immemorial—is a true miracle. Well ... sort of.

The more down-to-earth reason for the monastery's longevity lies
in a command given in a little-known document called the *Achtiname of
Muhammad*. Known also by scholars as the *Charter of Privileges*, this precious manuscript was ratified and signed with a handprint by the Prophet
Muhammad himself, and it granted till the end of time complete freedom
of worship, along with martial protection, if necessary, to the monks of

Saint Catherine. To this very day, Muslim leaders throughout the world still profess their confirmation of this document.

Visiting the sacred compound of Saint Catherine takes a bit of work, especially if you are an independent traveler. You must rent a car in Sharm-al-Sheikh and drive the long three-hour drive through some of the bleakest—but stunningly beautiful—lonely desert terrain on the planet. Although today the Sinai is controlled by Egypt, the peninsula uneasily exists as a sort of buffer zone between that country and Israel, and so the large presence of military in the region, unless you're used to it, can be quite intimidating. From the moment you pass through the first highly fortified military checkpoint leaving Sharm-al-Sheikh, and until you pass the fifth one on the outskirts of Saint Catherine (and even then, probably) you are under constant observation. But though this might sound like an ordeal, the bottom line is that it is safe, and I go down on record as saying that the two times we've made the drive, never have the soldiers been anything but courteous and welcoming.

With the exception of modern conveniences such as electricity and a couple of modest souvenir stands, the monastery and its surrounds exist in a state much like they did fifteen hundred years ago. The place functions primarily as place of worship and contemplation, and the Orthodox monks see to it that it remains so. A good deal of the grounds is off limits to outsiders, but what is available is quite interesting. The well-tended gardens, with their lush fruit and nut trees, grapevines, and vegetable patches are a miracle of existence. Nearby you can also visit the Chapel of Saint Trifonio, where you can look into the crypt beneath the building and see the rather gruesome but very practical, when you think about it, ossuary containing the bones of thousands of monks who have lived and worshiped and died in this desert oasis; it truly is something you don't see every day.

Inside the basilica itself are marvels upon marvels of ancient icons, dazzling mosaics, and a spiritual treasure trove of holy relics. As soon as you enter into the subdued candlelight of the sanctuary, you are overwhelmed by the pungent smell of frankincense, the almost two millennia worth of burning candles, and just the overall antiquity of it all. To add to the reverence of the moment, on the day we visited, a lone, gray-bearded monk stood beside the altar and chanted an ancient liturgy that the twelve Apostles themselves would very likely have understood. In a sarcophagus to the left of the altar lie the mortal remains of Saint Catherine herself. But as mysterious, holy, and spiritually alive as this sanctuary of God was, for me the highlight of our visit to the actual monastery itself was my being able to pray in the Chapel of the Burning Bush.

Located in a rather shabby looking, rather unpretentious building just off of the main basilica complex sits the Chapel of the Burning Bush. As the name implies, the building is built directly over the remains of the Old Testament's miraculous bush that "burned, but was not consumed," the bush out of which the voice of God spoke to the prophet Moses. A transplant of the bush still grows majestically up along the outside of the chapel.

Pilgrims enter the chapel one at a time from a short hallway leading from the church. A serious, stern-looking, old patriarch supervises and ruthlessly regulates who is allowed or is not allowed into the hallowed sanctum sanctorum of all of Judaism, Islam, and Christianity. If he said no, that was that! The old boy must have liked both Theresa and me, because he let us pass. Outside the unadorned actual doorway to the sanctuary stood a younger monk who, in perfect English, told us only one visitor was allowed into the tiny chapel at a time. He also reminded us to remove our shoes. Finally, when my turn came, I stepped barefoot (barefoot because I wanted the same holy physical connection to the earth that Moses felt) into the holy presence.

The soil floor inside of the small chapel was packed hard as concrete by the feet of millions of reverent pilgrims. All around me the walls were ornamented with oil lamps, incense burners, and candle holders. In front of the tiny space sat a small altar. And sticking up out of the consecrated ground under the altar were the stumps of what looked like a profession-ally pruned rosebush.

I now stood on holy ground! Because I was a little overwhelmed by the monumental meaning of it all, it took me a few seconds to fully understand that these small stalks of a long-dead, dried-up plant are the actual physi-cal remnants of Almighty God the Father's presence on earth. Realizing this, and probably just like old Moses himself, I fell prostrate onto the floor. I could not move, I could not pray, and I could not even sense the passing of time. All I could do was bask in the infinite magnificence and grandeur of that little room.

It was a few minutes before the young monk walked into the room to rouse me from my ecstasy. After assisting me to my feet, he walked me to the door so that Theresa and the other pilgrims waiting in line could have their turn. Completely drained from the experience, I waited in the dim light of the basilica on a chair set along the wall for that very purpose. The chanting monk continued singing out his eternal hymn to God. A warm, welcome dry desert breeze blew into the church and served to awaken me once again to the real world that existed outside of this holy place. It also reminded me that my visit to the area was not over yet. We still had to climb Mount Moses

Directly behind Saint Catherine's Monastery, rising to over seven thousand feet above the surrounding desert plain, is Jebul Musa. It was here on the lonely and desolate summit of this jagged red granite mountain that the Lord gave to Moses and the ancient Israelites the Ten Commandments. The climb we planned to make would be our second one.

There are two ways of getting to the top of Jebul Musa. The first is to climb the 3,500 steps carved out of the hillside by the monks. Climbing this trail in the heat of the midday Sinai desert sun would be foolish. The other climbing route, at least for the first two-thirds of its length, is fairly easy. I use the word *easy* only in the sense that the trail involves no great danger should you lose your balance and fall over the side. That having been said, the trail is still a grueling, three-hour walk, all uphill, with the last one-third of the climb narrowing down into a steep, zigged-zag path cut into the side of the mountain.

On our first climb up Mount Sinai six years before, we had walked the entire trail from the bottom to the top. Because we were several years older now (and because we'd never done anything like this before) we decided that this time we were each going to take a camel ride for the first leg of the climb.

For as long as there have been monks living and dying at Saint Catherine's, there have been Bedouin shepherds in the region residing side by side with the holy fathers. Moses' father-in-law, after all was a shepherd. Today, as in those early days, these desert nomads derive a large part of their livelihood from helping pilgrims and tourists to access and to visit the holy sites in the region, and the biggest money-maker of all is renting their camels.

We walked around to the back of the compound, and there, lying down and resting in the shade of the rear wall of the monastery were the camels, all contentedly chewing their cuds. Sleeping in a group next to them were about ten young boys. After only a couple of moments of standing there, in that mysterious way that always manages to happen in the Orient whenever a tourist seems the slightest bit interested in a financial transaction, from out of nowhere, a wise and savvy elderly gentleman appeared, ready to bargain. And this we did in only a half-hearted manner (because it's the expected thing to do), and only for just a couple of minutes; we knew what the probable cost would be and we were willing to pay it, just to save wasting time.

After reaching an agreement, he rousted two of the older boys from their slumbers. This was then followed by about ten minutes of violent hollering and raucous screaming between them and the old man. I swear that it sounded as if they were going to come to blows. One did not need to be a scholar of the Egyptian language to figure out that the last thing these two young men wanted to do on that hot afternoon was schlep up that big mountain guiding a couple of belligerent, cranky camels carrying a couple of unskilled American riders. Not quite sure what to do, and tired of them wasting our limited time, Theresa and I said 'the hell with them' and began the long trek up the mountain by foot.

And, of course, as is always the case, seeing that our resolve was about to win out over their theatrics, and more importantly, that they were all about to lose a sale, almost like a miracle, a quiet peace descended upon them and, very apologetically—and with great fanfare—they gestured for us to return. Upon doing so, the older man first had me climb onto a reclined camel and told me to hold on to the saddle horn. "Hold on very tightly, sir," he told me, and before I even started lifting my leg up over the back of the beast, he told me again—in no uncertain terms, "Please, sir, hold on very tightly!"

Once they were all convinced that I indeed had a good grip upon the saddle, the older looking of the two boys yelled something at the camel, and animal, with great reluctance and perturbation, began to stir. After letting out a cry that sounded like a cross between a long belch and a for-lorn plea for mercy, the poor beast started rocking back and forth from his front legs to his back legs in a desperate attempt to gain enough momen-tum in which to stand. After several seconds of this concerted effort, in one final push (as well as one big fart), the mighty critter rose to his feet. As for me, I was now tightly wedged into the narrow wooden horseshoe-shaped saddle, suffering a moderate degree of pain from the crushing compacting of my groin. In that moment, I came to the conclusion that, even if I someday might get around to doing so, I'd probably never ever be able to sire any children.

After watching Theresa's camel rise to her feet with surprising ease, I, she, the two camels, and both our boys started our trek up the hill. I'll say right off that riding a camel was not a carefree and painless experience for me, at least not right off. The constant forward and backward undula-tions of the great animal's gait demanded my full concentration and ef-fort to stay aboard. As we all chugged along up the hill, sometimes my boy walked ahead of my camel and at other times (mostly at moments when the trail was threateningly narrow and a potentially precipitous fall down the side of the mountain seemed—at least to me—a very real possibility) he ambled along behind us. For the whole of the trip, the child altered from singing a kind of a sweet sounding melody to uttering harsh, drill sergeant–like commands directed at my poor camel. I actually felt bad a few times for the poor critter.

But as life-threatening as some of the near falls might have seemed at the beginning, the camel turned out to be as sure-footed as a mountain goat. And once my rear end got used to the torturous saddle, the whole experience turned out to be quite an adventure. The views from the trail of the valley below as we zigged and zagged higher and higher up the hill were phenomenal. You could almost imagine what it was like for Moses as he descended the mountain so long ago carrying the stone tablets of God's law. Looking down he could see the assembled multitudes, the men and women, goats and sheep, all camped out on the wide plain that still exists at the base of the mountain. And, oh, how his heart must have broken when he saw that many of his Israelites now danced and bowed down to the golden calf.

About halfway up the hill, I saw Theresa offer a banana to each of the kids, which they both ate with great pleasure. Each boy, after finishing his banana, gave the peels to his respective charge that, in turn, gobbled them down with equal pleasure. After about an hour, and about two thirds of the way up the mountain, we reached the end of the camel trail. With the same jerky, rocking motion we had endure as we mounted the camels, the boys managed to get the beasts to lie back down so we could dismount. We then said good bye to each of them, gave the boys each a tip, and in no time, they were heading back down. After spending a couple of minutes to allow the blood to flow back to my benumbed rear end, we began tackling the last grueling third of the trail by foot.

As one approaches the top of a historic and sacred place like Mount Sinai, it is easy—at least for me—to be consumed by the moment and for a while at least to become emotionally overtaken by the grand and glorious meaning of it all. What I mean is that there I was, standing on the mountain of Moses, the very same barren, jagged, sacred mountaintop upon which the Lord of the universe Himself appeared in order to give to mankind His laws. The place was a genuine nexus between heaven and earth! This feeling of being overwhelmed actually did happen to me on my first visit here years before. But on this second time up Mount Sinai I knew better what to expect and was not disappointed.

Talk about the profane: one of the first things a climber notices as he approaches the summit is the smell of feces and urine emanating from the latrines near the trail's end. The next thing you see are a series of small sheds with local women and children selling water, Cadbury chocolate bars, and that most universal of all consumer products, good old American Coca Cola. On my first pilgrimage, I found the letdown as annoying as hell! But, in retrospect, if I had to be completely honest, I was kind of glad on both treks to be able to indulge in a cool drink of water and a (quite surprisingly) very tasty Cadbury chocolate bar.

Because of a strict edict from the monks of Saint Catherine's, the actual peak of Mount Sinai, however, remains unblemished by the hand of man and still remains in its original glory. If you, therefore, while standing on that spot, can manage to set aside and overlook the temporal world with all of its trash and consumerism, and instead open up to the sacredness of that awe-inspiring place, you can then hear and feel and see it all with a breathless clarity! In this moment of transcendence you'll come to understand why God chose this glorious place to fulfill His sojourn on earth. Words cannot describe it, but I believe that from that windswept red granite precipice, that if you look hard enough you'll see the whole world before your very eyes!

I loved being there on God's holy mountain again. It's rare that I ever say this, but one of my sincerest wishes is that before my adoring heart stops beating and my immortal soul once again unites with the Almighty, I can once again plant the soles of my feet upon the top of Jebul Musa.

When the time came for us to leave, we descended down the mountain on the steep stairway that over the past two millennia the monks of Saint Catherine's carved by hand from the living rock. Legend says that this was the actual goat trail that Moses used to ascend and descend the mountain for his meeting with God. (He must have been one tough and rugged dude!) After dusting ourselves off, we got into our little Toyota rental car and began the three-hour drive back through the desert to Sharm-al-Sheikh. It had been an amazing day: lots of gorgeous scenery to see, a large amount of truly ancient history for me to become "one" with, a great experience of the holy, all with just bit of the profane thrown in to remind us we were still among the mortals. But it wasn't over yet! We still had the long drive back through the desert, and one more experience to encounter at our hotel in Sharm-al-Sheikh.

The resort city of Sharm-al-Sheikh sits at the very tip of Egypt's Sinai Peninsula and is bordered by the two northern fingers of the Red Sea. On its east side, the city is bounded by the Gulf of Aqaba, a watery continuation of a huge crack in the earth's surface called the Great Rift Valley. This great split begins in northern Syria and extends southward from the

Sea of Galilee, through the Jordan valley and the Dead Sea, and eventually ends nearly four thousand miles later at Lake Tanganyika in the central highlands of Africa. On the city's western side she is bordered by the Gulf of Suez, a narrow passage of water that ultimately ends at the southern entrance of the famous canal of the same name.

The city draws tourists from all over the Middle East and Europe for its pristine Red Sea beaches and world-class scuba diving. The isolated location and sumptuous accommodations make Sharm-al-Sheikh a popular destination as well for world leaders to meet with one another in relative safety and comfort in order to discuss whatever crisis might be troubling mankind at the time. Although not completely immune to the terror that affects that part of the world (a few of the resorts have been the target of terrorists attacks) so many treaties have been signed in Sharm-al-Sheikh that its nickname is the 'City of Peace'.

After getting back to our room, we freshened up and went down to the hotel's seaside patio for supper. Like a lot of resorts throughout the region, the evening meal is usually in the form of a bountiful buffet, often with a theme. Our theme that night was—of all things!—an American Western barbecue. And overall, the management of the restaurant did a pretty good job interpreting the concept.

The entire spread was enormous: salads of every description, cheeses, Middle Eastern breads and cakes, fruits, and much to my wife's delight, fresh dates. As is my habit, I tried to sample them all. Most interesting were the small steaks grilled to order of both beef and goat meat, as well as lamb hot dogs (yuck), hamburgers, and kebabs. (Pork, of course, in a Moslem nation was an absolute no-no.) All were heavily spiced with a catsup-based barbecue sauce that was quite delicious. Quite cute as well were the costumes worn by the waiters. Both the women and the men wore red and black-checkered shirts with an orange triangular folded bandanna around their necks. The men had on stiff blue jeans and the ladies wore very modest faux blue jean skirts. Everyone wore a straw cowboy hat. In the background, a young Egyptian man discreetly strummed out old Merle Haggard, Hank Williams, and Slim Whitman ballads on a slightly out-of-tune electric guitar.

From our dinner table in the dimming light of that magical day we could look south out across the Red Sea and see way off in the distance the giant super tankers with their cargo of crude oil lining up to enter the Gulf of Suez. To the north we could see the last remnants of the setting sun still glowing on the mountains of Sinai, their jagged granite peaks blazing like a million bloodstained sharks' teeth. A steady warm breeze blew gently across thc patio bringing with it, once again, the earthy smell of the desert. Every sensual pleasure a traveler could ever hope for was there in that moment! It was truly enchanting. That is, until the stage show band began to play.

And this mother of all horrors began with the very first song. Now, I don't want to give the wrong impression here; the young Egyptian singers had heart, and they did the best they could. But the music these young men were belting out sounded like a combination of someone mercilessly torturing cats as well as someone at the same time rhythmically scratching their fingernails across a blackboard; all of it performed at eardrum-shattering volume. The poor lead singer had the shrill voice of the late Slim Whitman, just after Ol' Slim had been forced to ride a camel all day. To paraphrase, once again, Weird Al Yankovic: sticking a pitchfork in your brain would have been more humane than having to endure that agony. Oh! and the tune? Wow! You talk about the profane! I still can't get the darned thing out of my head!

"Don't tell my heart, my achy breaky heart ... my achy breaky heart ... my achy breaky heart ... my achy breaky heart ..."

The Dragon Bones

CHAPTER 3

A Tale of Two Cities

⸺◦◦◦⸺

Adventure is a path. Real adventure—self-determined, self-
motivated, often risky—forces you to have firsthand encounters
with the world. The world the way it is, not the way you imagine
it. Your body will collide with the earth and you will bear
witness. In this way you will be compelled to grapple with the
limitless kindness and bottomless cruelty of humankind—and
perhaps realize that you yourself are capable of both. This will
change you. Nothing will ever again be black-and-white.

–MARK JENKINS

IN THE MOTION PICTURE MUSICAL *Mame*, Lucile Ball, who played the eccentric,
fun-loving, and globe-trotting Auntie Mame, had a favorite saying, that
when I think about it, pretty much sums up the way I strive to live my life
as well: "The whole world is a banquet, but most poor people [*people* wasn't
the exact word she used] are starving to death!" Please note that I used
the word *strive*. I did so because first, I don't want to sound too uppity or
self-righteous about this whole living-life-to-fullest thing because it takes a
great deal of commitment and hard work to live such a life. I know there
are a lot of good people who, either because of family, work, or health demands; because of their personal temperaments or worldview; or because
of simple bad luck, just aren't able to fully savor all of the infinite wonders
this wonderful universe is waiting to offer us. Secondly, if the truth were to

be told, more often than I care to say, I find myself falling way, way! short of this idealistic mode of living one's dream life as well. Sometimes, just as the old poet (Wordsworth) said: "The world is too much with us!"

But until that moment when I breathe my last breath and bid fond farewell to this world as we know it, I plan with every ounce of my being to give Auntie Mame's philosophy of living my best shot!

Be it a trip to a local state park or a trek up the side of Mount Ararat, even after my almost sixty years of journeying to the far corners of our world, I never cease to be amazed at the seemingly limitless and unbounded diversity of experiences that living on this small blue dot of a planet we call home has to offer us. And even though our earth's overwhelming parade of animals, plants, minerals, sunsets, deserts, ocean beaches, and mountains' majesty oftentimes steals my breath away, it is being a witness to the accomplishments and the vast array cultural and behavioral peculiarities of my fellow man in which I find the most interest and pleasure.

My heart soars like an eagle when I'm the physical presence of the great works and deeds of great people who came before me. But on the other hand, just like sweet Auntie Mame after she tragically loses her husband in a skiing accident, I'm not blind to the sinister realities that so often exist side by side with the good in this world. Yes, I know from first-hand experience that we humans are capable of selfless acts of courage and love; yes, we are capable of monumental vision that can transcend our frequently mundane mortal existence; but as a species, we are also capable of the most abhorred and wretched evil imaginable.

And it was during a road trip on a gloriously sunny autumn day out into the surrounds of the city of Krakow, Poland that I got to see and experience both ends of the extreme of this incomprehensible two-sided nature of the human condition: examples of the most exalted of human goodness and the profoundest manifestation of all that is contemptible and depraved.

In the very heart of the modern-day city of Krakow, Poland, on a high ridge overlooking the Vistula River known by the locals as Wawel Hill, sits the historic Basilica of Saints Stanislaw and Vaclav. For a thousand years, this great church has been the traditional coronation site of Polish kings, and its catacombs under the basilica are the final resting places of many of Poland's heroes, monarchs, and saints. In more recent history, during the dark days of the World War Two Nazi occupation of the city, it was here in these underground caverns that a newly ordained Catholic priest named Father Karol Wojtya would conduct forbidden Catholic Masses. Twenty years later, while serving as the cardinal of the Archdiocese of Krakow, this formerly obscure country priest would be elected the first Polish Holy Father of the Roman Catholic Church and would take the name Pope John Paul II.

On the western slope of Wawel Hill just above the high-water level of the river, is a large cave and tunnel called 'Dragon's Den'. Legend says that in the old days before the founding of the city, a fierce dragon lived in this cave. Nicknamed the "whole-eater," this terrible creature demanded weekly sacrifices of cattle and sheep from the early settlers to this region to satisfy his insatiable hunger for meat. If, for whatever reason the farmers were unable to take animals to him, the monster would fulfill his craving by consuming human flesh.

Over time, a leader arose among the settlers who decided he would tolerate the demands of this ruthless creature no more. This man and his sons came up with an ingenious plan to kill the dragon by taking advantage of the beast's lust for flesh. First they would slaughter a cow and a sheep and removed the animal's skins. They then filled these hides with burning sulfur and placed them in the opening to the Whole-eater's cave. To make sure the deception went as planned, the brave sons stood just outside the creature's lair and one man bellowed like a cow, and the other bleated like a sheep. The greedy dragon, thinking he was about to feast on another easy sacrificial meal, gobbled the flaming sulphur-filled animal skins and was instantly consumed in his own fire. The wise patriarch who devised the ingenious plan to kill the Wawel dragon was named Cracus. The city that he and his family later went on to found was called Cracovia in his honor. Over the following centuries, the name became Krakow. Today, visitors to the old Basilica of Saints Stanislaw and Vaclav can look high up in the entrance to the great church and see several of the bones of the Wawel Dragon hanging in the archway. Legend says that as long as the bones hang there, the city of Krakow will always endure.

The first of our two planned destinations for the day's road trip would be the suburban town of Lagiewniki, just a short three-mile drive south of Krakow's Old Town district. Our driver/tour guide was a bright and ambitious young man named Andy. We were traveling to Lagiewniki to visit the world-famous Basilica of Our Lord's Divine Mercy and do a pilgrimage to the Shrine of Sister Mary Faustina Kowalska, Poland's newest saint.

> *"In the Old Covenant I sent prophets wielding thunderbolts to My people. Today I am sending you with My mercy to the people of the whole world. I do not want to punish aching mankind, but I desire to heal it, pressing it to My Merciful Heart. I use punishment when they themselves force Me to do so; My hand is reluctant to take hold of the sword of justice. Before the Day of Justice I am sending the Day of Mercy".*

–THE DIARY OF SISTER MARY FAUSTINA

Born Helena Kowalska on August 25, 1905, in the tiny Polish farming village of Glogowiec, the future Saint Faustina was not quite twenty years old when she received her calling to serve God and to enter the Congregation of the Sisters of Our Lady of Mercy. The directress of novices sent by the convent's Mother Superior to evaluate the new young applicant would years later recall her as "an unpromising, thin and poor weakling ... no one special really." But how wrong this short-sighted woman would be in her initial opinions of this humble and unassuming young girl, because in her short twelve years as a nun, as a blessed consequence of her visions and revelations of God's Divine Mercy, Sister Faustina would become the late-twentieth century's most beloved and most recognized saint in the world.

In 1936, blessed Sister Faustina contracted tuberculosis, and after two years of agonizing suffering, she died on November 5, 1938. Because of the late evening hour of her death, only one of her fellow sisters was at her side as she passed away. She was laid to rest three days later as just another devoted and loving servant of God in the tiny cemetery behind the Sisters of Our Lady of Mercy's Convent. As a rural, uneducated daughter of a poor farming family, Sister Mary Faustina's life at the convent had been filled with one mundane and menial task after another. To her superiors she was so ordinary that she never rose above the order's lowest category of membership. But while going through Faustina's personal effects in order to send them to the late nun's family, a very surprised Mother Superior discovered the future saint's diary.

And the rest as they say would be history.

When we arrived at the grounds of the Basilica of Our Lord's Divine Mercy sanctuary, Andy filled us in on some of the details of this holy site. The original buildings on the site were built by a wealthy Krakow businessman as a home for wayward young girls. Later on, they were given over to the Sisters of Our Lady of Mercy, who operate the convent to this very day. One of the first things I noticed as we walked on to the grounds was, not surprisingly, the newly built basilica itself. It was huge! When I asked Andy why the church was so big, he told me that such an enormous building was necessary to handle the three to four million pilgrims who visit the holy shrine every year.

The basilica was consecrated in August 2002 by Pope John Paul II himself. The building is elliptical in shape and of a modern glass-and-steel design. A fifteen-story-high bell tower/observation deck sticks straight up on its west end. From the outside it seemed like the crash site of a giant Goodyear blimp. In all, I thought it quite ugly. Inside the church, however, it was another story. The massive floor-to-ceiling windows created the illusion of being inside a giant light-filled crystal. The ceiling appeared like a big flying saucer hovering silently overhead. The effect was breathtaking. At the front of the church, behind the main altar, sat a giant bronze sculpture of Moses's burning bush. On the wall behind the sculpture, and appearing to be cradled among its branches, was hanging a reproduction of the famous *Jesus the Merciful* painting as envisioned by Saint Faustina.

After stopping for several minutes to pray in that magnificent house of God, Andy walked us around to the back of the basilica to the Cemetery of the Sisters. It was here, among the earthly resting places of her fellow "handmaids of Christ," that he showed us the former simple grave site of Sister

Mary Faustina Kowalska. As we stood there in that peaceful place, he told us more about her early life as a poor farmer's daughter who, because of her near illiteracy, had to originally endure countless difficulties and humiliations before finally being accepted into the Sisters of Our Lady of Mercy. He told of how she was constantly misunderstood and very much derided by her fellow sisters because of her visions, and, once again, of how she died a miserable, lonely, agonizing death at the young age of thirty-three.

As Andy related to us the details of this gentle and devoted innocent young girl's life, I silently wondered to myself (as I'm prone to do in these moments of conflicting emotions) why the Lord makes his loving saints suffer so much. Faustina's story is the same I hear told over and over again: Saint Thérèse of Lisieux dying at the age of twenty-two from a racking consumption, Saint Joan of Arc being burned alive at the stake, Jacinta and Francisco Marto, two of the three children who had a vision of the Virgin Mary in Fatima, Portugal, who both succumbed as teenagers to the 1918 worldwide flu epidemic, and most recently, Saint Gianna, an Italian mother whose refusal to get an abortion—even though it would have saved her life—died during the birth of her fourth child. The list goes on and on. No matter how hard I've tried, I've never been able to come up with an answer to this most seemingly unjust and unanswerable of questions, which is probably why I'll never make it myself into the realm of the heavenly saints.

Finally, Andy led us up the hill to the actual convent and the nuns' private chapel itself. It was here in this rather imposing, institutional-like, dark red bricked structure that Sister Mary Faustina Kowalska lived and served God in her final years. After her canonization, her mortal remains were transferred from the Sister's Cemetery and now rest in the convent's chapel. As we waited our turns to enter the building, he told us that the place was still being used as a convent and a home for wayward young girls. He pointed out a bronze plaque fixed underneath a second-story window which, in Polish, memorialized the room where Sister Faustina died. After our turn came to enter the building, we proceeded directly to the chapel. And as soon as I walked into that holy sanctuary, I was overcome with the reverent awe that often overtakes me when I'm standing in the presence of the truly divine.

In the end I believe the essential spirit that animates those
places animates me. If that spirit is God, then I found God
... If that spirit is life, then I found life ... If that spirit is awe,
then I found awe. Part of me suspects it's all three ... all I had
to do to discover that spirit and the resulting feeling of humility and appreciation was not to look or listen or taste or feel.

—BRUCE FEILER

I'm often made fun of when I try to put into plain words the overpowering sensations of wonder, of utter amazement, and feelings of *oneness* that
come over me when I find myself in the physical presence of the great
people of history or in the places where monumental events have taken
place. The same thing happens as well when I encounter the infinite majesty and overwhelming grandeur of nature and the natural world. Much
to the consternation of my wife, countless numbers of museum guards (I
was once thrown out of a gallery at the Metropolitan Museum of Art in
New York City for touching Vincent Van Gogh's *Starry Night* painting), and
a few of our private tour guides, I find that I'm never satisfied with just
looking: I have to touch, smell, hear, and whenever possible, even get a
taste of whatever experience I've been blessed to take part in.

Mystics, shamans, and other practitioners of the paranormal speak of
every person, place, or thing as having an anima, an aura, or some other
invisible live force. And as weird as this sounds, I believe these theories to
be true, especially in places and things already noted for their spiritual-
ity and human drama; places like temples, houses of worship, pilgrimage
centers, tombs, and great battlefields. However, the man of science in me
has another, more simple (sort of), way to answer what's going on. [My
apologies, in advance, if you think this sounds a bit weird.]

I prefer to explain away many these mystical sensations that often overwhelm me during my travels by a phrase I believe I invented: "*the commin-
gling of my molecules.*" I got the idea for this theory from a scientific article
I read somewhere many years ago about how each human being living on
the earth today has twenty thousand molecules in his or her body that

once were a part of Jesus. As a simple way to explain this very complex idea, let me give this example.

While He walked this earth as a man, Jesus breathed in oxygen and exhaled carbon dioxide. This carbon dioxide was, in turn, taken up by the surrounding plants, that then turned the molecule, via photosynthesis, into carbon (in the form of leaves, stems, and seeds) and oxygen. This plant material would then be eaten by an animal and then turned into food and fiber which would, in turn, be consumed by other animals. The oxygen would be taken up as well, continuing the cycle. And on and on and on. It's logical to conclude, therefore, that by eating an ear of corn, a lamb chop, or drinking a glass of local wine, that a traveler in the vicinity of the Holy Land could expect to incorporate into their body a greater concentration of Jesus' (as well as the biblical patriarchs) former atoms and molecules. [My apologies, again, if this sounds a bit weird.]

The same thing happens when I ate a piece of 100,000 year-old ice while walking on a glacier in Greenland. Locked in the ice are air bubbles that could very likely have been exhaled by the woolly mammoths. As I swallowed the melted water, I commingled these extinct molecules with mine. When I drank the water flowing down from the peaks of the mighty Himalayas, I took in and incorporated into every cell in my body the molecular essence of those mountains. In turn, as I voided my bladder on to one of the glaciers, I commingled my molecules back to the Himalayas.

When I inadvertently breathed in the smoke arising from a human cremation taking place at a Hindu temple next to the river in Kathmandu, Nepal, I took into my lungs carbon, magnesium, calcium, and nitrogen that once were a part of another life, and that departed soul and I, in that small way, commingled our molecules and are now "one." (I read in the city's newspaper the next morning that the deceased had been a great Nepalese poet, but as of this writing, no great poetical talent has been made apparent to me. That part of the man's essence must have blown past me.) This theory, although perhaps sounding quite bizarre to those with whom I share it, makes a lot of sense to me.

The sensation of awe I had when I walked into the Sisters of Our Lady of Mercy's chapel on that late summer morning, however, was strictly of the spiritual variety. The feeling of exaltation that came over me of being in the same small sanctuary where Saint Faustina worshiped God, received Holy Communion, and now ultimately lies in eternal rest was a blessing I cannot describe. After mentally returning to the earthly realm of the room in which we now stood, I started to look around. One of the things I noticed was that every square inch of the walls from floor to ceiling were covered with crutches, leg braces, letters, and votive offerings of hearts, lungs, and other body parts sent in as thank-you gifts from people from all over the world who had undergone miraculous medical cures as a result of their devotion to this humble Polish nun.

When our turn finally came, I knelt down with Theresa in front of the altar over which the relics of Saint Faustina now rest. Above her, fastened to the wall, is the painting of *Jesus the Merciful* which she as a young nun saw in her vision. Painted on a scroll on the bottom of the picture are the Polish words *JEZU UFAM TOBIE* ... "Jesus, I trust you." After a few short prayers, I removed from a bag a small handful of religious medals with pictures of Faustina on them, which I'd earlier purchased at the shrine's gift shop, and placed them on a small glass reliquary on the right side of the altar that contained a few actual finger bones of the saint. I then picked them up, placed them reverently back into the bag, and bent over and kissed the precious relics. I could have lingered there for hours, but a long line of fellow pilgrims were waiting.

In her diary, Sister Mary Faustina Kowalska spoke of God wanting her to share with all of mankind three things. The first (from the Vatican's Saint Faustina Web site) was to remind the world of the truth of our faith revealed in the Holy Scripture about the merciful love of God toward every human being. Secondly, He wanted her to impress upon mankind God's mercy for the whole world and particularly for sinners, through the practice of new forms of devotion to the Divine Mercy as presented by the Lord Jesus. Lastly, He asked her to help initiate an apostolic movement of the Divine Mercy that undertakes the task of proclaiming and entreating God's mercy for the world and strives for Christian perfection.

Through her visions and her encounters with the divine, Sister Faustina shared with the world the good news of God's Divine Mercy and of the boundlessness of His infinite love that's available to all of mankind. All you have to do is place your life in His hands and say, "Jesus, I trust you!"

With few exceptions, however, both back then and to this very day, the world has almost universally chosen to ignore her message. On that day as well, my own personnel, rapid descent from a pinnacle of transcendent benevolence and love downward into the utter bowels of depravity would be just a short half hour drive away.

The Stolen Child
Come away, O human child!
To the waters and the wild
With a fairy, hand in hand,
For the world's more full of weeping than
you can understand.

–W. B. YEATS

About thirty miles west of Krakow is the Polish farming town of Oswiecim. Surrounded by her bountiful orchards, her checker-board fields of wheat and barley shining golden in the early autumn sunlight, with her green pastures full of fat and contented grazing dairy cows, this quiet and rather unassuming rural community would today look to anyone who might not know of her dark past like any of the other tens of thousands of rural towns that dot the landscape all over Eastern Europe.

But Oswiecim *is* different! Because of the geographically unfortunate accident of being located at the confluence of several European railroad lines in the early years of World War Two, the town will for all of eternity bear the stigma of her horrific past. Until the last human being walking on this planet breathes his or her last breath, and even until the sun burns its last precious molecule of hydrogen fuel, Oswiecim, or, as she is better known by her German name, Auschwitz, will forever be the symbol of everything that is most vile and wretched and evil that could ever possibly spew forth from the mind of man.

The death camps at Auschwitz were conceived and ultimately built to be nazi Germany's answer to "The Jewish Question." Between the years 1940 when the first prisoner arrived and 1945, when the camps were finally liberated by Allied forces, an estimated 1.1 million to 3 million European Jews, Polish nationals, Gypsies, homosexuals, Jehovah's Witnesses, and all other "undesirables" were put to death with a cold-hearted, mechanical precision never before seen in history.

According to tourist officials, up to half a million people visit the Auschwitz/Birkenau complex every year. Their motivations range anywhere from doing a pilgrimage in which to honor fallen relatives and friends, all the way to simple curiosity. I wanted to visit the camps for two reasons: First, I firmly believe that we as humans, living on this otherwise amazing planet, must occasionally *look into the void*. That is, we must confront the darker sides of our natures, to see firsthand all that we, as a species, are capable of perpetrating on our fellows, and, ultimately, to attempt to grasp—with the simple goal: to control—the raw and savage power of hate.

Be it at Tiananmen Square in central Beijing, Ground Zero in New York City, the epicenter of the nuclear bomb blast in Nagasaki, the killing fields of Cambodia, or anywhere else that intentional slaughter of innocent people has taken place, it must never be forgotten that those who planned the murders, those who carried out the orders, and even worse, those who stood by in silence while holocaust all happened around them were, for all intents and purposes, us!

Until near the very last moment of my visit, my second reason for wanting to visit the death camps was a little harder to pin down. I was somehow being drawn to the place. I seem to remember hearing about Auschwitz for as long as I've been alive, and I'm not sure how or why. I don't recall my parents or relatives talking to me about it. I don't recall hearing my teachers telling me about it. It was something I just knew about and that one day I'd have to visit.

One of the first things we did upon our arrival was to get something to eat at the cafeteria. As Andy and I ate our hamburgers and French fries, I noticed that my wife was just sitting there looking at her food. When I asked her what was wrong, she simply said she had no appetite. It would be my first indication that she wasn't all that thrilled about visiting this terrible place.

The camp that we were now exploring was known simply as Auschwitz One, and was the first death camp to be put into operation by the nazis. Andy told us that what we were looking at (with the exception of the trees and garbage cans and tourist signs) was pretty much the same way it looked in its heyday. The former barracks have all been converted into one big museum with each of the barracks highlighting a different aspect of the repugnance. Exhibits, display cases, and various other relics filled each room. Photographs, too graphic and horrific to describe, of life in Auschwitz covered every square inch of wall.

The stories of the medical experiments, the tortures, the poison "showers," and the cremation ovens—those ruthless, all-pervasive, and consuming ovens—are all part of modern mankind's collective consciousness, and so I won't say any more about them. I'll just mention a few of my more graphic memories. I recall one glass-enclosed room with thousands of victims' suitcases stacked behind the clear wall, all of them labeled with the names of various countries: United States, Canada, Australia, Israel. Andy told us that prisoners were told they were being deported to the various countries written on their luggage as a further way of deceiving them into believing they were going to be safe. Of course it was just a sick ploy by the nazi bastards; the country names were really just code words for the various death camps. Another room contained thousands of pairs of eyeglasses, another shoes, another hair combs.

I remember being especially sickened by what I read as part of a collection of letters in a display case. According to the English translations next to the letters, they were contracts and receipts for the purchase of human hair collected from the victims. Human hair! The letters proved, at least to me, just how ingrained and accepting the German people were of what was going on in these death camps. Their money-hungry titans of industry even figured out a way to make money from this most base of German innovations!

After about two hours more of exploring the various other different sights to be seen at the camp, Theresa told me—in no uncertain terms—that she'd had enough; Auschwitz was making her physically sick. I told her OK, but on our way out, two other exhibits caught my eye. Sensitive to her discomfort, I came very close to just passing them by. But for reasons that to this very day I can't explain (and my hands tremble as I write these words), I found myself uncontrollably drawn into their presence. And what I saw and what I felt afterward drove the horror of Auschwitz home personally for me, forever.

We next traveled a couple of miles up a back country road to Auschwitz Two, better known by its colloquial name, Birkenau. When we pulled into the parking lot, Theresa—and for very good reasons—refused to get out of the car. And if the truth were to be told, for just a second I kicked around the idea of cancelling the whole thing. But I couldn't; after what I read and experienced at the museum at Auschwitz One, my visit to these depraved factories of death had now become sort of a family pilgrimage.

Theresa's instincts were correct: As difficult as the brutality of Auschwitz One was for any rational human being to comprehend, Birkenau would be completely unfathomable! Although most of the camp is in ruins, the size of this aversive and repugnant patch of ground dwarfs its smaller partner in crime. In no uncertain terms, Birkenau was enormous!

At its peak, the death camp had over three hundred barracks in which to temporarily house the prisoners, four football-field-sized "bath-houses" in which the prisoners were gassed and murdered, and enough crematoria capacity to handle up to twenty thousand corpses per day. As we stood there amid the rotting ruins of the former barracks, Andy told me that even though it also had crematoriums and was responsible for its own ghastly share of killing, the Auschwitz One we had just visited was mainly reserved for political prisoners, medical experiments, and other non-Jewish undesirables. Even though a prisoner's life at Auschwitz One was a living hell, there was a chance that he might just be able to live another day.

Birkenau on the other hand, was strictly an all-consuming killing monster. The camp's sole reason for existence was the complete, abject, systematic extermination and efficient disposal of every Jew, Pole, Gypsy, and—in the words of Adolf Hitler himself— "worthless eaters" on the European continent. Period! In just one of the hundreds of shocking examples of this madness, nazi records indicate that between May and July of 1944, the methodical butchers of Birkenau exterminated over 438,000 Hungarian Jews! That is 438,000 innocent men, women, and children in just three months!

Andy and I explored a couple of the camp's still-standing barracks. Where the grass hasn't completely covered the ground, you can still see flecks of bone and ash from the ovens that had been emptied of their precious remains and then dumped between the buildings as human landfill. He said that the whole property is like one giant unmarked graveyard. We then started to walk to the rear of the camp to look at what is left of the infamous "death showers" and giant crematorium complexes, but about halfway there I asked Andy to stop. I, too, simply couldn't take it anymore.

Just before walking out the main gate, however, we lingered for a few minutes at the grassy banks where the unloading docks were located next to the incoming railroad tracks. From the pictures I'd just seen on the walls of the museum at Auschwitz One, I could imagine in my mind's eye the millions of victims as they once stood on this very spot. The poor souls were cold, filthy, exhausted, hungry, and scared to death; most had no idea they were just hours away from violent and inhumane slaughter at the hands of their nazi, rat-bastard captors. The silence of the place chilled me to the marrow of my bones. As we walked out the front gate and got into the car, even though it wasn't on the list, Andy said he had one more place he wanted to show us.

> This was how it was with travel: one city gives you gifts, another
> robs you. One gives you the heart's affections, the other destroys
> your soul. Cities and countries are as alive, as feeling, as fickle and
> uncertain as people. Their degrees of love and devotion are as vary-
> ing as with any human relation. Just as one is good, another is bad.
>
> –ROMAN PAYNE, *CITIES AND COUNTRIES*

As we drove back into Krakow, Andy exited from the expressway into one of the outer industrial sections of the city. Thinking we were just passing through the area on our way to crossing over the river, I just sat there in the front passenger seat taking it all in and said nothing. But as we drove along, it became obvious that this was not yet to be the case. Looking quizically toward Andy, he just smiled and said once again that he wanted to show us something before we headed back into town. Knowing from experience that most guides usually know what they're doing, I left it in his able hands.

The area we were driving through looked no different to me than any other industrial district in any other city in the world: block after city block of rather nondescript, ugly, postmodern-style concrete-and-steel factory buildings, grimy smokestacks, and run-down, windowless warehouses. As we drove silently along, Andy suddenly pulled the car over to the curb and stopped. "There it is," he said as he rolled down his window and pointed towards a building across the street. Looking like any other building both up and down the street from it, I, at first wondered what he could be talking about. And then I saw written in big block letters the sign above the entrance to the factory compound: Fabryka Oskara Schindlera.

For people who saw the movie *Schindler's List*, the story of this otherwise nondescript factory building and this extraordinary man will already be familiar. For all others who may not be familiar with the work of Oscar Schindler, the story needs to be told and told and told, over and over again.

As the son of Roman Catholic parents, Oscar Schindler's early life was rather uneventful. Growing up in what is now the Czech Republic, his primary occupation was that of an industrial salesman. After being bankrupted by the Great Depression, he worked—until being arrested as a spy—for German military intelligence. Upon his release from jail, he joined the nazi Party. Always the businessman and opportunist, when Germany invaded Poland in 1939, he took advantage of his party membership and purchased an abandoned enamelware factory, the very factory we now stood in front of.

To provide workers for his new business, he made use of what he in the beginning, thought would be a seemingly unlimited supply of Jewish slave laborers. In no time, with his keen and incisive business skills, combined with the constant aid of a Jewish accountant named Itzhak Stern, Oscar Schindler prospered and became a multimillionaire. But as the war lingered on, and as he became painfully aware of the vile, demented horror of all that was going on in the world around him, something extraordinarily wonderful happened in the mind of Oscar Schindler. Or, more likely, as those workers who were most closest to him firmly believed were his original intentions from the very beginning of his enterprise, this profit-driven?, nazi(?) capitalist? began accomplishing his plan.

For reasons known only to himself, he made it his mission to do everything in his power to save the lives of the twelve hundred-plus Jewish workers in his employment. Under the very weak pretence of needing to preserve his workforce for the German war effort—and at great risk to his own life—Oscar Schindler cajoled, lied, bribed, and eventually spent his entire fortune to induce local government officials and nazi SS officers to turn a blind eye to the workers' existence. Relentless roundup after roundup for the sole purpose of exterminating every last Jew in all of occupied Europe dogged their daily existence, and when the slaughter finally came to an end, Oscar Schindler was financially wiped out. But he'd pulled off a miracle. In this ugly, characterless, factory building, Oscar Schindler managed to hide and keep every single one of his workers from the death camps.

There is a trend in society today, an offensively selfish and somewhat slothful trend, to advance the moral, intellectual, or financial standing of certain self-centered individuals by minimizing and/or bastardizing the accomplishments of those people who have come before them. Both modern-day university scholars speaking from the safety of their ivory-towered citadels as well as pissant armchair cynics pontificating in our newspaper editorial pages have tried their damnedest in recent years to belittle and denigrate the accomplishments of Oscar Schindler. They babble on and on, using vague and demeaning words like *greedy capitalist, amoral slave owner, nazi operative, financial opportunist,* or even *egotistical hedonist* to try to explain away his motives for saving his Jewish workers. But as much as these naysayers may try to spout their meaningless drivel, the facts say it all!

Literally, in the very shadows of the death camps at Auschwitz and Birkenau, Oscar Schindler was all that existed between living and annihilation for more than 1,200 Jews. He was an ordinary man, full of flaws—just like the rest of us—who under the worst possible circumstances, accomplished extraordinary things ... things matched by *NO ONE* at the time. The numbers tell it all. The Jewish population of Poland in the years prior to World War Two was 3.5 million. As I write the first draft of this chapter in 2013, there are only an estimated 3,500 Jews left in *all* of Poland. But thanks to this amazing man, the surviving Schindler Jews and their descendants throughout the world number well over 7,000!

When we returned back to the car, I thanked Andy for his thoughtful effort to help restore my faith in humanity.

Postscript

> Every journey is personal. Every journey is spiritual. You can't
> compare them, can't replace, can't repeat. You can bring
> back the memories but they only bring tears to your eyes.

> —Riana Ambarsari

While we were still at Auschwitz One, and just after Theresa asked if we could end our visit, I saw a sign and an arrow that had the word *Poland* written on it and pointing to yet another former barracks structure. I asked Andy about it, and he said that several of the former barracks had additionally been converted into memorial centers for a few of the more victimized European nations such as Poland, Hungary, Yugoslavia, and Russia. Even though I'd just told Theresa we'd be leaving, my curiosity got the best of me, so I asked her if I could check it out. She said OK but said she'd wait outside. Andy and I went in.

There were more of the same pictures and artifacts of the Holocaust that we'd seen all over the camp. However, in the back of the building on several shelves were large ledgers. These books contained of the names of the Polish citizens murdered by the Nazis at this camp. With great trepidation, I slowly leafed through the pages, and I looked at the names. And there I saw what I was hoping not to see. There, in the perfect penmanship of some sad and long-forgotten file clerk, were listed fifteen victims whose last names were Orzechowski (my father's father's family name) and twenty-one slaughtered souls whose last names were Karpinski (my father's mother's family name).

I found myself completely struck dumb. I never in a million years would have guessed that I would have seen either of these two family names. Although there are the occasional family rumors to the contrary, for at least four generations back in time, all my family has been Roman Catholic. Andy, seeing my bewilderment, offered me a possible explanation.

He said that most people in the world looked upon the nazi genocide during the Second World War as strictly a Jewish genocide. But he reminded me that up to a million non-Jewish Poles were murdered as well. Andy said again that Auschwitz One's primary function was the incarceration, torture, and execution of political prisoners and medical experiments. Therefore, even though it was possible that various lines of the old-world family could have been both Jewish and non-Jewish, it was very likely that the family's connection with this horrible place had its origin as political prisoners or freedom fighters—or Gypsies, or Jehovah's Witnesses, or homosexuals.

For some diabolical reason, the German SS troops who ran this camp felt that political prisoners better deserved execution with a bullet(s). On our way out of the camp, the last thing Andy showed me was the section of prison wall where most of these political executions took place. And this would be my most enduring memory of my visit to Auschwitz: that of standing next to and actually touching the numerous bullet holes that scarred the stone and brick. Just looking at the wall, I was overwhelmed by the realization that each wretched bullet hole upon bullet hole upon bullet hole constituted another extinguished life.

I remember how it took me several seconds—especially now with the likely context of there being a potential family link!—before finally mustering the courage to touch the wall. In spite of the early afternoon summer's heat, there was a clamminess, a cruel coldness to the touch. I swear I could feel the stones throb and almost wince with pain as I brushed my hand across its pitted and tormented surface. It was as if the long-ago fallen wanted their anguish to be felt and for their collective voice to be heard, to tell me their stories, their hopes and dreams, their passions and fears.

Resting my head upon the stone, I whispered to them: "Hello Cousins! Hello Uncles! Hello Great-Great-Grandfathers! Please speak to me!" I knew from deep within the very core of my being that these long ago fallen were begging me to tell their story to the world, but the distances between us in both space and time were just too great. I tried and I tried, but to no avail; all I could hear were the chirping of the birds in the tree behind the wall, the far off sound of a farmer's tractor, and the pounding sound of my broken heart.

Huu Tiep Lake and Her Sacred Relic

CHAPTER 4

A Vietnam Journey

⟨⟨⟨

Deep As The Sea
War
has wounded me
invisible wound
deep as the sea
invisible wound
deep as the sea

—Lamont Steptoe

Untitled
On this land
Where each blade of grass is a human hair
Each foot of soil is human flesh
Where it rains blood
Hails bones
Life must flower

—Ngo Vinh Long

Just west of the capital city of Hanoi, in the small suburban village of Ngoc Ha, there is a small and rather unassuming body of water called Huu Tiep Lake. Actually, the term *lake* is a grand overstatement: a large, grungy, algae-choked pond would be a more correct description of this diminutive square-sided body of water. As just another of hundreds of similar ponds and scenic lakes that dot this region of northern Vietnam, Huu Tiep Lake would have existed in relative obscurity, as it has since time immemorial, were it not for one titanic event that literally rocked its world. In 1972, just a couple of nights after Christmas, a crippled American B-52 bomber plummeted headlong from the sky and crashed directly into the lake.

Vietnam. VIETNAM!!! Just the sound of the word conjures up so very many confusing memories for me. At a time that today seems like so long ago, an entire generation of my fellow American countrymen and women grew up hearing about a faraway place called Vietnam and about a divisive and contentious war that was being waged there. For most teenagers and young adults of that frantic period in our nation's history—if they were lucky—the war was mostly an abstraction, a rallying cry, a cause, or just something to rebel against. For many, depending how they felt about the whole damn mess (or, as it often turned out, how their parents, their high school sociology teacher, or their college political science professor told them they *should* feel), the war would influence their political ideology and worldviews for the rest of their life.

For others who were not so fortunate, for those men and women who actually had to leave home and do battle either on the land or on the sea or in the air, the war was a palpable and bewildering nightmare (as all wars are!) that would shatter forever their lives and the lives of those who knew and loved them (as all wars do!).

And it was in this latter context that my wife Theresa and I found ourselves on a Vietnam Airlines Airbus 320 jet airliner flying from Hong Kong to Hanoi, the capital city of a modern-day united Vietnam. I was returning after more than thirty years later to a land and a people that I had spent the majority of my fleeting youth helping to bomb into oblivion and a country I never intimately got a chance to ever know. This was because I spent almost all of my four-year military commitment in the Weapon's Department on board a U.S. Navy aircraft carrier, cruising the Tonkin Gulf and the South China Sea, helping to facilitate the assembling, handling, loading, and arming of bombs and rockets and missiles and then sending these weapons off to war on F-4 Phantom fighter jets. For the sake of simplicity (because there was much, much more involved that I still do battle with), I was a veteran of the Vietnam War who never spent any serious time in Vietnam.

Subconsciously, there was to be more involved in the visit, sort of an undefined yearning for something that at the time I couldn't wrap my mind around. I was a little bit afraid, but I knew the trip was something I had to do; and I had to do it now. I'd waited long enough. Consciously, however, as I planned the journey, I really had only three goals in mind: I wanted to be a guest at the world-famous Hotel Metropole, I wanted to make a day trip up into the mountains to see the Perfume Pagoda complex, and I wanted to make a pilgrimage to Huu Tiep Lake. I had absolutely no interest in visiting Ho Chi Minh's mausoleum, the infamous Hanoi Hilton, the old French Quarter, or any of the hundreds and hundreds of ubiquitous embroidery shops that clog the tourist sites.

My wanting to stay at the world-famous Hotel Metropole was to be a tribute to one of my most-admired authors, and fellow traveler, William Somerset Maugham, who said it was one of the best hotels in the Far East. And indeed it was. The hotel even honored Mr. Maugham with his own memorial library and reading room. My homage to this great writer (I've also stayed at the same places he's stayed in London, Singapore, Cambodia, and Bangkok) is part of my never ending earthly quest to be "one" with the great people and events of history and to discover and savor the inspiring metaphysical concept known as *authenticity of place*. For me, to stand in and to smell and to touch places where great men and women and deeds have actually taken place is a thrill I'll never tire of.

Located right in the heart of Hanoi, the Metropole (now part of the Sofitel Hotel chain) is a grand old dame of French Colonial architecture. And even if Mr. Maugham had not graced her with his presence, I probably would have picked her as a place to stay anyway. Her comfort and service were everything the guidebooks claimed. We dined in her sumptuous Vietnamese-style Spices Garden restaurant and splurged one evening as well on genuine French cuisine in her Le Club bar. The hotel is also the birthplace of the Graham Greene martini, and in honor of this other great world traveler, I drank a couple of these sweet martini-like drinks. The only problem I had with my stay at the Metropole was that I found out later that the hotel's otherwise great reputation had been soiled (in my opinion anyway) by being home to the infamous "Hanoi Jane" Fonda during her traitorous visit to the then country of North Vietnam in 1973.

The day trip to the Perfume Pagoda was suggested to me by a fellow traveling friend. Located about fifty miles southwest of Hanoi, the trip by private car was a great way to see some of rural Vietnam's fantastic countryside and her stunningly gorgeous Marble Mountains. As an additional bonus, our trip took place during the rice harvest. Being farmers ourselves, we found it interesting as well to see how other farmers brought in the hard-earned fruits of their labor. All of the rice harvesting and drying was still being done with hand tools. Most of the heavy hauling was accomplished by huge, lumbering water buffalo.

The Perfume Pagoda temple complex turned out to be truly awe-inspiring, especially when you consider that pious Buddhist pilgrims have been journeying to this holy place for over five hundred years. (Some Buddhist scholars feel that the region has been a place of worship for over two thousand years and that the great Buddha in person had rested there!) The pagodas themselves are inaccessible by any way except a one-hour boat ride down the Yen Vi River. By hundreds of years of tradition, the boats are all paddled by teenage girls. Our girl was named Rita, and she was very shy. The boat voyage was hot and exhausting. We passed by fisherman working the shallow river with nets and electrical prods. The views of the surrounding mountains as we floated down the river were breathtaking. Most Buddhists spend four or more days at the temple complex because there are so many pagodas and shrines to visit at the site. We had time for visiting only the main attraction, the ancient Huong Tich Grotto. This holy cave is on the top of Perfume Mount and can only be reached by a long hike on a well-traveled mountain trail or, conveniently, by a handy cable car ride. Owing to our short schedule and to the fact that a three-mile, all-uphill hike in the unrelentingly humid tropical heat of midday just didn't sound all that appealing to me or our guide, we decided to take the cable car. When we reached the top, we had to walk down several hundreds of steps into the holy cave.

The place was alive with the solemn worship of a thousand devout Buddhist pilgrims. The damp musty air of the cave mixed with the smell of burning butter oil lamps, bundles of intoxicating incense, and of cheap tobacco, and its coolness brought a welcome relief from the oppressive heat. Our guide told us that the place is so adored and venerated that the Vietnamese believe that the whole mountain complex is Buddha's heaven. Seeing and feeling the stunning natural beauty and splendor of that holy place, I could understand why. It's not often I get this urge, but I think someday I'd like to return to the Perfume Pagoda and spend the required four days there.

My reason for wanting to visit Huu Tiep Lake was somewhat more personal. Even though I can't recall the exact moment in time that I got the notion to do so, it seems that for nearly all of my adult life I've wanted to visit this hallowed place. I do remember, sometime during my sailor days, seeing a newspaper or magazine picture of the downed B-52 bomber resting nose-down in that North Vietnamese lake. There was something about that haunting image that just seemed to linger on the edge of my conscious thought, and without trying to sound too corny or melodramatic about the whole thing, something told me that this was where I would discover (for lack of a better term) a profound truth.

That afternoon, as Theresa, I and our guide were being driven from the hotel to the crash site, I couldn't help but marvel at how well the people of this former Communist country had so exuberantly embraced capitalism. Driving along the beautiful tree-lined streets and passing by a park complex that surrounded the huge concrete mausoleum containing the body of North Vietnamese leader and war hero, Ho Chi Minh, all I could think of to myself was how the poor old Communist was probably turning over in his grave at the sight of all of this detestable consumerism.

Everywhere there were new Ford Taurus's, Lincoln Town Cars, Chrysler minivans, Citroën compacts, Mercedes city buses, Toyota pickups, and Daewoo dump trucks. I recalled to myself how, a couple of days before, as we were driving from the airport to downtown Hanoi, I commented to my wife that you could barely see the countryside because of the deluge of billboards that lined the new four-lane highway and all blaring out the now universal message of flagrant consumerism: Coca-Cola (Coca-Cola is everywhere in the world!), Pepsi, Marlboro cigarettes, Gucci handbags, Cottonelle toilet paper, Chevy cars, Quaker oatmeal, Ralph Lauren suits, Nestlé's chocolate drink, Canon cameras, and on and on.

I also made an observation that baffled me at first. As seemingly important to me as the visit to this relic of a long-ago war may have been, it apparently wasn't that big a deal to either our young guide or the even younger limo driver. Our guide (whose name, quite ironically, was Charlie) said that he'd only been there once before in his life, and that was on a field trip as an elementary school student. The driver had never even heard of it! On our drive to the crash site, they had to stop three times in order to ask local residents where the place was. This apparent indifference—or at least what I interpreted as indifference—for what I felt should have been a monumental part of their country's history shortly turned out to be the first of many revelations I would have on this personal pilgrimage.

After an hour of zigging and zagging through narrow boulevards clogged with buses, motorcycles, bicycles, and even the occasional donkey cart, we turned down an alley that was barely wide enough for a motorbike, much less our Mercedes sedan. But the driver insisted on giving it a try. And sure enough, after about five minutes of honking and hollering at oncoming bicycles and motor scooters, the alley opened up into a large, sunny square. After letting us and our guide out, he drove over to the far side of the square, parked the car, leaned back, and began to take a nap.

The city square in which we now stood was about three hundred feet on each side. It was rimmed by a cracked and crumbling concrete sidewalk. Private homes, storefronts, and several small restaurants and many bars lined every square inch of the plaza. All had seen better days. Probably intended originally as a memorial park to the glory of their nation's defenders during the great *American War*, the place was now dirty and run-down and, in the subdued late-afternoon light, seemed somewhat forbidding. In the center of the whole thing was Huu Tiep Lake. And still visible in the center of this slimy, green, algae-clogged pond, protruded the remains of the crashed B-52 bomber. This was what I had come to see. While Charlie took a seat at one of the cafés, Theresa and I walked around the square.

I thought I'd be a little nervous about walking along unescorted, being an American and all, but as we strolled around the square, we were only greeted with smiles and the occasional giggle from everyone who walked past us. Even the couples who sat at the restaurants' outdoor tables looked up and graciously nodded and smiled as we passed by. My first guess was that they didn't very often see that many Westerners who had gone through all the effort to visit their little area of the world. And this indeed may have been the case. But as I ambled on, I soon realized that there may have been a little bit more to their cordiality. It was like they all had a shared secret that they weren't going to tell me, but rather were going to make me discover on my own.

As we walked around the lake, I made sure to photograph the fallen bomber from every angle. There wasn't too much of the old aircraft left, and very likely, in another ten years it will be gone completely. There was a part of the fuselage still sticking up as well as a small chunk of wing. Most prominent was a completely intact landing gear. The sight looked nothing like the picture I had in my memory. On the far side of the lake there was a large rusting plaque that said: "At 22:00 hours on December 27, 1972, the capital's anti-aircraft forces shot down this B-52 in the area of Ngoc Ha Village."

And before we knew it, we were back around again to where our guide was enjoying a cup of tea. He offered to buy us both a cup as well. Theresa, glad to get off her feet and rest, accepted. Finding myself in the throes of reflectivity (as I am prone to do in these situations), I politely declined and said I'd like to go for another walk around the lake by myself. The guide, looking quite serious, said that he understood.

I slowly walked one more time back around the pond to the spot where the crippled B-52 was closest to the railing. As I stood there looking at this relic of a long-ago war, I became for the moment completely oblivious of the crowds of evening strollers and patrons enjoying their respite from the tropical heat of the day. I found myself drifting back in time to that December evening and wondering what the scene may have been on that dreadful night when this behemoth fell from the sky. What awful and deadly carnage there must have been! To have a disabled jet over 160 feet long with a wingspan of over 185 feet, probably still filled with tons of flaming fuel, fall from the sky in the very neighborhood where I now stood must have been the physical manifestation of hell on earth. Besides the stricken American aircrew of the bomber itself, the death toll on the ground must have been staggering.

It was at this moment as well that I discovered the "secret" the kind hearted people all around me were graciously keeping to themselves. Standing there on that hallowed ground, I could now see the whole story, and discern for myself the complete experience from both sides. Although it haunted me somewhat at first, this realization, once it all sank in to my confused consciousness, quite surprisingly gave me a little bit of comfort.

The evening strollers and diners who went about their lives all around me may indeed have been genuinely welcoming to me with their smiles and friendly greetings; for the Vietnamese people, generous hospitality toward strangers was, I was learning, an integral part of their cultural heritage. But these lovely people all had one other bit of profound knowledge in common with one another: they knew they were the winners. They were able to accept the sad memory of this place because they knew that the destruction of this *American instrument of death* that was rusting away in the water in front of us ultimately helped lead to their country's victory.

There was also something else that came to me in that moment: the people of Vietnam have moved on. A new generation, represented by both Charlie and our driver, has taken on the role of leadership. The Vietnam War to them is now just something they learned about in school or, much to their tedium, something their grandparents occasionally ramble on about. The only battle the young people of Vietnam have to fight today is that of the pursuit of prosperity and happiness. And, who knows, perhaps that's how it should be.

The peach trees once again grow on the blood-soaked battlefield of Gettysburg. Although its floor is still pockmarked by the explosions of over six million World War One artillery shells, the forest has reclaimed the hillsides surrounding the tragic French village of Verdun. Today, coral reefs thrive and teem with every form of marine life imaginable as the unwearied sea gnaws away at the steel hulls of the ships resting on the sea bed of Pearl Harbor. And so it will be that someday, Huu Tiep Lake will swallow up the remainder of its most sacred charge, becoming then just another algae-clogged pond. This, in my mind, is perhaps the greatest lesson the story of Huu Tiep Lake can offer our world.

The next day of our stay in Vietnam was Sunday. We were scheduled to leave later that evening to fly down to Bangkok and then push onward to another destination. And being a Sunday, one of our great pleasures while traveling this glorious planet is to attend Catholic Mass. When asked the night before, our hotel concierge told us that the nearest Catholic Church was only a "romantic and very lovely" twenty-minute walk away. From past experience, we got a good forty-five-minute head start that morning because we nearly always get lost in these impromptu excursions. (We did.)

The walk was indeed lovely. The route took us past several parks where, like people all over the world on beautiful holiday mornings, were out enjoying the coolness of the new day. A good part of the stroll took us around a large—and this time genuine—lake whose shoreline was dotted with many Buddhist temples and pagodas. I'd had no idea that old Hanoi would be such an attractive city.

As Theresa and I walked along on that beautiful morning, I remembered the night before being a little disappointed when the hotel concierge first told me that the nearest church was St. Joseph Cathedral. My personal feeling has nearly always been that the very grandeur and hugeness and magnificence that makes a church a *cathedral* sometimes interferes with my ability to experience real closeness to God during the holy Mass. There is often too much ostentation, too many distractions. I much prefer, whenever possible, to attend services at the local parish church.

But this disconnect would not be the case on this morning at St. Joseph Cathedral. As a matter of fact, it turned out that the good men of Hanoi would bless me with the absolute greatest spiritual gift that a former enemy could ever bestow upon a former foe.

We arrived at St. Joseph's about ten minutes before Mass began. One of the first differences we noted from our own churches at home was that the congregation was divided by sex: women on one side of the aisle, men on the other. We saw that throughout the congregation were scattered a few Western-looking (probably French) couples, and they chose to sit beside each other. Not sure what to do, but mostly not wanting to stand out any more than we already were, Theresa went to the right side with the women, and I went to the left with the men.

This was not the first time I'd attended Mass with people from Vietnam.

In the early summer of 1975, about two weeks after the falls of Phnom Penh (the capital of Cambodia) and of Saigon (the capital city of then South Vietnam), and the subsequent forced end to the Vietnam War, our ship had pulled into the naval base at Subic Bay in the Philippines. We needed to disembark a hundred or so South Vietnamese refugees who'd managed to make their way out into the Tonkin Gulf and onto our ship. We needed also to do some much-needed repairs and to prepare the ship for an upcoming cruise to Australia. On one of the Sundays we were in port, my friend Grover and I got together with several of our Filipino friends and rented a small boat to take us out to a private island located just off the coast owned by an American expatriate named Mr. Blaine.

Mr. Blaine [I have intentionally modified his actual name] was the quintessential beachcomber/beach bum. He was a large-bellied, solid, slightly balding man with a weathered red face and a gentle, devious smile. He'd long ago gone native, wearing only a well-worn grass skirt and white crew-necked T-shirt. His tattooed arms were the size of a fireman's battering ram. A retired naval chief who, as a very young sailor, came ashore on the Philippines with General MacArthur, Mr. Blaine (who insisted on being called Mr. Blaine) had created quite a nice little hospitality enterprise on his private island. His well-stocked bar and his quarter mile of immaculate, white, sandy beach were the envy of the whole Seventh Fleet. And other than the costs of the food and drinks at his bar, or of paying rent for one of the few overnight bungalow units he let out to welcomed guests, the unlimited use of the whole of his facilities were free to all navy men and their guests.

That is, of course, if he liked the looks of you. Mr. Blaine made it a point to personally meet every arriving boat to his island—boats that, with the supreme authority granted to all master chiefs in the U.S. Navy, he covetously controlled. If for any reason he didn't like the look of you or anyone in your party, he sent you packing back to the mainland. And nobody ever dared mess with Mr. Blaine!

No one I met was ever able to exactly say what his specific criteria were for approval or disapproval. Mr. Blaine had two large, powerful telescopes, one behind the bar for when he worked and one in his private lounging area, both of which overlooked his gorgeous beach and the surrounding coconut groves. And he spent a lot of time with his eye glued to these scopes. My personal feeling is that he was quite the voyeur and liked to watch all of the young sailors (mostly) and/or their young Filipino girlfriends as they swam and occasionally cavorted naked on his beach.

On this particular Sunday, after having passed Mr. Blaine's muster, we all set up our picnic fare on a far corner of the beach. Grover and I had both been here before, and all was fine, except that we noticed that about two hundred yards offshore toward the leeward side of the island was a large, single-masted, wooden sailboat. When we asked our Filipino friends what it was, no one seemed to know. And for a while, that was that. For the next couple of hours we ate our freshly killed delicious barbecued chicken and drank ... and drank ... and drank large quantities of local San Miguel beer, and we gave the vessel anchored off our beach no more thought.

But as the late morning slipped into mid-afternoon and it became unbearably hot, Grover and I went for a swim in the becalmed ocean. I wore a bikini-style bathing suit. Grover wore his white cotton, navy issue boxers, which when wet, very likely pleased Mr. Blaine! We floated and swam around in the immaculately clean and clear and refreshing sea like we had not a care in the world. All the while, however, as we had not paid a bit of attention to what we were doing, we'd unconsciously floated out to within about twenty yards of the sailing boat we'd seen earlier. Aroused by our proximity to the vessel, or because of the lack of inhibition resulting from our state of mild intoxication, we both decided it would be fun to swim out to the craft and to see what it was.

As we swam closer, we could see that a large crowd of people had gathered onto the port side of the boat to watch our approach. When we'd finally managed to swim up alongside the ship, mildly exhausted, I managed to holler out a friendly, "Hello."

One of the men answered back, "Are you boys Americans?" Grover answered that we were both American sailors. Upon hearing this, several men on board the ship laid down a wooden ladder over the side so that we could climb aboard. Thankful for the opportunity to rest, first I and then Grover climbed onto the boat.

My first impression of the ship was that it looked in pretty rough shape. The vessel was a motor/sailor about fifty feet long with a beam of about twenty feet. The partially rolled-up sail tied at the base of the solitary mast looked to be torn to shreds. There were planks missing from the deck and railings, and a couple of the hatchway doors looked to have been violently ripped from their hinges. Most strikingly of all, it looked like the crew and passengers had been living on board the boat for a long time. Makeshift shelters of shipping crates and wooden pallets covered with canvas and plastic sheets consumed the whole aft two-thirds of the main deck upon which we now stood. As we stood there taking it all in, more and more people began emerging from below decks, including an elderly woman with a pot of tea.

After we introduced ourselves to what I took to be their leader/spokesman, he told us the following sad—gut-wrenchingly sad!—story. It turned out that Grover and I were on a Vietnamese refugee boat, one of thousands that were dispersed throughout the length and breadth of the South China Sea. I remembered seeing several vessels similar to this ragged one over the course of the last few weeks as we sailed about the Gulf of Tonkin trying to tie up the "loose ends" of what had been a long and controversial war.

The group of people with whom we now shared tea had managed to escape from the North Vietnamese Communist forces just one week before the fall of the South Vietnamese government. They left their homeland with fifty-two people aboard. Only one of their members was a fisherman who, it turned out, knew very little about sailing ships and nothing at all about being out on the open ocean. All of the rest of them were government workers and bureaucrats who were completely ignorant about operating a boat. Hoping to make it to Indonesia, they had motored due east by following the sunrise. When they ran out of fuel, they were only about fifty miles from where they had started. From that point on, they were at the mercy of the wind and their sail. That is, until the sail had been obliterated to mere shreds in a violent gale.

After enduring twenty-four days of violent seas, two severe squalls, incessant heat, and interminable hunger, they managed to be spotted by a U.S. naval destroyer, who then towed them and their boat to where they were now anchored. Along the way they suffered the loss of four of their young children and two of their elderly grandparents.

And to make matters devastatingly worse, when they had finally arrived to safety, they were denied landing rights by the Philippine government. They were now in a state of political limbo and being cared for temporarily by the U.S. Navy. The rumor circulating on board the fragile ship was that they were soon to be forced back out to sea in order to try to reach Hong Kong. I shuddered with profound sorrow as they told me of their wretched plight.

Before we knew it, however, an hour had passed. Worried that our friends might think us drowned, Grover and I told our guests that we had to start swimming back to shore. Even though we were quite sad-dened by their woefully wretched story, we knew there was nothing we could do to help them. But just as we were getting ready to jump over-board, we saw that a small navy boat was motoring toward us. Curious as to what they were going to do, Grover and I decided to stick around a few more minutes.

The crew of the launch was bringing these *boat people* several hundred pounds of food and personal sanitary supplies. They also had on board a U.S. Navy Catholic chaplain. After helping with the unloading and stow-age of the cargo, we were invited by these lovely people to attend Mass with them. Being Catholic, I jumped at the opportunity. Grover, an admitted agnostic, said he'd like to stick around just to have the experience. Before beginning the Mass, a tiny, serious-faced, elderly lady passenger brought us a couple of towels to wrap around our nearly naked waists and to cover our bare shoulders.

The entire group of passengers and the crew of the navy launch all gathered on the bow for the service. The priest, even though he was an American, spoke the Mass in French (mostly) with a little bit of English (probably for my and Grover's sake). As we stood on that ragged and tired little life-giving ark anchored off of that island paradise, in the by now late-afternoon sunshine, with a steady, gentle sea breeze providing us all with a much-needed cooling respite from the sweltering heat, I looked at the faces of the men and women around me who had so generously invited us to join them in their private worship.

All I saw in their eyes were looks of pitiful sorrow for the loss of their families and their homes, the looks of the terror and horror of war as well as that of their grueling ocean crossing, and their looks of bewilderment and complete disbelief that the world was once again going to throw them into the howling infinite. The weight of the unbearable pain and anxiousness and inexorable fear of their unknown futures hung in the stifling hot and humid equatorial air like an all-consuming nightmare. But through all of their trials and hardships, these brave people still took the time to take pause from their shattered lives and thank God for what they had left and to simply ask him to grant them a safe passage. After partaking of the holy Host, I prayed along with them all as the priest gave them his final blessing. And for just a moment, a look of divine serenity won out over their formerly troubled expressions. For now at least, these kind and much-troubled people had peace. Looking over toward Grover, I saw that he, too, had bowed his head, as if he was praying with us.

Back in Hanoi, even though the church was packed, I managed to find a small space in a crowded pew next to the center aisle. Although I'm not normally too self-conscious in these situations, I did, indeed, stick out like a sore thumb. Even though I am just shy of six feet tall, I seemed to tower over every man around me. Plus they were all rather formally dressed in their long-sleeved white cotton shirts and their neatly pressed black trousers. I, however, although not looking too much like an utter slob, had on a plain old pair of blue jeans and a light blue striped short-sleeved shirt. It was also at this moment that I realized with great horror that my big, bold navy tattoos on my bear-like arms could not have been more obvious. There was no way in the world that I could not be taken for anything but an American ex-serviceman … an older ex-serviceman, at that. I could only hope for the best.

And for a brief moment, I had a flashback to that tired and battered little wooden sailboat anchored in the unrelenting equatorial heat off of the Philippine coast upon which I'd last shared a Holy Communion with people from Vietnam. There were really only two differences between then and now: The first was that the peoples of the former countries of South Vietnam and North Vietnam were now one united nation. Second, and probably most important of all, was that instead of the men and women around me having the look in their eyes of horror and despair, all of them seemed to exude a confidence and contentment. For now, and hopefully forever, they were at peace. And when this last thought crossed my mind, I closed my eyes for a second and smiled. I truly was happy for them!

The holy Mass was, of course, this time entirely in Vietnamese. But one of the nice things about the Catholic Liturgy is that it is basically the same all over the world. My wife and I carry with us from our home church a small prayer book that has all of the readings for the upcoming months, so we usually can get the basics of the Mass, no matter what the language or where we are. When we separated, however, Theresa took the book with her, so all I could do is stand there attentively as the Gospels were read and the priest gave his homily. I have no idea what his sermon was about, but he spoke it with a great deal of passion and just a little bit of brimstone.

We all then knelt as the priest recited the Liturgy to prepare the bread and wine for the Eucharist. When he finished, the congregation stood, and we all recited the Lord's Prayer. I quietly whispered along in English. For non-Catholics who may not be familiar with the order of holy Mass, the Lord's Prayer is then followed by an injunction for participants in the service to experience and then go forth and spread the good news of Jesus' love as well as his wish for eternal peace. It is called the Sign of Peace, and the words for the ritual are as follows:

The Priest: Lord Jesus Christ, you said to your apostles: I leave you my peace, my peace I give you. Look not on our sins, but on the faith of your Church, and grant us the peace and unity of your kingdom where you live forever and ever.

The Congregation: Amen.

Priest: The Peace of the Lord be with you always.

Congregation: And also with you.

Priest: Let us offer each other a sign of peace.

At this time, depending on local custom, everyone offers up to their near neighbors a gesture of loving friendship and peace. And throughout my travels of the world I've seen this gesture be as hollow as an indifferent glance from a neighbor (San Francisco), to a slightly formal bow (Kuala Lumpur), to a firm handshake (most places), to an enthusiastic, hearty handshake that nearly rips your arm off (Usa River, Tanzania), all the way to exuberant, potentially life-threatening bear hugs (Tonga).

Throughout the whole of the Mass I had been just a trifle anxious about this moment. My worry wasn't a fear or dread or some weird foreboding of an impending doom. It was more like the awareness of the intense sadness of it all: of my sadness, of the sadness of the people around me, and of the sadness of all of our fellow generation for having to have suffered with that terrible war. Standing in that packed-to-overflowing house of God, the whole awful mess became crystal clear to me: the war was Catholics bombing Catholics and Catholics defending their homeland against Catholics who were determined to annihilate them from the face of the earth. What a terrible realization!

I don't know if the good men of Hanoi sensed this in me as I stood in that holy sanctuary that day, or if it was just in their nature to be gracious to strangers. I would like to think that maybe, just maybe, they felt the same way as well! Because, when the time came to exchange gestures of peace, I found myself being physically and emotionally overwhelmed by their outpouring of affection. For at least the next two minutes I was bowed to, hugged, shook hands with, and had "Peace be with you" wished upon me by probably fifty different people. The men were nearly knocking themselves over in an attempt to share their peace with me.

I am not one to be overly emotional in situations such as these; it's just not in my nature. But this time, as I looked into the eyes of my fellow Christians as they wished me peace, I could not hold back the God-given power of that moment. The tears that welled up in my eyes that morning were those of joy and of an overpowering relief, the blessed relief of having had a great and crushing burden lifted from my soul. The good men of Vietnam, either on purpose or not, on that glorious morning had given me a sincere and heartfelt gift that I did not expect, but one that I was hoping beyond all hopes to someday receive.

They gave me the precious gift of forgiveness.

Moses' Spring - - Or So I Thought!

CHAPTER 5

Mt. Nebo and Moses' Spring

—∞∞∞—

Then Moses climbed Mount Nebo from the plains of Moab to
the top of Pisgah, across from Jericho. There the Lord showed
him the whole land—from Gilead to Dan, all of Naphtali, the
territory of Ephraim and Manasseh, all the land of Judah as far as
the Mediterranean Sea, the Negev and the whole region from the
Valley of Jericho, the City of Palms, as far as Zoar. Then the Lord
said to him, "This is the land I promised on oath to Abraham,
Isaac and Jacob when I said, 'I will give it to your descendants.' I
have let you see it with your eyes, but you will not cross over into it."

–Deuteronomy: 1-4 NIV

High above the valley of the Dead Sea, in what is today known officially
as the Hashemite Kingdom of Jordan, stands the summit of Mount Nebo.
Located about twenty miles south of the capital city of Amman, it was from
the top of this barren and desolate mountain that the Lord allowed the
prophet Moses to look out upon the land that He had promised to give to
the ancient Israelites. The irony, of course, of this poignant event was that
this rock-strewn and lonely mountaintop would be as close as Moses would
ever get to the promised Land of Milk and Honey. Tradition also contends
that it was here (in a 'secret' location) that God Himself buried the great
prophet.

At a height of 2680 feet above sea level, Mt. Nebo is the highest point in the Moabite Mountain Range in this region of the Middle East. For almost two thousand years—and probably much, much longer—pilgrims and travelers, kings and paupers, priests and popes, have journeyed to this sacred spot to be *one* with the great prophet. It was on this clear and sweltering hot summer day that we, too, now stood taking in the sacred history of this grand panorama.

And what a glorious view it was! To the north and west was the valley of the sacred Jordan River, a lush green sliver of agricultural land boxed in by a forbidding desert wasteland. A little bit to the right of the view you could see where the river emptied into the Dead Sea; this was the spot where John the Baptist baptized Jesus Christ. There also, on the Israeli side of the river, was the city of Jericho, one of the oldest continually inhabited settlements in the world. Directly below us, and filling up the entire valley to the south, lies the great Dead Sea. On the western shore of this vast inland body of water you could just make out the community of Qumran, home to the mysterious Dead Sea Scrolls caves. Farther south, somewhere buried beneath the salt plain, rests the doomed cities of Sodom and Gomorrah. We were told by our tour guide that on certain days of the year when the haze rising up from the Dead Sea wasn't so thick, that if you look straight ahead to the west toward the hills of Judea you can actually see the white rooftops of the holy city of Jerusalem! Wow! As Theresa continued her explorations, all I could do at that moment was stand there in reverent awe.

Seeing that I was most likely having one of those over-whelming moments of rapturous bliss that travelers/pilgrims tend to fall prey to when the sights and sounds and smells and the sensations of history all come together, the tour guide left me alone so that I could take it all in. (He actually just wanted to go off and smoke a cigarette.) As I stood there on that very spot where Moses himself had stood over three thousand years ago and looked out over the Promised Land, I could imagine the profound heartbreak that burned within the bosom of the great prophet when almighty God told him he would be denied this final prize. After forty years of leading his beloved Israelites through the desert of Sinai, the sorrow of it all must have killed the great man.

When the guide returned, he told us a little bit about the church that was behind us and of the ground upon which we now stood. Like a lot of the major sights of pilgrimage in the Near East, he told us that this one was owned by the Catholic Franciscans. When I asked him how it came about that this was the case, he told us that the tradition goes all the way back to the time when St. Francis himself visited the Holy Land. Despite the fact that he was a devout Moslem, the caliph in charge of this region of ancient Palestine at the time was so impressed by the piety of the great saint that he assigned Francis and his Order the rights for all perpetuity to protect both the Old and New Testament holy sites. In all of my trips to the area, I'd not heard that before.

Besides the viewing area we just left, there were a few other interesting sights to see. Nearby was a tree planted in the year 2000 that commemorated the visit of the late pope, John Paul II. There was also a large bronze sculpture of a snake coiled around the top of a high pole. Our guide told us it was a representation of the talisman that Moses had his sculptors create to help protect the frightened Israelites from dying from the bites of the relentless desert snakes that kept harassing them. I read somewhere that Christian scholars say that the symbol prefigured the Cross as mankind's future path to salvation. As a medical person, I was struck by the similarity of the sculpture to the modern-day symbol of the Staff of Aesculapius painted on every doctor's office, hospital door, veterinary clinic, and ambulance in America.

We then went inside the large church that the Franciscans had built over the historical Third and Fourth century basilicas that previously existed on the site. Inside, besides the modern chapel, there were many well-preserved ancient ruins from these former churches. In several rooms, still visible on the floors, were beautiful ancient mosaic panels of hunting scenes, birds, gazelles, bulls, and flowers. Many had Greek inscriptions.

The highlight of the visit to this church, however, was our stop at a simple altar built out of large limestone blocks located to the right of the main chapel. This simple altar sits on top of the exact spot where ancient tradition says lies the grave of the prophet Moses himself. So important is this little piece of the world that John Paul II made this spot one of his first stops during his initial pilgrimage of the new millennium. On the bare stone altar is a framed picture of the pontiff kneeling in prayer. I, too, then took several minutes to pray along with the Holy Father upon that sacred rock in solemn reverence and with grateful heart for the man who softened the heart of the Pharaoh of Egypt, who delivered from bondage people of Israel, and who stood in the physical presence of God here on earth.

> In the spring of AD 384, the wandering monastic, Egeria, while on a pilgrimage to the Holy Land region of Mt. Nebo, met with several monks in the Duyun Musa Valley. The holy men of that desert wasteland region showed her a local spring that miraculously seemed to flow forth from a large rock. In her journal Egeria wrote, "Between the church and the monk's cells was a plentiful water source which indeed bubbled up from a huge rock, beautifully clear and with an excellent taste." The monks told her that this was the very site that the prophet Moses brought forth water from the rock to slake the thirst of the wandering children of Israel.
>
> -M.L. McClure, *The Journey of Egeria*

After we exited the church, I took another moment to once again walk back to the overlook area in order to just one more time take in the overwhelming immenseness of this sacred place. As we all turned to walk away, I then noticed that directly off toward the east, that in the distance, there was a small strip of vegetation starting from about halfway up a small valley that began as a point, and then expanded slightly more and more as it went downhill. The green strip seemed absurdly out of place in the endless barren rock and desert wasteland from which it had originated. The guide told us that this was the Uyun Musa Valley, the valley of Moses' spring. He then said there was a good road that led down the mountainside to the spring and that it would be a shame for us to miss such an important and historical place in the life of the great prophet.

Getting back into our rental car, we then drove down the winding and twisting dusty gravel road into the upper end of the valley, thankful that the brakes on our Citroën sedan worked well. We were in the burning heart of the ancient wilderness of Moab. With the exception of the small strip of land watered by the spring, there was not a tree or bush or sign of life anywhere; just inexorable heat, dirt, sand, rocks, and nothingness! After about twenty minutes of non-stop downhill, we saw a small sign in both Arabic and English pointing down toward an even smaller dirt road that said, *Moses' Spring.*

We drove to the end of the small road and parked our car under a large sycamore tree and the ruins of an old church. We then got out of the car and walked over to the edge of a deep ravine, where I assumed the spring was located. It was god-awful hot. Not a cloud was in the sky, and the sun beat down without mercy. But being bound and determined and moderately enthralled by the sanctity of the place, I started to walk down the bolder-strewn trail (it was more like a sheep path than a trail). As I started down, I noticed Theresa hesitating at the trail rim. She said that the wall of the gully seemed a little bit steep and that it was not only dangerous to climb down into the hole, but that in this scorching early afternoon heat, it was quite stupid as well. She also reminded me of the deadly vipers that the ancient Israelites had had to contend with in this area. Taking more time to survey the area than I did, she thought that she could get as good a view of the spring from farther up the ravine.

Still determined to satisfy my need to be once again "one" with the great prophet, I fibbed somewhat and told her that it didn't look from where I stood like such a bad hike down into the ravine. As for the snakes, I told her that it was probably too hot for them to be out. (That was wishful thinking on my part; as a veterinarian I knew that if any vipers were down there in this gully, we would soon be interacting.) But this was Moses' Spring! I could not come this close and not make the attempt!

When she brought up the point of not having any water to drink for the walk, I pointed out to her that I'd be able to refresh myself with the cool, sweet water that gushed forth from the rock when I got down there. Theresa, after all of our years of traveling together, knowing of my insistence upon authenticity of place and of having to become "one" with every darned thing I encounter on these journeys, said she'd wait for me up top. She knew that no force on earth would keep me from clambering down that hole.

And clamber I did. The hike down into the gorge turned into a small challenge. As I've done so many times before in situations like this, I momentarily had to stop and ask myself, "Richard, what in the heck are you doing? This is stupid!" But no sooner had this thought crossed my mind than just down the ravine I caught sight of a large growth of vegetation springing from the center of a small twenty-foot-high rock face. And bubbling down from beneath this tangled mass of small trees, bushes, and green slime, was flowing water.

I'd found Moses' Spring!

Either out of pious zeal or just plain exhilaration, the remainder of the hike down the gorge went quickly without a single slip or fall. I'd even forgotten all about the snakes, the scorching desert sun, or even how I was going to climb back up out of this gully. All I could think about was that spring, that cherished life-saving trickle of cool, clean water. And as I hiked closer and closer to the small pool of water that had formed around the base of the cliff face, I looked up slightly and saw that it indeed emanated from a crack near the top of the huge rock.

Before doing anything else, however, I backed up a few feet and scanned the rim of the ravine to see if I could see Theresa. I wanted to let her know that I was safe. When at last I caught sight of her, I could see that she had walked farther up the rim of the gorge and was now looking down at me. I also noticed she was frantically waving both of her hands. I also thought that I could almost make out a tiny cry. Seeing that she saw me, I waved back. And satisfied that she knew I was safe, I walked back up to the pool and knelt down beside the flowing water.

For several minutes while refreshing myself in the coolness of the shade of that rock face, I did nothing but just take in the sanctitude of the moment. Here I was, about to drink from the same water well that the God of Abraham, Isaac, and Jacob had personally provided the ancient Israelites. Looking up at the water flowing from out of a crack in the rock, I could almost imagine the weary and bone-thirsty prophet, following God's direct command, striking the rock with his staff and calling for the precious water to flow forth. Oh! What a blessed event it must have been.

> God must love stupid people because he
> sure made an awful lot of them!
>
> —AUTHOR UNKNOWN

Returning back into the moment, I got ready to carry out what I'd come to do. The air was full of the grass-like smell of wet vegetation, the only sound in my ears the gurgle of flowing water. I then reached down and, cupping my hands, scooped up as much as I could of the cool and sweet water and reverently drank of the precious liquid several times. Just like Egeria said, the water was "beautifully clear and with an excellent taste." From that moment, in every possible sense of my existence, I was now truly "one" with the great Moses. Or so I thought.

I stayed for a few minutes more to savor again the raw beauty and divine sacredness of that holy place. When I finally stood up, the reality of my situation once again kicked in. I still had the arduous task of climbing back up out of the ravine. But, either because of the natural high of my recent ecstatic experience or simply because sometimes it's just easier to clamber up a steep bank than to descend, the trek back didn't seem all that bad. When I reached the rim of the gully, I saw Theresa several hundred feet up the rim trail to the left. She was waving for me to walk up to her. I started to do so, and when I got about halfway to where she was standing, I looked down into the now much shallower ravine, and my heart sank.

Somewhat disillusioned by what I saw, I still kept walking toward Theresa. As I approached her, and before I could even get a word out, she asked me (quite bluntly), "You didn't drink from that stream, did you?" Meekly, I told her that I did.

Somewhat frustrated—and perhaps a little worried as well—she then said, "Gosh darn it Richard (not here exact words), didn't you see me waving my hands trying to get you to stop?" I told her that I did, but that I thought she was just trying to congratulate me for making it down the ravine wall safely. After telling her this, she calmed down somewhat and gave me that look of resignation and disbelief that I've seen a hundred times before when I'd gotten myself into situations like this. "I knew it," she said. "I *just knew* you were going to drink from that little stream. All I was trying to do was to stop you before you went and got yourself sick!" And then she pointed toward the place that I had already seen on my walk toward her.

Directly in front of us was a ten-foot-wide and thirty-foot-long area of flat rock over which a small stream flowed from right to left and then disappeared down into a big crack. I had been out of sight down in the ravine just below this drop-off point. What I had thought was the spring appearing miraculously from the front of the rock face was actually the water flowing down from the crack at the left end of the stream we now stood in front of.

This realization, in and of itself, wasn't all that bad. What made it all somewhat nauseating, however, was that the flat section of the stream appeared to have served, probably since time immemorial, as a convenient watering hole for all of the nomadic farm animals of the region. The reason we knew that animals frequented the waterway was because upon closer examination of the streambed, we saw that not only had the nomadic goats, sheep, camels, donkeys, and probably the occasional cow used it to drink from, it looked like most of them had decided to answer the call of nature and to defecate into the water as well! Yuck!

As a veterinarian, I knew full well what nasty parasites and other critters could be found in those piles of feces and what terrible diseases I had now potentially exposed myself to. By drinking the water that had flowed over and under and through all of that crap, I'd essentially mainlined the microbes into my system. Theresa was quite concerned, but after a couple of seconds thought, I found myself not worrying at all, not even a little bit.

We then walked to our right about a hundred feet to where we could see the stream was flowing from the hillside. There, from between two large boulders, the water gushed forth in all of its precious glory. And stuck into the ground to the right of the water source was a small sign, again written in both Arabic script and English with the words, *Ayun Musa*. We had finally, officially, found Moses' Spring.

I knelt down next to the flowing water, took several big drinks, and once again for the second time that afternoon became "one" with the great prophet. And Theresa, knowing with complete confidence that unless some miniature goat or lamb or camel had somehow managed to squeeze itself up into the hole under the gigantic mountain in front of us and pooped, the water emanating from this holy place would be perfectly safe to drink. She, too, would now be "one" with the great Moses.

Walking back to the car, Theresa began to worry again and to question me on the possible illnesses that I potentially might have to face. I told her very plainly that I wasn't all that worried. But being the realist of the two of us (and also knowing she would have to ultimately bear the burden of my care), she continued to press me for a few of the symptoms that she should look for just in case I did get sick. I mentioned to her mostly we'd see intestinal signs such as profuse vomiting and/or diarrhea. In a worst-case scenario we'd see possible longer-term diseases of liver, brain, or lung parasites. Pretty scary stuff, if you take the time to think about it.

But I reminded her of something that I knew with absolute certainty in my heart of hearts and that she knew also but had probably just forgotten: that the mother of Jesus, the most-holy Virgin Mary, always protects her children while on pilgrimage, and that I had not a thing in the world to worry about.

I refreshed her memory of the time we were on a pilgrimage to Assisi, Italy, to visit the shrine of the great St. Francis, and of how, when we hit a cinder block in the road in the middle of a crowded, darkened, highway tunnel, that the Good Mother miraculously held back the traffic until we could exit the tunnel and safely pull over to the side of the road. Of how, when returning from a visit to Mt. Sinai in the middle of nowhere in the Egyptian desert, she softened the heart of a well-armed, overly-zealous security policeman who was hell-bent on arresting us for not having our passports. Or of the time we were on a pilgrimage to her shrine in Medugorie, that she, in the guise of our limo driver, a former Croatian mine-removal expert, first alerted me and then safely guided me back from a Bosnian minefield I'd innocently stepped into in order to go pee.

"No," I told my dear wife, "I wasn't worried a bit."

As I write this recollection of this journey some five years later, I have not suffered so much as a burp, at least with regards to this adventure.

The Navel of the World

CHAPTER 6

Navel of the World

———⁂———

...To be away from home and yet to feel at home anywhere; to
see the world, to be at the very center of the world, and yet to
be unseen of the world, such are some of the minor pleasures
of those independent, intense and impartial spirits, who
do not lend themselves easily to linguistic definitions. The
observer is a prince enjoying his incognito wherever he goes.

—CHARLES BAUDELAIRE

FOR READERS WHOSE RECOLLECTION OF our world's geography isn't too great,
the speck of land known as Easter Island is located in the absolute middle
of nowhere in the Southern Pacific Ocean. Situated halfway between Tahiti
and South America, this tiny triangle-shaped island, just seven miles wide
and fourteen miles long, has the distinction of being one of the loneliest,
most isolated places on earth. In ancient Polynesian folklore, Easter Island
was historically known as Te Pito o te Henua, the "Navel of the World."

As a die-hard traveler ever since my youthful—and now very distant—four-
year stint with the U.S. Navy, and on all of my hundreds of journeys ever
since here and there all over the face of this planet, I often find myself in
the stimulating company of other dedicated and obsessive travelers. One
of the many things I've noticed most about these fellow wanderers who I've

been blessed to meet in the assorted far-flung corners of the world is this: those who travel, often tend to travel a lot.

Like me, they are rarely content to ever sit still in one place for any length of time. Sure, when asked by well-meaning people who don't quite understand why we continue to do what we do, we'll instinctively say that it's always a pleasure to return home, to eat safe and familiar foods, to rest our weary bones, to reconnect with our roots, and to once more take shelter and find sanctuary within the bosom of our own kith and kin. Indeed, all of the truly great travelers in history have had a home base they could return to; that's what separates a traveler from a simple vagabond or bum.

But something always happens to us when we attempt to grasp this bit of imagined contentment: All will be fine for a week; it might be fine for two weeks; or if we're lucky, maybe for a month. Soon, however, as we finally begin to settle in from a journey, our inborn feelings of wanderlust start to creep into our consciousness. We stout-heartedly attempt to do the best we can to hide our disquietude by working harder (all of these travels must be paid for somehow!), by applying ourselves to our readings or studies, or maybe even by watching reruns on *The Travel Channel* or perusing the Sunday *New York Times* travel section. All, of course, is to no avail.

In several of his travel books and essays the late British writer, Bruce Chatwin (quoting the French poet Baudelaire), even had a name for this malady: *l'horreur du domicile*, the horror of the home. For the lucky ones, this urge to leave behind the loving embrace of home and return at once to the road is just a minor annoyance, a distraction, an uncomfortable itch on the bottom of their feet that he or she can co-exist with until an opportunity arises to get away; for most habitual travelers, however, the urge is a choking, a stifling, a—for lack of a better term—a horror! It's like there exists a great disconnect with life, and living, that has unmercifully engulfed us, and we fear we'll lose our lives—or worse!, our souls—if we can't achieve an escape.

However, in speaking with my fellow travelers, most of us also have a purpose or a story that they'll use to rationalize to non-travelers the reason(s) why they can never sit still. For example, as I write this book, I tell people that a life's goal of mine is to do pilgrimage to the final resting places of the twelve apostles of Jesus. A good deal of the people that I meet are out in the world to accumulate platitudes: that is, to climb the highest climbable mountains, to see every bird or beast on the planet, to journey to the most southern or northern cities, to experience the most number of countries or to trek to the most isolated islands. Many are on pilgrimage, either to sacred holy sites, famous battlefields, or the graves of famous people. I've even met a man who collects United Nations World Heritage Sites.

There are only two ways to get to Easter Island. The first way is how the original Polynesians settlers arrived around sixteen hundred years ago: by a treacherous, ungodly long sea voyage on the brutal and unforgiving southern ocean. Or, as we did, travelers can arrive on a regularly sched-uled jet airline. Lan Chile Airlines flies two times a week on what their pilots refer to as a "milk run." That is, they fly from their home base at Santiago, Chile, to Easter Island and then onward to the warm and sensu-ous island of Tahiti. There, they fill the plane back up with fuel and pas-sengers and return to Easter Island and then onward again to Santiago. I rode on the Tahiti-to–Easter Island leg, round trip. The flight to from Tahiti to Easter Island leaves about midnight and then flies eastward over the vast cold emptiness of the southern Pacific Ocean. I remember waking up after a short and fitful nap and looking out the window of the 737 jet into an incredibly bright moonlit night and just seeing nothing, nothing, and more of nothing. And then, just as the sun was starting to rise, the three volcanic peaks, whose co-joining lava flows helped form this far-off patch of land, started to come into view. There was something primeval about how, as we got closer and closer, the morning fog came rolling down the sides of the island's largest peak like some forbidden elixir overflow-ing the rim of a kettle of witches' brew. "Ain't that something?" I said as I pointed out the view to Theresa. It really was one of those travel moments that often leave me breathless. "Wow!"

But the magical spell was somewhat broken as we continued our flight over the island. Because of the prevailing westerly winds, our pilot had to overshoot the island, fly a few miles eastward over the sea, and then turn back around to make our approach to land. This gave me a chance to really scope out the whole island. It was at this time that I noticed the strangest thing: there, on this island—an island literally in the middle of nowhere—was this gigantic almost 10,000-foot-long runway! The thing was almost as long as the island was wide! (A tour guide would later tell us that the runway was built by the United States government's NASA as a potential emergency landing site for the space shuttle.)

The history of Easter Island is as shrouded in mystery as are the silent stone statues that famously dot her landscape. The original settlers were probably Polynesians who most likely arrived from the Marquesas Islands. Why the islanders began their cult of carving and of worshiping the giant stone statues is still a complete mystery. Archaeologists know *how* the moai (the Polynesian name for the statues) were carved because to this very day, you can still see the statues in various stages of doneness in the quarry on the side of the volcanic peak, Rano Raraku. When I first had a close-up look the moai, the poor stone creatures reminded me of giant Frankenstein's. Even more incredibly, while standing on the sides of the volcano, you can look across the wide, sloping plain down toward the seashore and see hundreds of moai—some weighing up to seventy-five tons!—dotting the landscape like so many titanic children's toys.

And this leads to the most important question of all: why, after all of their wondrously hard, ball-busting labor and toiling, did the builders of the moai suddenly stop their obsession with these stone behemoths? To an objective outside observer, it looks to all the world like just one day, all of the islanders woke up and said to their selves, "To hell with it all," and just laid down their tools and ropes.

Theories abound: everything from some kind of epidemic, all the way to intertribal warfare. One very real possibility for the halt to the cult of the moai, and a theory strongly touted by modern-day social scientists, is the breakdown of the island's infrastructure and environment. In their frenzied and fanatical zeal to create the behemoth statues and the monumental bases that supported them, the inhabitants of this isolated and fragile speck of real estate neglected to care for their food crops or to tend to their domesticated animals. They also literally cut down every single tree on the island. By 1877, the population of the island had decreased to eighty-one men and thirty women.

> The metaphor is so obvious. Easter Island isolated in the Pacific
> Ocean—once the island got into trouble, there was no way
> they could get free. There was no other people from whom
> they could get help. In the same way that we on Planet Earth,
> if we ruin our own [world], we won't be able to get help.

—Jared Diamond

But things are beginning to turn around for the good people of Easter Island. The moai, who nearly made possible the extinction of this isolated race of people, are now the islanders' biggest source of prosperity. Tourism and development on this tiny island are at an all-time high. Also, the recent addition of Easter Island to the United Nation's list of World Heritage Sites will only help insure this trend to prosperity, and to further serious scholarship and conservation of these invaluable treasures. And I'm glad. Easter Island is an astounding and wondrously magical place.

Speaking of magical places, Theresa and I discovered in our three days of traveling on every road on the island and exploring every nook and cranny of her barren shoreline, a place that at the time was not yet mentioned in any tour book I'd seen. I don't think this place even has a name. Because we had plenty of time to spare until the Lan Chile Airlines jet made its return from Santiago, we ended up making three visits to the place. With the exception of our first visit to the spot, we saw no other tourist.

It was on this first visit that as we were driving the coast road that circles a portion of the island, we saw on the north shore a small tour bus parked at the end of a long rugged driveway leading down to the sea. Curious about what was going on, we decided to check the situation out. After parking our car and walking down to where the people were, we noticed that a small group was sitting inside a small stone circle with their hands resting on something big and round. They appeared to be praying or to be chanting some sort of mantra. What appeared to be the group's driver stood off to the side. Again, because I was curious, I quietly walked over to where he was and asked him what was going on.

The man turned out to be quite a sociable chap. He told us he had absolutely no idea what it was his group of tourists was doing. All he could say was that they were New Zealanders and that they were a strange bunch. I asked him if he himself was from Easter Island. He said that he was, and that with the exception of a short stint in the Chilean Navy, he'd never left the island.

After watching the people for a few more minutes, he and I came to the conclusion that they appeared to be worshiping or perhaps somehow paying homage to something in the center of the square. When I asked him what that big round thing was that they appeared to be revering, he smiled and told me that it was a very powerful and magic stone. And then for a second, he was very quiet. He appeared to be having second thoughts about what he had just said. When he started to speak again, his voice assumed a reverence he hadn't had earlier.

"I'm not sure what these silly people are doing," he said, "but the *Old Ones* say that this important stone is the *actual* navel of the entire world. All of the earth they say came forth from this stone; it has existed since the earth was born, and it will exist long after the world is consumed by the void!" Of course, I hung on his every word and found what he had to say quite fascinating. When he finished, we then continued our small talk: where Theresa and I were from and what we did for a living and how we were enjoying our visit. When his group finished whatever it was they were doing, we shook hands and said good-bye. I thanked him again for the great story.

When the group and their driver finally drove away, we walked over to the small stone square. And sure enough, exactly in the center of it was a large—about three feet in diameter—perfectly round grayish pink rock, just like my new friend had told me. Indeed, it looked just like a giant "outie" belly button! Of course, as is my wont to ceaselessly and obsessively become "one" with every possible experience on this planet, I sat down on one of the rock seats that surrounded the stone, and I slowly laid both of my hands on it. Smoothed by hundreds of centuries of people caressing the stone with their bare hands, it looked to me like no other rock I'd so far seen on the island. It was also surprisingly warm to my touch. But other than the feeling of being part of the cosmic parade of all of those who have sat in this very spot before me, I can't claim any universal insights bestowed upon me by the rock.

I got up and let Theresa sit down. I then walked slightly up the hill away from the stone in order to take a few pictures of the place. It was at this time, as I was alone with my thoughts, that I was struck by the rugged beauty and splendor of this sacred place. The ocean waves crashed unrelentingly against the rough and rocky shoreline as they have since the day this lonesome landmass first burst forth from the sea floor millions of years ago. The cool, sea mist–filled air that I now breathed was un-fouled by any other living creature on earth. The whole scene before me was one of primordial newness, as if the world was indeed being born over and over again before my very eyes. As I found myself overcome by the majesty of it all, I thanked *my* God for giving me this chance to glance into this glory of His creation.

After walking back down the small knob, I rejoined Theresa. But before walking to the rented car, I walked back over, sat back down, and laid my hands once again on the rock. I said no prayer or mantra to this legendary "navel of the world," but I thanked it for helping to make this enchanting moment possible for me.

I mentioned earlier that nearly all of the travelers who come to Easter Island are on a singular quest to see the island's famous stone statues. Before flying out on our last night on the island, I met one exception to this rule. We were sitting in the small lounge area at the airport that served as a restaurant, waiting room, ticket counter and bar. The place to me had the same feel and atmosphere as the interplanetary barroom scene from the first Star Wars movie. But instead of bizarre looking aliens, this room was filled with every possible race and nationality of people on the planet.

All of us had just been entertained by having the chance to watch the local airport officials chase a pack of the island's feral dogs off of the gigantic runway so that the jet from Chile could safely land. With their racing jeeps and whooping and hollering, it was like watching something from out of the Wild West. As we were waiting for the plane to discharge a new group of visitors and then to refuel, a rather short and stocky, slightly balding older man sat down next to me and introduced himself. After some small talk of the sort that travelers always indulge in, he told me his name was Johannes and that he was a retired lawyer from Israel. When I asked him what he thought about the moai, he gave me a bit of a smile and said that even though he gave the statues the obligatory cursory look-over, they were not the main reason he had come to Easter Island.

Excluding many New Age notions such as extraterrestrial intervention and the strange lost continent of Atlantis theories, Easter Island is still a place shrouded in great mystery. Although modern genetics has partially proven that the natives of the island are of Polynesian descent, no one can say how these intrepid and courageous sailors managed to end up on that speck of rock over two thousand miles from anywhere else. Though archeologists think they know how the great moai were carved, no one can say absolutely how these multi-ton giants were moved around the island and then lifted-up onto the seaside platforms. Or for what reason! But what Johannes told me about Easter Island still to this very day just fascinates the daylights out of me.

Long before his retirement, he said he'd been captivated by the written alphabet of the ancient Easter Islanders. The reason for his obsession was the uncanny similarity of the Rongorongo script (the name given by linguists for the Easter Island writing) and the three-thousand-year-old symbols being then recently excavated by archaeologists in a newly discovered Indus River valley civilization on the subcontinent of India. As we waited in that bar in that little airport so very far away, he showed me a few of his notes, and indeed, when placed side by side, over one hundred of the figures matched identically. Johannes had come to Easter Island to try to get a feel for how the two writing systems, separated by six thousand miles and by the landmasses of Australia, Indonesia, and Southeast Asia, could have come to be.

After half an hour of listening to his fantastic theories, we had to say good-bye. We promised to keep in touch, swapped e-mail addresses, but— as is often the case with wanderers—we never got around to talking again.

POSTSCRIPT

> Just as the navel is found at the center of a human being, so the
> land of Israel is found at the center of the world ... Jerusalem is
> at the center of the land of Israel, the temple is at the center of
> Jerusalem, the Holy of Holies is at the center of the temple, the ark
> is at the center of the Holy of Holies, and the Foundation Stone is
> in front of the ark, [and this] spot is the foundation of the world.

–MIDRASH TANHUMA, KEDOSHIM 10

During a pilgrimage to the holy city of Jerusalem, we lucked out in two ways: Our first bit of luck was that right at the beginning we met an enterprising Palestinian guide named Hamad who, because Jerusalem was his home, knew all there was to know about the city and her surrounding holy and historical sites. Better yet, he knew how to gain us unchallenged entrance into many of the otherwise restricted places. His expertise at getting us past the various guardians and doorkeepers turned out to be especially valuable during our visit to the city's Temple Mount. The other blessing that graced our visit to Jerusalem was that we had managed to visit the city at one of her rare moments of peace; it was a tenuous and uneasy peace, and our visit was not without incident, but it was a peace none the less.

When newspapers or travel magazines want to show their readers a picture of the old city of Jerusalem the image they show us first is often that of her Temple Mount region with its majestic, golden-domed, Dome of the Rock mosque dominating the scene. They call this roughly rectangular-shaped, thirty-seven acre chunk of land the *Temple Mount* because this is where King Solomon built the First Jewish Temple to honor God and to house the biblical Ark of the Covenant. After the building's destruction under Nebuchadnezzar, a second temple was constructed by King Cyrus of Persia; this building, in turn, was then greatly expanded upon by King Herod the Great. Five hundred years after the Romans destroyed this second temple during the first Jewish-Roman War, Abd al-Malik, Caliph of the new Islamic Empire, built the present-day mosque the world now recognizes as the Dome of the Rock.

There are many places on the planet that are said to be "navels of the world" and they lay claim to the title by using one (or both) of the common meanings of the word *navel*. Some cultures use the word to mean *the center*, as in the phrase *center of the world*. Examples of this are the Oracle of Delphi on the mainland of Greece, Mount Kailash in Tibet, and the entire Inca city of Cuzco in Peru. I should mention also that the written Chinese characters for the modern day nation of Red China, Zhong guo, mean *middle* and *kingdom,* in the rather egotistical belief that China was/is the center of all the civilized world.

Other places use the word literally to mean a human navel, the belly button, the place where an umbilical cord at one time connected a mother to her child. These are places on the planet (or in mythology) where various peoples believe that the earth and heaven were at one time—or still are—attached to each other. The navel stone on Easter Island is an example of this meaning.

But there exists one place, however, that claims both meanings of the word: The Foundation Stone of Jerusalem. Profoundly sacred to both Judaism and Islam (and to a lesser degree, Christianity), the stone itself is a large outcrop of limestone rock and was at one time in Jerusalem's ancient past the former summit of the biblical Mount Moriah. It is over this rock that the present-day Dome of the Rock mosque now stands. Jewish tradition says that it was here upon the Foundation Stone that God formed the first man, Adam. Biblical tradition states that Father Abraham passed God's supreme test of loyalty by being willing to sacrifice his son, Isaac, upon the rock. (In one of those great debates that always clouds the Divine Word, Islamic tradition says rather that it was actually Isaac's step-brother, Ishmael, who Abraham had offered up for sacrifice.) Moslems to this day also believe that it was from upon this rock that the Prophet Mohammed ascended on his Night Journey to heaven.

The Foundation Stone's most important significance, however, and what makes it the most holy place on the planet for all of Judaism is that the rock is believed to be the location of the Holy of the Holies of the former Temples in Jerusalem. Also, at least during the first Temple period, the biblical Ark of the Covenant once sat upon the stone as well.

The sanctity of the entire thirty-seven acre Temple Mount area is still so overwhelmingly sacred that there are signs posted at its entrance gates forbidding Orthodox Jews not to enter the region, least they accidentally step upon and defile the ancient Holy of the Holies. The closest they may approach to what is still believed the Divine Presence is the plaza near a section of Temple Mount's western retaining wall known as the Wailing Wall.

> How can we sing the songs of the Lord while in a foreign land?
> If I forget you, Jerusalem, may my right hand forget its skill.
> May my tongue cling to the roof of my mouth if I do not remember you, if I do not consider Jerusalem my highest joy.

–Psalm 137:4-6 NIV

My first impression upon approaching the Dome of the Rock mosque was its sheer grandeur. "This is the most beautiful building I've ever seen," I reverently said to Hamad as we approached one of its entrances. The eight-sided structure is a masterpiece of wood, stone, ceramics and gold. One little discussed theory regarding her construction by Caliph Abd al-Malik that the world—intentionally or otherwise—chooses to ignore is that the ruler intended the building to rival that of the glory of King Solomon's first temple.

My initial awe, however, would be short-lived as we became distracted by a commotion a short distance from the building's entrance that we were about to pass through. A small group of angry, taunting, Palestinian men had formed around a pair of twenty-ish, Western European-looking women who had somehow slipped passed the Israeli Temple Mount security guards whose job it was to control this kind of access to the area, and who were now being shamelessly screamed at by one of the mosque's holy men for being indecently dressed. That is, they had the audacity (and disrespect) to wear shorts, tank-top blouses, and to not cover their heads in such a holy precinct.

Hamad, sensing my instinctive impulse to come to the aid of any fellow human being in distress, gently grabbed my elbow and said, "Mr. Richard, please Madame, it's best we hurry." He then cautiously, but with great haste, herded us past the disturbance. He seemed quite upset by it all. As for myself, all I could think of as we passed was that how could these young women be so foolish—or worse, arrogant. When we got to the entrance, Hamad told us that these girls were in serious trouble and, because non-Palestinians have no authority to intervene in these matters, and that the Israeli police would not be able to help. (The crowd had dispersed by the time we exited the mosque.)

Allahumma salli ala rasullika wa'abdika 'Isa bin Maryam. "In the name of the One God, Pray for your Prophet and Servant Jesus, son of Mary"

−A QUOTE FROM THE KORAN WRITTEN IN ARABIC SCRIPT AROUND
THE BASE OF THE DOME IN THE DOME OF THE ROCK MOSQUE.

The inside of the Dome of the Rock mosque was as impressive as the outside! The walls were covered in a kaleidoscope of golden and buff and turquoise ceramic tiles. Circling around the base of the dome were bands of stunningly elegant black and delft-blue Arabic script quoting verses from the Koran. All of the geometric designs the imagination could possibly dream up filled in the gaps. There were several elaborately carved columns supporting the outside wall and another interior ring of columns with light and dark archways which supported the actual golden dome itself. Hamad told us that many of the limestone and marble columns were saved from the rubble of King Solomon's original temple. In the center of it all was the Foundation Stone.

The surface of the original limestone mountaintop was difficult to actually see completely. Either due to construction or by intention, there was a woven wooden screen around it hiding a clear and unobstructed view of the surface of the stone. About three-quarters of the way around the building there was a doorway leading to a subterranean chamber beneath the rock. It lead, Hamad said, to a small room called The Well of Souls and is thought to be where the Ark of the Covenant was hidden during the Babylonian Captivity.

The highlight for me of the visit to this holy sanctuary was (of course) when I was blessed with the opportunity to touch the actual stone itself. Thanks to our dear friend, Hamad, who pointed out to me the possibility of me being able to do so, I reached my hand through a hole in the marble wall built around the Foundation Stone and actually laid my hand upon the living rock! The small area of limestone I felt had been smoothed to the touch by the hands of literally billions of the believers who had come before me who also desired to become one with the Holy Presence of Almighty God. The rock felt cool and moist without being actually wet. And all I could do was stand there taking it all in. I'd like to be able to say that I experienced some sort of energy flow or divine insight, but I didn't; all I felt (and when I say *all*, I mean *All* with a capital "A") was a sensation of pure and overwhelming sense of transcendent calmness. Other-worldly would be an understatement! I literally didn't want to pull away!

But after some time passed, Hamad gently laid his hand on my shoulder and told me it was time to go. I remember afterward my hand smelling like rose pedals or possibly even vanilla cookie dough.

After leaving the mosque, we walked a short distance to a nearby café bordering the Temple Mount area owned by one of Hamad's cousins, and there the three of us all were given a glass of hot tea. We didn't speak much at first, probably because I was still in the grip of the exhilaration and the downright holiness of it all; Hamad still seemed distracted, perhaps by the earlier episode regarding his countrymen's rough treatment of the two European women. When we did finally talk we spoke mostly of the history and politics of the Temple Mount.

"Mr. Richard," said Hamad, looking across the expanse of the Temple Mount that lay before us toward the Dome of the Rock, "there are many men who, in the name of Almighty God, seek to create chaos and unrest by trying to destroy that beautiful building." I was aware of what he was about to say, but only on one level. I recalled at that moment the screening and interview process that had taken place at JFK Airport in New York before our El Al flight to Tel Aviv. Both Theresa and I were summarily separated from each other before we could get in line to be served by the airline's ticket agents and were individually grilled with a barrage of questions regarding the intentions of our visit to Israel, our personal religious beliefs, our opinions of world events, etc. by Israeli security agents. I knew in advance this would take place because we had been warned of these security interviews by our local ticket agent.

Although it seemed to make little sense to me at the time, one of the primary reasons for the comprehensiveness of the El Al security agents interrogations —other than to thwart a potential hijacking—was (and still is) their fear of on-going threats to the security of Jerusalem's Temple Mount from several radical fundamentalist, Christian sects. From their studies of both ancient Jewish texts and the Old and New Testaments, these groups believe that by destroying the Dome of the Rock and then rebuilding a third Temple the act will facilitate and clear the way for Jesus' promised return.

But Hamad told us that there were many Jewish groups as well, both religious and secular, who wished to bring down the Dome of the Rock and establish in its place a Third Temple. Devoutly religious Jews, he said, see the rebuilding of the Temple as a way to unify the various factions of their religion not just in Israel, but the whole world as well. This reestablishment of the purity of their faith will, in turn, open the door for the promised return of the Messiah and will provide redemption for all of mankind. The secular Jews, on the other hand, see the rebuilding as a rallying point for the cultural and political fulfillment of their dream of a true Jewish State.

Hamad also said that there were reports that some of these fundamental Christian groups are in collusion with some of the hardcore Jewish Third Temple extremists to bring about the destruction of the Dome of the Rock. All I could think of to myself was, "No wonder this place is so screwed up!"

As our time together drew near its end, Hamad asked us a question. "Madame; Mr. Richard: do you know what the word Jerusalem means?"

I told him I did. "It means The City of Peace."

"That is correct, sir" he said. "It word has the same Semitic root as salaam and shalom, the Arabic and Hebrew words for peace." But what he said next really boggled my mind. "You know, Mr. Richard," he said, the muted tone of his voice reflecting the seriousness of the statement he was about to make, "it is said that this area before us (the Temple Mount), as well as all of Old Jerusalem, is one of the most bloodiest pieces of ground on earth."

Hamad then went on listing the times Jerusalem has been sacked and laid to waste by her enemies: By the ancient Israelites themselves during their conquest of the region, to the first Jewish Diaspora perpetrated by the Babylonians; from the purging of the land by the Roman empire to the wanton slaughter and plunder during the Crusades, where it was said the blood flowed as high as the horses knees; from the final Moslem conquest of the Holy Lands and continuing to this very day during the various Palestinian uprisings, all Jerusalem has ever known—with the few exalted exceptions of when the actual Presence of God was upon the people—is weeping.

Wow! A profound, but poignant thought, by a profound and holy man. And sadly, his message is one in which the world still grapples with to this very day. Even as I work on this chapter's final re-write during the summer of 2014, blood still being spilled over the City of Peace

The Tree Of Life

CHAPTER 7

The Tree of Life

~oø~

In Memory of Martha
Last of her species, died at 1 p.m.,
September 1st, 1914, age 29,
in the Cincinnati Zoological Garden.

WHEN EUROPEAN SETTLERS FIRST ARRIVED on the shores of North America, it's estimated that there were over five billion passenger pigeons on the continent. There were so many that in the 1700s, the American Puritan minister, Cotton Mather, wrote in his journal of witnessing a flock of the birds over a mile wide. However, by the year 1900, in spite of this seemingly limitless quantity, no passenger pigeon was ever again seen in the wild.

What made this deplorable extinction so sad and so very pathetic was that it was brought about by the hand of man. We, mankind, did it, mostly as a result of commercial exploitation of the pigeon for meat and fertilizer, as a result of totally unregulated sport hunting, and to a lesser degree, from willful destruction of the bird's habitat. People who paid attention to this stuff in the last half of the 1800s saw the bird's decline coming. Laws were futilely passed in an attempt to end the slaughter, but they were totally ignored. In1896—*knowing full well what they were doing*—frenzied hunters, in one final collective act of human stupidity and bloodlust, wiped forever from the face of the earth the last wild flock of 250,000 passenger pigeons. Martha, the last surviving passenger pigeon in captivity died in 1914.

Nothing in the world is more dangerous than sincere ignorance and conscientious stupidity.

–Martin Luther King, Jr.

Sitting directly on the equator 450 miles west of the South American nation of Ecuador are the Galápagos Islands. This isolated, distant chain of volcanic islands and the oceans surrounding them are home to some of the most amazing (and strangest) animals I've ever seen: iguana lizards that swim, cormorants that don't fly, penguins that don't require any ice, a tool-using finch, and of course, the giant Galápagos tortoise. It was the biological uniqueness of these islands, along with their thirteen distinctly different species of finches (buntings, actually), that inspired a then very young naturalist named Charles Darwin to propose one of the profoundest and most controversial theories in the history of science: the theory of evolution.

At the Charles Darwin Research Center on the main island of Santa Cruz lives a Galápagos tortoise named Lonesome George. As we stood outside his pen in the equatorial sun watching the magnificent tortoise as chomped away at a head of cabbage, Faustus, our tour boat's naturalist, told us Lonesome George's story. The haunting history of this poor creature turned out to be just another version of the same sad story that has darkened mankind's legacy on this planet since we first picked up our first tool and smashed it over the head of another living being: that of wanton environmental destruction for our own—and mostly selfish—desires.

Charles Darwin noticed in his landmark study of Galápagos Island finches that each isolated island of the group had its own separate and distinct species of this bird. And so it is with the Galápagos tortoise as well; each island has its own unique species. Lonesome George had the misfortune of being a native of the ecologically ravaged island of Pinta. For a hundred years, sailing ships would come ashore on the island and gather up as many of George's brothers and sisters as their ship's storage capacity would allow. The tortoises would stay alive in the ship's holds for months and thereby provide a source of fresh meat for the sailors. When the tortoises' number became too low to bother with, ship captains would set loose goats on to the island to forage and multiply. These goats, in turn, ate all of the grass and plants the remaining tortoises needed to survive, and one by one each died off until there was just one left..

In 1971, a biologist discovered Lonesome George near death and brought him to the research center where he lives to this very day. He is the last of his kind on the face of the earth. For the last forty years, his caretakers at the institute have been trying to mate him with what they feel are closely related species, but all of the eggs he has fertilized have proven to be infertile. Barring a miracle of biological science, when Lonesome George dies, so will his species.

And that will be that.

[Lonesome George died on the 24th of June, 2012. His autopsy said he died of simple old age. He was embalmed and placed on display at the Biological Field Station on Santa Cruz Island. And like his feathered counterpart, Martha, sitting in a glass case in a zoo in Cincinnati, Ohio, there he will look out at us and the generations yet unborn with his innocent—but dead, dead, dead—dark eyes, and ask that most damning and eternal of questions: Why!, why did you let this happen?]

But there's a part two of the madness that I'd like to share with regards to my Galápagos Island story. It's yet another example of mankind's self-centered avarice—a really pathetic example!—that I got to witness first-hand. And, sadly, this is only one of hundreds of examples that I could mention!

The tragic story of Lonesome George played itself out forty-some years ago when our world was just beginning to take the notion of man-made environmental destruction seriously, and so our fellow humans could (in a half-assed sort of way) be forgiven for their foolishness. Since that time, however, you'd think that with the Galápagos archipelago being on the United Nation's UNESCO Endangered World Heritage list, that all life would finally be safe and well cared for on the islands; you'd think that with over forty years of being hammered by all of the science educators, biologists, naturalists, and environmentalists all over the world doing their utmost to teach the citizens of our planet what a wonderful gift we all have with regards to this amazing place, that life on the islands would now be bountiful and carefree; you'd think that with all of the television specials, wildlife fund-raisers, and do-gooder, worldwide, animal welfare awareness campaigns that have been presented over and over again that the plants and fishes and all of the other various critters that live in the Galápagos would finally be left alone to live out their lives as nature intended; but this is still not the case! Not even close! The specter of human stupidity continues to this very day to raise its ugly head.

Around the sixth day of our ten-day expedition of sailing around the islands, Faustus took our small group ashore on the island of Isabella. He wanted to show us a mangrove swamp. As we drifted in the Zodiac boat among the densely packed, tree-like vegetation lining the shore, he told us about how mangrove swamps throughout the world were the second most biologically diverse regions (after coral reefs) known. He told us of how the tangle of roots that anchored each tree acted as sort of nursery and sanctuary for hundreds of species of young marine animals. To illustrate the point, he pushed back a large overhanging branch with one of the oars, and we could see hundreds of little finger-sized fish swimming away.

As we continued drifting up the small tidal channel, we rounded a bend and glided into a large, sheltered cove. It was here that we got a firsthand glimpse of a senseless form of destruction that the government of Ecuador— and all of the other environmental watchdogs charged with protecting these islands—seem helpless to prevent. All around us were huge one- hundred-foot-wide sections of bare, exposed, jagged coral shoreline with short stumps of what once were mangrove trees protruding from its surface.

Faustus told us that hunters cut down the mangrove trees for firewood in order to process illegally harvested sea cucumbers. Considered a delicacy and an aphrodisiac in some cultures, this marine invertebrate is being wiped out throughout the Galápagos. (But before anyone gets too self-righteous and condemns some poor old Chinese businessman for simply wanting to maintain his manhood and virility, it must be noted that in the West, sea cucumbers are sometimes used as an ingredient in some joint supplements we give to our dogs for their arthritis!) He continued on by pointing out the obvious:

not only are the poachers decimating the native sea cucumber, they are also condemning hundreds—if not thousands—of other species to early deaths by cutting the mangrove trees and depriving them of a place to grow up.

After wheat, corn, and rice, the lowly potato is the fourth largest source of food in the world. Originating in the high Andes mountains of Peru around the body of water known today as Lake Titicaca, it is estimated that there are over 6,000 different varieties of the tuber, many of which, have yet to be discovered. In charge of helping to preserve the huge genetic diversity of this important food source is the International Potato Center based in Lima. As one of hundreds of gene banks located all around the world, the center maintains 3,000 varieties of the plant that originated just from Peru alone. It serves as not only a repository for maintaining the bio-diversity of potatoes but also supplies farmers in need with seeds to plant their own crops.

But in the early 1990s, even though human beings have been grow-ing and consuming potatoes for over 8,000 years in the region, the High Altitude Research Station of the International Potato Center had to make arrangements to transfer its precious potato collection to a center in neighboring Ecuador. Why? Not because of earthquakes or avalanches or any other natural disaster; not because of finances; and not because of the outbreak of some devastating pestilence or disease.

They had to seriously curtail activity at the center because of two malicious attacks on the installation by a Maoist rebel group who called themselves Shining Path. Consider the logic (illogic?) of these "brave" warriors: As terrorists—in that demented sort of way that all terrorist think—you can see their point in "valiantly" attacking their unarmed fel-low farmer and peasant countrymen, by killing innocent unarmed French women tourists, or by "courageously" slaughtering teenage schoolchil-dren and Catholic priests, because that's what terrorists do. Their goal is to create mayhem and chaos by terrorizing innocent people. But attack-ing a potato research center???, operated by unarmed scientists who've dedicated their lives to trying to save the very people and the national heritage they (these big, brave warriors) perversely claim to represent?

As far as I'm concerned, there are three mystical places in the
world: The desert outside Santa Fe, the tree of life in the Arab
emirates of Bahrain, and the restaurant at Sunset and Crescent.

–Harris K. Telemacher (Steve Martin): *L.A. Story.*

Time and time again in my travels about this vast and glorious world of ours,
I often find myself in reverent awe of the overall basic goodness of my fellow
men and women. Therefore, whenever curious friends and acquaintances
ask me what I think of a group of people that I've met in this country or
that country, I'll tell them that with very few exceptions, most people on this
beautiful planet of ours are just trying to get by and make a living the best
way they can. People everywhere are just trying to find someone to mate
with, to care for and feed their families, and to improve their given stations
in life. To the best of their abilities, most people will do whatever they can to
help a stranger or the downtrodden living among them. And nearly all just
want to be left alone to worship (or not) their god(s) in peace.

However, having just said all that, more often than I'd like to say, there
are other times that I find myself completely baffled by my fellow human
beings' acts of—for lack of a more delicate term—downright stupidity.
The stupidity I'm referring to is not about the average person's foray into
the silly or dumb because of youthful (or not) inexperience, ignorance,
or intoxication. It seems predestined that part of our human condition
dictates that most of us have to learn things the hard way. And I'm not talking about those Darwinian acts of stupidity where boneheaded individuals
do something so cockamamie and lethally dumb that they benefit all of
mankind by removing themselves from the breeding pool. This behavior,
I believe, is just part of the normal selection process.

Nor am I talking about that most wanton of waste and brutality that is
war. This form of stupidity is something we human beings just can't seem
to get ourselves past. Despite the unceasing efforts of the saints, diplomats,
educators, and all of the other great humanitarians whose bones have long
since turned to dust, we are—as a species—un-capable, or unwilling, of getting over the fact that we're still tribal in our social organization. Strangers

and those outside of our common circles are generally regarded as threats. And until we learn to accept—and embrace!—our differences and strive to overcome our ignorance, wants, and common selfishness, we may (if we're not careful) end up the way of poor old Martha, the last of the passenger pigeons.

The stupidity that I'm talking about is that of individuals (or groups) who, with complete awareness of what they are doing, either out of lust, expediency, greed, egoistic want, or zealous ideology, continue to wield whatever destructive force they may possess to deprive the rest of the world of its heritage. Whether it's the hunter who shoots the planet's last passenger pigeon for the mundane purpose feeding it to his pigs or the Hong Kong businessman who—even in this day of Viagra—selfishly insists on consuming his precious sea cucumber appetizer because he can no longer satisfy his mistress or the "heroic" warriors who kill unarmed farmers, priests, and schoolgirls, and who purposely do everything they can to wipe out their country's agricultural legacy, the end result is the same: our world becomes a far darker place.

Sitting in the Persian Gulf on the east side of the Arabian Peninsula is the tiny island nation of Bahrain. Somewhat unique among the other Islamic nations of the region, Bahrain is noted for its social and religious tolerance, safe political environment—at least by Middle Eastern standards—and its thriving middle class. The best example of this relative personal freedom was a warning given to me by the concierge at our hotel. I had asked him how careful we had to be (as Westerners) in and around the tourist sites. He laughed somewhat and said that the biggest problem we had to watch out for was especially around the roads leading to the causeway that connected Bahrain to Saudi Arabia. It seems that it's quite common for "pious" Moslem men to make day trips to this country for the sole purpose of getting intoxicated.

Bahrain has its own Formula One racetrack, publishes more books than any other country in the Persian Gulf, and—as of this writing—is the home-in-exile of Michael Jackson. More so than any other place I've seen, flagrant, unabashed wealth in the form of automobiles, seaside villas, and brand-new, ultramodern, high-rise hotels exists tastefully side by side with lovingly cherished traditional Arab culture. A delight that my wife and I had the pleasure to enjoy on each of the three nights we stayed on the island was to watch from the man-made jetty behind the super-glitzy Ritz Carlton hotel the sunset departure of hundreds of ancient felucca-type fishing boats heading out into the Gulf.

We really enjoyed our stay in Bahrain.

> And the LORD God said, 'The man has now become like one of us, knowing good and evil. He must not be allowed to reach out his hand and take also from the tree of life and eat, and live forever." ... After he drove the man out, he placed on the east side of the Garden of Eden cherubim and a flaming sword flashing back and forth to guard the way to the tree of life.

> —GENESIS 3:22, 24 (NIV)

Our main purpose in visiting this tiny Middle Eastern nation was to visit what ancient local tradition says is the biblical tree of life spoken of in the Book of Genesis. My interest in this relic from the Garden of Eden was first aroused when I heard the actor Steve Martin's character in the movie L.A. Story mention it as one of the three most mystical places he'd ever seen.

Located in the middle of the desert about twenty miles south of Bahrain's capital city of Manama, the tree of life is an absolute miracle of survival. Surrounded by nothing but endless sand dunes and mile after mile of inhospitable nothingness, all the while being constantly bludgeoned by the oppressive, unforgiving blazing sun, the tree somehow survives—and actually manages to thrive. It's an amazing sight to behold; there is nothing but the brutal, scorching desert and this tree!

Our driver/tour guide, Hassan, a slightly rotund, middle-aged, lifelong native of Bahrain, told us his version of the story of the legendary tree under whose cool, refreshing shade we all now stood. He told us the story from the Bible—which most people sort of know—of how there existed in the Garden of Eden the now-famous tree of the knowledge of good and evil, which was forbidden to Adam and Eve. Forgotten by most people—or completely unknown to some—however, was a second tree, the tree of life, which God had placed in the garden so that the human creatures he created on the sixth day, and so very much loved, would never have to suffer the agony of death. Of course, as the story went first Eve and then her husband Adam disobeyed the Lord and ate from the tree of the knowledge of good and evil. For this they were eternally banished from the Garden of Eden. And to further prevent them from becoming godlike as well by consuming also from the tree of life, the Lord blocked their way to the tree with angels and a flaming sword.

Looking around at the desolation and barren wasteland that surrounded the tree for as far as the eye could see, I could almost imagine this fiery desert scenery as a metaphor for a divine flaming sword. Our driver continued the story by telling us of how scientists and plant experts are completely baffled by the tree's ability to live without any obvious water source. Hassan smiled slightly as he told us this last detail probably because he knew something that those learned and objective men of science didn't: he believed with all of his heart, as do most people who've ever stood in the presence of this awesome and holy creation, that this is the very tree of life spoken of in the biblical scriptures.

When Hassan was finished with his story, I took a small walk out into the desert to get some photos of the tree. As I took pictures of the tree from different vantage points, I found myself (as I am often prone to being) completely overwhelmed at what I've had the gift of being able to see and touch and to be in the presence of something sacred. I literally stopped everything I was doing and thanked God for this blessing.

When I got back to the tree, and as Theresa and Hassan waited patiently, I walked around it, rubbing my hands on the papery bark and just simply becoming "one" with it. I noticed down near the base of the front of the tree that previous visitors had left several small bouquets of orange and white flowers lying there in the sand. Also, to my surprise I noticed as I got around the back side of the tree that there was a level line of what looked like recently bored-out insect holes, maybe about a hundred of them. Hassan, seeing my curiosity was aroused, walked around to where I stood and, with an air of resignation and acceptance so common in the Middle Eastern Moslem tradition, told me what happened.

"Mr. Richard," he said, "those are bullet holes. Last year, a couple of soldiers emptied several clips from their AK-47 machine guns into the trunk in order to try to kill the tree." He then pointed to several area of some of the lower limbs that looked like they had been in a fire. When I asked him what had happened, he told me that another group of men had tried to burn the tree down.

For a couple of seconds, maybe even minutes, all I could do was stand there completely dumbfounded as to who would want to destroy such a resplendent example of God's creation. Incredulous and stunned to the very marrow of my bones, I looked over at Hassan, and nearly broke into tears. Clearly their intentions were not to obtain firewood or obtain lumber to build a house. When I finally got myself under control, the only question I could muster up was, "Hassan, why would these men want to do something so brainless? What could they possibly be thinking?"

"Mr. Richard," he calmly said, "Please, come with me." I then followed him around to the front of the tree. When we got there, he pointed down to the flowers lying on the sand near the base of the tree. "We have guest workers from India and Nepal who visit this old tree on their days off from work. As a gesture of respect, they will leave small offerings behind. It's a

Hindu tradition." Hassan then paused for a second, as if he was trying to put off as long as possible what he now needed to say, took a deep breath, held it in for another second, and then let it out; I could tell that it genuinely pained him having to say it.

"Islam," said Hassan, "strictly forbids the worship of idols. Both the men with their fire bomb and the soldiers with their bullets, overwhelmed by their fundamentalist zeal, all interpreted these offerings of respect as a form of idolatry. Therefore, they believed with every ounce of their being that by killing this innocent tree, they were doing God's work." And then the dear man said no more.

> Our lives on this planet are too short and the work to be done
> too great ... But we can perhaps remember—even if only for a
> short time—that those who live with us are our brothers, that they
> share with us the same short moment of life, that they seek—as we
> do—nothing but the chance to live out their lives in purpose and
> happiness, winning what satisfaction and fulfillment they can.

–Senator Robert Kennedy

I remember for few minutes just the feeling of numbness, blown away by the lunacy of it all. Neither of us said a word. We just stood there, two men, Moslem and Christian, believing ultimately in the same God, both us saddened beyond further words by the wanton act of destruction perpetrated upon this old patriarch. For me, it would be several days later, somewhere over the Atlantic Ocean as I was flying home, that would reach some clarity on the whole incident.

As I typed out a few thoughts on my laptop into the rough outline of what would eventually be this chapter, I came to the realization that what I'd seen in Bahrain was just one more tragic example of how otherwise reasonable and rationally thinking people can be driven to madness in the name of politics or religion. And it doesn't matter who they are or when they live, whether they're barbarians plundering the Catholics and heathens of ancient Rome, the European Roman Catholic crusaders sacking Byzantine Christians of Constantinople, the Church of England ransacking Catholic monasteries in Scotland, the Chinese Communists consciously trying to wipe from the face o the earth Tibetan Buddhism, the Tamil Tigers of Sri Lanka blowing up Hindu temples, and on and on since the dawn of humankind, their story is always the same: it's all just a senseless waste.

But Hassan, seeing my obvious bewilderment, put his hand on my shoulder and looked me in the eye and smiled one of those beautiful, all-knowing smiles that people who are at peace with the world seem to be so capable of. He then said to me, "Mr. Richard, as young boy I remember my grandfather bringing us to this tree for picnics with our family. He often told us of how *his* grandfather brought him and his parents to picnic under this amazing tree when they were small children!" He said that he still brings his wife and children to this spot for family picnics.

"Don't worry about this old tree, Mr. Richard. God is protecting it. I have every faith that my great-great-grandchildren will someday share in the cool and refreshing shade of this miraculous creation of God, just as we are right now.

Monte Cassino

CHAPTER 8

The Polish Cemetery at Monte Cassino

＊＊＊

... Years will pass and ages will roll,
But traces of bygone days will stay,
And the poppies on Monte Cassino
Will be redder having quaffed [consumed] Polish blood.

—Author unknown

I READ AN ARTICLE A few years back written by the food editor for one of the major New York City newspapers. In the piece, the author shared with her readers the story of her attempt to research the history behind a traditional Jewish onion roll pastry, that I'd known as a kid growing up just north of New York City, called a bialy.

As part of her quest, she traveled to the city of Bialystok, Poland, where local custom said the bialy originated. But her research trip turned out to be in vain. The problem was, that once she arrived in Bialystok, she discovered a horrific truth: there was not one single Jew left to be found—much less be interviewed—in the whole of the city. Every last single one of Bialystok's Jewish citizens had been consumed or dispersed by the Holocaust.

Shortly after reading this article, either by Fate or Divine Intervention, this morally reprehensible annihilation of the originators of the bialy was further pounded home into my awareness by a chance visit with a friend to a Polish military cemetery on a mountaintop in of all places, the country of Italy.

> Traveling is a brutality. It forces you to trust strangers and to
> lose sight of all that familiar comfort of home and friends.
> You are constantly off balance. Nothing is yours except the
> essential things: air, sleep, dreams, sea, the sky—all things
> tending towards the eternal or what we imagine of it.

–Cesare Pavese

On a lovely late Italian summer day a few years back Theresa, our friend Richie, and I were all motoring northward on the Autostrade (the principal north/south highway of the Italian peninsula) back to Rome's international airport after a week- long visit to Naples and the Amalfi Coast. I was driving. We were still about eighty miles south of our destination when we noticed a highway exit sign for the city of Cassino. Upon seeing the sign, Theresa reminded me that just a few weeks before, we'd watched a really good television special about the monumental World War II battle that had taken place in the surrounding mountains to recapture from the nazis the hilltop fortress of Monte Cassino. As an extra bonus, she said, we could also visit the old Benedictine monastery on the summit of the mountain founded in 524 AD by old Saint Benedict himself. We made the spur-of-the-moment decision right then and there to exit.

Our friend Richie riding in the front passenger seat gently made it known that he wasn't overly thrilled about taking the detour. Having survived a minor car crash in a pitch-black highway tunnel earlier in our trip near the city of Assisi, as well as having to just endure a week's worth of maneuvering among the absolutely crazy, daredevil, audacious, Neapolitan drivers and motorcyclists, he just wanted to get back to Rome as quickly and safely and uneventfully as possible. I assured my good friend that in my many years of travel, that often, some of our greatest discoveries and adventures occurred when we'd ventured unplanned off of the beaten path.

It would turn out that our diversion to Monte Cassino would prove to be the case for all of us this time as well ... especially for him.

Located in Italy's fertile Liri valley, the little city of Cassino would be otherwise just another busy farming community located along the ancient Roman Appian Way were it not for two special attributes relating to her geography. The first of these features had to do with the superior military importance of Monte (Mt.) Cassino itself. This steep, enormous rocky hill located just north of the city dominates everything around it for miles.

The second reason Cassino proved so valuable—and, ultimately what would prove most disastrous for the city, her Benedictine monastery on the summit of the mountain, and for the unfortunate soldiers who had to do battle there—was its specific strategic location. A quirk of geological bad luck situated the town and its mountain fortress directly upon a line drawn on a map at the narrowest portion of the "waist" of the Italian peninsula between the Tyrrhenian and Adriatic seas. In the dark days as the Second World War raged on, and because the Germans needed to do something drastic about the rapidly advancing Allied troops marching their way northward from southern Italy, a desperate Hitler and his generals devised a massive line of defensive emplacements to be built on this narrowing. This line of defensive bunkers and gun emplacements would later be known as the Gustav Line. It was the city of Cassino's fate to be sitting directly on the western edge of this defensive line.

The actual Battle of Monte Cassino (known also as the Battle for Rome) began on January 4, 1944, against a well-entrenched, heavily armed, elite grouping of German paratroopers and Panzergrenadiers (better known at the time as Hitler's "supermen.") For over four months, the nazi defenders of Monte Cassino managed to successfully repulse three major assaults by combined units of United States, British, New Zealand, Indian Gurkhas, and French soldiers.

Ultimately, in one of those ironic twists of fate so abundant in the history of our world, 40,000 Polish troops under the command of the Polish General Wladyslaw Anders, on a five-day, bloody, all-out final assault of the hill, ultimately managed to break through the Germans' defenses and plant the Polish flag on the site of the former monastery. By May 19, when the bloody campaign was finally over, 54,000 Allied and 20,000

German soldiers were dead. The Benedictine monastery, having been bombed by American B17 and B26 bombers to prevent the Germans from using it as a spotting station for their artillery barrages, lay before them in total ruin.

After wasting many frustrating minutes of fruitlessly driving around the city trying to find the road that would lead us up to the top of Monte Cassino, we by chance stumbled upon a British military cemetery (the final resting place for the New Zealanders, the Indians, and the Gurkhas killed in the battle of Monte Cassino). It was one of three military cemeteries in the vicinity. As it's been with all of the military cemeteries I've ever visited all over the world—especially those like this one on the site of a former battlefield—when I see the stark simplicity and precise placement of the simple grave markers, I once again feel a profound sense of peace and of overwhelming gratitude for the men (mostly) lying in this sacred place for their ultimate sacrifice on behalf of freemen everywhere.

I wasn't sure of it at the time, but looking over at my friend Richard, I had the distinct feeling that this may have been his first visit to a military cemetery of this sort; to my surprise, he seemed to be exceptionally moved by it all. He examined each grave marker with great interest, studying the soldiers' units, the dates of their deaths. When he did speak, he seemed to be especially taken in by all of their young ages (and these poor guys were indeed all only about eighteen and nineteen years old). After about fifteen minutes of paying our respects, we started walking back to our rental car. As we walked out of the cemetery's gate, Richard stopped, turned back around, and thanked out loud the fallen heroes one more time for their services and for their supreme sacrifice.

As we drove out of the cemetery's parking lot, we saw a much-welcomed sign giving directions to a nearby government tourist information center. By following the directions on the sign we successfully managed to find the place. However, because of this annoying habit that the Italians (and all of the other Mediterranean countries as well) have for closing down their businesses between the hours of one o'clock and three o'clock for siesta, by the time we'd gotten there, the place was closed. Fortunately, there was one redeeming benefit that made the effort of finding the tourist kiosk worthwhile: they had a map nailed to the outside of the building that showed in clear detail—or so we thought at the time—how to find the road that led up to the monastery at the top of Monte Cassino.

After about fifteen more minutes of wrong turns, one-way streets, and false starts, we managed to finally find the monastery road. And what a road it was: All hairpin turns, switchbacks, no shoulders, and worst, oversized tour buses with crazy Neapolitan drivers all hogging the road. But it was a blast to drive! The scenery of the valley below and of the distant mountains in the background was absolutely gorgeous. Being late summer, the bright yellow harvested wheat fields contrasted sharply with the dark green cornfields on the valley floor like the patterns on an antique patchwork quilt. The air was full of the smell of drying hay and freshly harvested grapes. We stopped about two-thirds of the way up the mountain at a pull-over spot to snap some photos and for me to have a few moments to take it all in.

After a couple of minutes of standing there, I was able to give some thought (as I am so prone to do) to the long and harrowing struggle that had taken place on this very spot over sixty years before. I could now understand why the German military command had chosen this piece of tragic earth upon which to make their final stand in their desperate attempt to protect their strategic position on the Italian peninsula. You could indeed see everything that moved for at least forty miles to the south and east and west. Also, as I looked both below us and above us at this steep, boulder-strewn, rocky-outcropped, treeless mountain, I remember thinking to myself that a person would have to be part mountain goat in order to *just* climb this damn hill under normal conditions!

And no sooner had this thought crossed my mind than I was struck with the question I always ask myself whenever I stand on a titanic, history-altering battlefield such as this. It's the same question I asked myself as I stood upon Gettysburg's Seminary Ridge at the site of the beginning of the Confederate army's famous/infamous Picket's Charge and looked uphill across the mile-wide, naked, merciless, hayfield of death toward the Union's defenses on Cemetery Ridge; it was the same question I asked myself as I stood on the coverless, wide-open strip of bloody sand that will be forever know as D-day's Omaha Beach and looked upward toward the German army's thick reinforced concrete bunkers and their unforgiving machine gun nests resting upon the impenetrable French cliff top. The question is always: "How did those soldiers find the courage, the sheer fortitude, or just plain have the *balls* to pull it all off and do what they knew had to be done?" I am in awe of their brave and heroic deeds every time I stand on one of these hallowed pieces of ground.

When we finally got to near the top of the hill, we parked the car and walked the rest of the way up to the monastery. The only problem now, however, was that the front gate leading to the building's main entrance was locked. It was still the damned siesta break! They would not be open for an hour. And so not knowing what else to do, we sat down for a few minutes under a big cypress tree in the garden next to the parking lot. After talking the situation over, we decided that if we were to wait the hour for the monastery to reopen, we'd be getting back to Rome after nightfall, a fate for a foreign driver in Italy worse than death!

Driving in Italy is challenging enough in the daylight hours; we didn't want—if we could at all help it—to drive any more than we had to in the dark. We were quite disappointed and a little bit annoyed about the whole situation, having worked so hard to get there, but we decided it would be best if we left. However, as my friend Richie would soon find out, some of the most profoundest moments of any journey often occur when you travel off the beaten path.

> You must regard this deviation from your plan as part of the adventure that you sought when you decided to embark on it in the first place ... absence of certainty is its essence. People ... who choose to shun the mundane must not only expect, but also enjoy and profit from surprises.
>
> —ADAM YAMEY, *ALIWAL*

About a quarter mile down the hill from the monastery, we noticed a plain roadside sign visible only to downhill traffic, pointing drivers to a road to the left that simply said "Polish Cemetery." Not knowing anything at all about it, I made an impulsive decision to turn onto the side road and take a few minutes to check it out. This road ended after another half a mile in a small parking lot packed with six giant-sized tour buses. "Gosh," I said to Richie as I was locking up the car, "this must be a real popular place."

We then walked down a long tree-lined walkway toward the cemetery. Flanking the entrance to the cemetery were two large bulletin boards that listed the names of all of the known soldiers that were buried there. There were over a thousand of them. I scanned the names quickly, looking to see if any of my family names were there. There weren't. After we finished looking at the list, we walked into the cemetery.

The graves of the Polish Cemetery were arranged in a large semicircular pattern that rose steadily upward like seats in an amphitheater. In the very center of the cemetery was a central stairway that led to three additional, larger, and highly decorated graves. One of these was the final resting place (as we later found out) of General Anders, the commanding officer of the Polish Second Corps. A Catholic Mass was being held at that very moment we arrived over the general's grave, and nearly all of the passengers from the tour buses we'd seen just minutes earlier in the parking lot were attending the service.

Not wanting to disturb them, we circled toward the lower right side and just silently walked among the graves looking once again at the names of the fallen soldiers. I was instantly struck by the family names of the men resting under the gravestones; they were the un-mistakably Polish names I'd heard all my life such as Bukowski, Kowalski, Grabowski, Jankowski, Sienkiewicz,

and Tumilowicz.

As we made our way to the very lower, right-hand corner of the cemetery, there were eighteen graves that were slightly different from the other one thousand or so graves. Rather than each being inscribed with a Christian cross, these gravestones were instead inscribed with Stars of David, and the family names were ones like Lipschutz, Lieberman, and Szapiro. I would later learn, these soldiers were a small group of the eight hundred fifty Polish Jews of the Second Corp who fought and paid the supreme price for this sacred piece of Italian mountaintop upon which we now stood and under which they now rest for all eternity.

These courageous men were a small part of the vanguard of hundreds of thousands of brave fighters who would ultimately defeat Hitler and his cohort of maniacal, bloodthirsty murderers. But as my friend Richie would soon point out to me, the poignancy of this group of Jewish soldier's sacrifice was more tragic than anything any human being should have had to endure.

After a few minutes of silent meditation, we continued our tour of the cemetery. Walking among the graves, Theresa and I talked about some of the names we saw written on the stones, and we wondered out loud if the possible relatives of some of the family names we recognized from home knew their potential kinfolk lie resting here. Attempts to bring our friend Richie into the conversation proved difficult; although normally quite the chatterbox, he seemed distracted and distant. After several more minutes, he told us that he wanted to go back—alone—to the area of the Jewish soldiers. Knowing that he was Jewish himself, and that he most likely wanted to have some kind of private moment with these fallen heroes, Theresa and I told him it would be no problem at all.

By now the Catholic Mass had ended, and the busloads of visitors were dispersing throughout the cemetery. Many of the people grouped around various soldiers' grave sites. Many kneeled in prayer. It was obvious that they were members of the fallen soldiers' families. As we made our way to the center stairway and the tomb of General Andes, I glanced down toward the area of the Jewish graves and I saw Richie standing there all by himself. About a half hour had passed since we left him, and being as we needed to get back on the road, I decided to walk down to tell him that it was time to move on to Rome before dark. Theresa said she'd meet us at the front gate.

I'd known Richie as a classmate from our starving days at veterinary college. He's been a treasured colleague and good friend ever since for over twenty years. I'd always had the impression of him as a gentle and generous man, but with a straightforward and objective temperament. But I knew the moment I returned back to where we had left him earlier and saw him standing there by himself in that lonely corner of that sacred ground that he was being visibly moved by this whole visit.

The next thing I noticed was that he had placed upon each of the Jewish soldiers' gravestones a walnut-sized rock. Before I could say a word, he pointed toward the headstones and he asked me, "Richard, out of all of those busloads of people that we saw wandering around this cemetery, how many of them did you see stop and visit these soldiers?"

Thinking about it for a second, I remembered as Theresa and I walked around the cemetery that we both had noticed several of the people approach the Jewish graves, but none had ventured anywhere near as close to them as Richie and I now were. Not knowing what else to say, I said, "You know, Richie, I don't recall a single person other than you and me and Theresa spending any time here."

There followed a couple moments of curious silence as he once again looked down at one of the gravestones. "And do you know why?" he asked me.

I didn't know why, but one obviously sinister answer came to me instantly: that of anti-Semitism. However—and such to my relief—before I could even attempt to answer his question, he answered it for me. "It's because any family these men may have had back in Poland are probably all gone themselves! Every last one of them was probably killed in the death camps or dispersed to who knows where. Even if the whole world knew or cared that these soldiers were resting here on this lonely hill, it's very possible that there's no one left alive to grieve for them or to acknowledge their sacrifice!" Richie then raised his arm, turned around, and made a broad, sweeping motion toward the majority of the graves, "At least not like the rest of these men!"

Turning back toward the Jewish graves, he said, "By placing a stone on each of their graves, they can now rest in peace knowing someone at least one time acknowledged their existence." And he said no more.

Wow, you could have knocked me over with a feather. I never in a million years would have realized the sorrowful reality of the fate of these departed soldiers had not Richie shared his point of view with me from a Jewish perspective. I even felt a little bit of guilt about my first thought of these Polish citizens walking about as to their possibly being anti-Semites. Their only sin—if you could call it a sin—was they probably didn't know any of the soldiers.

I thanked Richie for setting me straight. We then got into our car and successfully made the trip back to Rome's international airport in one piece. The next day we would be off to the Greek island of Nisyros for the wedding of his beloved cousin. But as we drove up the Autostrad, I thought about the Polish Cemetery and about the Jewish soldiers lying there in their eternal rest in that quiet corner of that hallowed earth and about what I could do to tell the whole world the deeds of these brave men. From the notes that I made later that evening in our hotel room, I ultimately decided to write this story. And even though no one may ever buy, or much less read, this humble book, it will contain forever (as a gift to my friend Richie) the names of his Jewish soldiers, in sacred memory of their sacrifice.

—⟨≈≈⟩—

Roll of Honor:

Aleksander Grunberg

Eljasz Szapiro

Marek Szapira

Hersz Zygman

Stanislaw Lipschütz

Leon Pastor

Jakub Lieberman

Chuna Sztybel

Wilhelm Knobloch

Abraham Wurzel

Maurycy Unger

Dr. Adam Graber

Józef Thiebeger

Leon Simon

Mordko Chaskielewicz

Herman Mauer

Henryk Zegrze

Teodor Baum

Photo by Kamil Bulonis

Postscript

Several days later, we all arrived on Nisyros, an absolutely gorgeous, still very traditional and seldom visited island located a thirty minute ferry ride south of the tourist island of Kos. Here at the ancient Greek Orthodox monastery of Panagia Spiliani (Blessed Virgin Mary of the Cave) we would be graced with the opportunity to attend the wedding of Richie's cousin. On the day before the ceremony, after helping the family set up the tables and chairs in the town square, we borrowed Richie's uncle's car and went on a drive around the island.

Other than its natural beauty Nisyros's biggest claim to fame is its volcano which is still active. As Richie drove us all up the winding road to the mountain's summit, we passed terraced fields of corn and tomatoes (some of the most delicious tomatoes I'd ever eaten), vineyards, and lemon trees that thrived on that rich volcanic earth as far as the eye could see. Here and there were small paddocks of goats. It was all so, so beautiful. After reaching the top of the crater rim, we then drove down as far as we could into the caldera. Walking down the trail the rest of the way into the crater the first thing we noticed was that the floor was very hot. Looking around at the crater's sides we could see steam venting from its active fumaroles. The place reeked of sulfur and could have served to all who stood there as an earthly vision of Dante's Hell. We didn't stay long.

When you read in the ancient Greek myths of the buffoonery and often soap opera-like melodramas of the old gods, one of the first things that's obvious is just how unbelievably dysfunctional those divine families were. The antics on display every weekday afternoon on our modern day bastions of contemporary culture—i.e., talk shows such as *Jerry Springer* and *Judge Judy*—don't hold a candle to the shenanigans of the grand pantheon of old Mount Olympus! Those Greek gods and goddesses really knew how to misbehave!

And it all started off at the very beginning of time. In Greek mythology, the goddess Gaia, the original earth mother, brought forth (I'm not sure *giving birth* would be the correct term) her husband, the god Uranus. This method of obtaining a husband was a bit of a different take on a normal courtship ritual, but not really all that odd. With her new son/husband as their father, Gaia then gave birth to the Titans. Afterward, and for reasons that are not completely clear (probably to keep them from gaining his power) their father, Uranus, chose to lock away these children deep within the earth at a place called Tartarus. This, in turn, greatly displeased his wife/mother, Gaia.

Cronus, the youngest of the sons, full of hatred of his father (and being goaded on all along by his mother Gaia) waited until his parents were both lying together in connubial bliss, and then with a sickle made of flint (designed by his mother!), this youngest of the Titans castrated his father and threw the severed testicles into the sea.

As bizarre and maladjusted as that all sounds, it's not over yet. From his father's gonads that Cronus threw into the sea there arose Aphrodite, the goddess of love. Also, the droplets of blood that flowed from Uranus's wound fell to the earth and they, in turn, gave rise to the Gigantes—the Giants. There were about twenty named giants, but the only one that pertains to this story is the one named Polybotes. An interesting point to ponder with regards to this story of Polybotes's birth is that it gives new meaning to the term *blood relative*. For just a moment this brings us to the end of part A.

For part B we need to go back to the bizarreness by talking some more about Cronus, the last offspring born to Uranus and Gaia. I know this is a bit complicated to follow, but recall he's the one who neutered his dad with the flint jack-knife. Anyway, Cronus ends up marrying his sister—and fellow Titan—Rhea, and together, this brother and sister team would gave birth to the Olympian gods we all learned about in our high school litera-ture classes: Demeter, Poseidon, Hades, Hestia, Hera, and, important to this story as well, Zeus.

This brother marrying sister, once again, is not all that unheard of in our time. But like his father Uranus before him, Cronus feared, almost to the point of mania, that his children would someday overthrow him as well. To prevent this from happening, he devised the rather gruesome plan of eating them all as soon as they were born. Which, of course, se-verely upset his wife/sister Rhea.

When the last of her children, Zeus, was born, Rhea (along with the help and full knowledge of her mother Gaia) devised a plan. First, in order to trick Cronus into thinking he'd eaten this last-born child, Rhea wrapped a large rock inside Zeus's swaddling cloth and then fed both the rock and birthing cloth to him. This unusual tactic worked surprisingly well.

Rhea then stole her son away to the island of Crete where she hid him in a deep cave on Mount Ida. What happened to the infant afterwards is somewhat lost in the mists of time. The is most likely that Zeus was suckled and raised to young adulthood by the she-goat, Amalthea. An interesting side note to this episode in Zeus's life—and one which fits perfectly with the weirdness of it all—is that to hide the child's crying from his father, his grandmother Gaia enlisted the Kouretes Daktyloi, armor-clad male spirits who sang and banged cymbals and performed nonstop frenzied and rollicking dances, thereby creating enough noise to cover over the infant Zeus's weeping.

[Yet another aside: In true spirit of the Jerry Springer television show, the five male Daktyloi married their five female sisters (the Hekaterides.) When added up, their number totaled ten, exactly the number of human fingers, and it is from the word *Daktyloi* that we get the term *dactyl*, the Greek word meaning *finger*. Another interesting bit of information is that from the offspring that were born from the union of these ancient spirits arouse the first men of Crete.]

Zeus survives, of course, into adulthood and it is here where the parts A and B of this story reunite. The god, again with the help of his grandmother Gaia, concocts an emetic with which together they forced Cronus to drink, which in turn caused him to vomit up all of Zeus's brothers and sisters. The story from here on, however, dwarfs anything modern man could ever imagine seeing on daytime television.

For all of the usual reasons, after some time had passed, war broke out on Mount Olympus between the children of Gaia and Uranus (the Titans) and the children of Cronus and Rhea (the Olympians.) The fighting seemed to involve a little bit of everybody including their "blood brothers" the Giants; and any attempt to follow the conflicting details of this war would be like trying to stay on top of the sordid details of one of Judge Judy's court cases: not possible to accomplish by any mere mortal.

However, for the sake of this short postscript (and to keep the story short) I'll just talk about one easy-to-understand episode as it pertains to this chapter. One of his brothers that Zeus forced Cronus to regurgitate was the sea god Poseidon. As the war drew near its close, Poseidon became engaged with his cousin/blood brother, Polybotes the Giant in a titanic (no pun intended) battle, with Poseidon being the ultimate victor. He won the fight by cornering the giant on the Greek island of Kos.

When at last he gained the upper hand, Poseidon grabbed the giant by the ankle and flung him out into the Aegean. As he held his cousin/brother fast to the sea floor with his trident, the Olympian then grabbed the biggest mountain peak on Kos, ripped it from the island, and placed it on top of Polybotes, trapping the giant forever. This newly formed island became present day Greece's only active volcanic island: Nisyros. And it is said that when the volcano on the island rumbles, it is actually the Giant struggling to break free.

The Road Less Traveled

I shall be telling this with a sigh
Somewhere ages and ages hence:
Two roads diverged in a wood, and I,
I took the one less traveled by,
And it has made all the difference.

–ROBERT FROST

After driving back up to the top of the volcano, rather than returning back to his cousin's village, we turned southward to explore some more of the tiny island. The view of the sapphire blue Aegean Sea all around us was breath taking and we stopped many times to photograph the glory of that day. When about a half an hour went by, we came to a small road that looked like it would take us down to the seashore. Not able to resist the *road less taken* anymore than the mighty Odysseus could refuse to listen the Siren's song, I said to Richie, "Let's go down there and see what we can see."

Richie, in the worst way, didn't want to drive down that hill. I don't remember exactly what his reasons were to not go down that steep mountainside road. I do however, remember they were many and most were probably quite valid: the road was too steep, the brakes on his uncle's car might not be that good, we were tired. I persisted anyway, and after refreshing his memory about our recent adventure at the Polish Cemetery, and reminding him of the often very rewarding benefits of being spontaneous, he relented. The little harbor at the bottom of the hill was called Avlake (Richie looked the name up when he returned to the States) and reflecting back upon that moment, I have the feeling, that even though he did put up a bit of token protest, he, too, was finding himself drawn to this spot as well.

The drive down the mountainside was full of the usual hairpin turns, switchbacks, and forbiddingly shear drop-offs. At the bottom of the hill was a tiny, circular, harbor, the only one (we would later find out) on this south end of the island. Partly man-made, the original builders took advantage of a natural indentation in the ancient lava flow that originally formed the island and added a stone and concrete curved breakwater to protect the quay from the crashing waves of the sea. The sheltered water was deep and maybe seventy feet across.

We parked the car, got out, and walked out to the end of the breakwater. There, alone on that rock we stood silent, taking it all in: the wind blowing the salt spray from the unrelenting sea crashing upon the leeward rocks onto our exposed faces and the sight of the bright blue sky blending effortlessly on the distant horizon with the white-capped, deep aquamarine of the eternal Mediterranean; it all combined with the smell and pungent taste of fish and seaweed and churning water.

Then shortly after our arrival, as if on cue in some Anthony Quinn/ *Zorba the Greek* fantasy, a solitary small, brightly-painted, red and blue and white-trimmed fishing boat spurred along by an old man passed by us through the harbor's narrow opening and tied up to the far side of the quay. He unloaded several large baskets of something, timing his work with the pulsating rising and falling of the waves. He then untied his boat, waved modestly as he drove past us, and headed eastward up the coast.

Gosh, it was incredible! Breaking the silence, and in that fantastical way I'm prone to doing so at magical moments like this, I speculated out loud on how that old fisherman could have been Alexander the Great, perhaps leaving tribute to the gods of Nisyros; or the old Argonaut Jason leaving behind, in the safety of this protected cove the coveted Golden Fleece; or, maybe it was old Odysseus himself depositing upon the shore for all the world to see, the remnants of his battle with the Medusa. Richie seemed to hear none of it. He simply seemed overwhelmed by it all.

What I am in search of is not so much the gratification of a curiosity or a passion for worldly life, but something far less conditional. I do not wish to go out into the world with an insurance policy in my pocket guaranteeing my return in the event of a disappointment ... On the contrary, I desire that there should be hazards, difficulties and dangers to face; I am hungry for reality, for tasks and deeds, and also for privation and suffering."

–HERMANN HESSE, *THE GLASS BEAD GAME*

After a time, we started our way back to the car. But while still only about short way back on the breakwater, Richie said he wanted to sit down and just rest and take it all in a bit more. I joined him a few feet away. Theresa said she was going to explore the rest of the harbor. After several minutes of small talk in which we had spoke of his family and the wedding and how delicious the fruit of his uncle's lemon trees was, I noticed that he had become suddenly quiet. Looking over at him, I then saw that he had laid down in the shade of the seawall and had fallen asleep! Thinking it a real good idea, I propped my head against the rock wall where I sat and immediately conked right out as well.

And there alongside that harbor, lulled by the crashing waves and warm, gentle, sea breezes, we relented to the Sirens' call, and crashed dead tired from our weeks of hard traveling. There we would have stayed an eternity were it not for Theresa reminding us that we had to drive back to town and get ready for yet another bountiful pre-wedding feast. I mentioned to Richie how I couldn't believe how refreshing that small nap was. He agreed saying that it was one of the best naps he'd ever had.

Walking back to the car, I thought I detected a bit of melancholy in Richie's voice. After Theresa and I got into the car, he continued to stand there gazing out over the harbor; it was like he'd found something, maybe a break from the world, some kind of inner peace he'd forever longed for, and now that he had it in his sight, didn't want to let it go.

The harbor at Avlake has since, indeed, become that inner place where Richie goes when the relentless oppressiveness and the occasionally overwhelming weight of the world bears down hard upon him. It's a place we all have—or at least we should have. To a small degree, in his personal travels since our trip together to Italy and Greece, he's even ventured out and has taken his own "roads less traveled."

We talk at least once a month on the phone. I'll ask, "Richie, how goes the battle out there in Arizona in veterinary medicine?" He'll tell me (and you can just hear the frustration in his voice) about how there are times when dealing with an irate, neglectful, or mean owner that he wants to just smack them silly. I'll agree, and then we'll spend the next ten minutes sharing horror stories.

He always ends our conversations the same way: "Richard," he says, "Thank God for Avlake!"

Saint Joseph's Cathedral (Photo by Boris Kester: www.traveladventures.org)

CHAPTER 9

The Roosters of Vava'u

—◦⊷◦—

There are two ways to live your life. One is as though nothing
is a miracle. The other is though everything is a miracle.

—Albert Einstein

The best and most beautiful things in the world cannot
be seen or touched. They must be felt with the heart.

—Helen Keller

No matter where my wife and I find ourselves on our various trips around this amazing planet, one of our great pleasures, especially if it's a Sunday, is to attend Mass. This obligation to partake of the Eucharist is, of course, expected of us, but even if it wasn't, we'd probably still go anyway. This is because it doesn't matter where you are, the Roman Catholic Mass follows a pretty strict and easy-to-follow universal format. With the exception of a few minor local traditions that may be added for a region's cultural tastes, a Mass in Kuala Lumpur, Malaysia, is the same as Mass in Usa River, Tanzania, is the same as a Mass on the island of Tahaa in the northern Society Islands, is the same as Mass at the Vatican. It's like a little bit of home away from home.

The most memorable Catholic Mass I've ever attended happened when we were traveling the northern Tongan island group of Vava'u. We had been sailing around that spread-out cluster of islands for the previous four days and, knowing we'd be near land on the upcoming Sunday morning, we made arrangements with our crew to attempt to attend church. This not-so-small task required us to anchor in a cove on the eastern side of the group's main island and row a dinghy toward shore as far as we could into the shallow inlet. We then rolled up our pants, waded in the shallow water for a couple of hundred feet to the beach, and took a private car belonging to one of the crewmen's cousins into the main village of Neiafu.

Our destination, Saint Joseph's Cathedral, sits on a tall hill in the center of town majestically overlooking the Port of Refuge (I just love that name!), the main harbor of Vava'u. We arrived at the church about twenty minutes early so we would be able to leisurely observe the congregation as they arrived for their worship. And what a sweet sight it was to watch those lovely people. The beautiful brown-skinned Tongan women were all clothed in their modest but vibrantly colorful skirts and muumuu dresses. The young boys all wore white long-sleeved shirts with black ties, and the girls wore pastel-colored Western-style dresses; all were barefoot. Most of the older men, and some of the women as well, wore what looked like large woven coconut frond mats that extended from their chests down to their ankles. But aside from the visual delight of seeing these gorgeous people dressed up in all of their glory, what made the experience of that morning's Mass in Saint Joseph's so memorable (blissfully transcendent would be a better phrase) for me was the singing.

Before going any further I need to make a disclaimer. If the truth were to be told (and my wife will confirm this), in the majority of cases, I'm actually not too crazy about singing at Mass. I know that a lot of people take pleasure in it, and yes, I know that the good Saint Augustine said that "prayers sung are prayers said twice," but for me, it's a distraction—especially in congregations where there's no local long-standing tradition of singing—and a lot of times, to me, the discordance often sounds as if somebody somewhere is torturing cats. But in that Tongan Mass that I felt so graced to be able to attend, the congregation's singing seemed like part of the landscape, like it was part of their culture ... it was like part of their genetic makeup! When I think about it, it wasn't the perfection of the choral presentation that so much blew me away, but rather it was the complete and unabashed harmonic exuberance with which they sang that so bedazzled me!

These big (very, very big) and beautiful people sang with every ounce of the blissful love of God that they had in their bodies. It may seem to some like a bit of exaggeration, but I can think of no way else of putting it into words: On that morning, in that weather-beaten old church sitting gloriously on that little knoll overlooking that peaceful, sheltered, South Pacific harbor, as I shared the exalted honor of worshiping our Lord with all of those lovely Tongan women and men, I genuinely felt at that precious moment that I was actually standing in the sanctified presence of God's heavenly angels.

> While you are proclaiming peace with your lips, be care-
> ful to have it even more fully in your heart.

> —Francis of Assisi

In the early years of thirteenth-century Italy, Francis Bernardone, then still a young penitent, was walking alone in the valley below his former hilltop home of Assisi when he happened upon the ruins of an old country church. As this future Saint Francis of Assisi stood in front of the collapsed building, an internal voice told him to go inside and pray. Obedient to this voice, a voice that he was becoming more and more accustomed to hearing, he entered what was left of the abandoned building and cleared away enough rubble so he could approach the sanctuary's ancient altar. Above this decrepit and broken-down altar hung the intact crucifix that is now known and revered throughout all of Christendom as the San Damiano Cross.

As young Francis knelt down and began his prayers, he happened to gaze up at the face of the Lord painted upon the cross, and as he did, he saw the suffering Jesus' lips begin to move. The Lord then spoke the words that would guide Saint Francis's every ounce of being for the remainder of his earthly life, and that, in turn, would change the face of Christianity forever: "Francis, go repair My House, which as you see is falling into ruin." The obedient saint would, of course, not only go on to repair the actual physical building in which he had found himself on that day but would also go on to institute an order of brothers and sisters, the Franciscans and the Poor Clares, who would oversee and lovingly nurture many of the then much-needed reforms to the Catholic Church. A copy of the San

Damiano Cross hangs above the altar in the present-day Church of Saint Damiano, the very same church that Francis and his early followers rebuilt stone by stone with their own hands. The original crucifix can be seen in the Church of Saint Clare just up the hill in the town of Assisi.

The San Damiano Cross is classified by scholars who study such things as an icon cross. By this they mean that images and messages that the crucifix's artist intended to communicate to his viewers are illustrated on the flat surface of the cross as if it was a painter's canvas. The San Damiano Cross has a little bit of everything with regards to its iconography. First, of course, it has the image of the crucified Christ, triumphant, his eyes open, and with no crown of thorns upon his head. Legend says that originally, Jesus' eyes were closed, but upon hearing Saint Francis's voice, he opened his eyes in order to behold this sweet and devoted man. The icon also has images of the five major witnesses to the crucifixion (Mary, mother of Jesus; Mary Magdalene; Saint John, the apostle whom Jesus loved; Mary, mother of James; and the Roman centurion), several minor witnesses, a welcoming committee consisting of a chorus of heavenly angels, the six patron saints of Umbria, and at the very top, a representation of the right hand of God the Father. As well, the iconography of the cross contains two representations of what I consider universally-found animals. Near Jesus' left thigh, there is painted a small rooster; on the lower right side of the shaft there is a small and very difficult to see (at least for my eyes) cat.

In most world mythology the rooster always acts as a harbinger of danger, that is, he warns us that something dreadfully wrong is about to happen. This was probably the intention of the artist of the San Damiano Cross in placing the little bird on the crucifix right next to Jesus. Just like he did on that dark night in Jerusalem after the terrified Saint Peter denied the Lord three times, this rooster is placed there to remind us of our own potential weaknesses and to help keep us ever vigilant.

The cat's presence on the crucifix baffles the scholars. The best possible answer they can come up with is that the cat, just like the devil, is forever lurking in the background, always ready to pounce upon the unaware soul. With my apologies in advance to these great men and women of letters, I think this is academic lunacy at its most slothful. My personal feeling is a little more realistic, and people who know and love cats will surely agree with me on this theory: I believe that just as the sweet breath of the cows in the stable in Bethlehem helped to warm the infant Jesus on that first freezing cold Christmas evening of His birth, so did the rhythmic purring of this loving cat cuddled around His feet helped to soothe our Lord on the night of His Passion.

> A cat has absolute emotional honesty: human beings, for one
> reason or another, may hide their feelings, but a cat does not.

-ERNEST HEMINGWAY

In my many travels around this world—this stunningly beautiful world—I've observed many universal absolutes. And what I mean by an *absolute* is that there exists predictable phenomenon that a traveler can take for granted that he or she will likely encounter almost any place they go. (The Arctic and Antarctic are two partial exceptions to the general rule.) A first and foremost example of an absolute, and perhaps the easiest for most non-travelers to understand, is that of mother's love. I don't believe too much needs to be said about this one. Be you a Tanzanian Bushman or an Inuit fisherman living on the frozen tundra of Greenland, a Sri Lankan elephant or Kazinga River (Uganda) hippopotamus, a Pacific Ocean red-tailed tropicbird or an Antarctic king penguin, without mothers (both biological and adoptive) and the critical and live-giving nurturing that they lavish upon their offspring, our species—as well as all of the other sentient beings on our planet— would have long ago vanished.

A second absolute is, of course, the availableness and universal format of the holy Catholic Mass

And without a doubt in my mind, a third worldwide phenomenon that travelers can expect to encounter in nearly every occupied region of our globe would be that of the prevalence of cat ladies. Every city, town, village, or outback crossroads has one—or more—of these special ladies: women whose whole mission in life is to care for their appreciative feline charges.

These loving ladies and their hordes of cats are everywhere! I've seen cat ladies at a lonely desert gas station in the Jordan valley on the road from Jericho to the Sea of Galilee, at a carpet shop located within the shadow of the great Blue Mosque in Istanbul, at the colossal cemetery in Buenos Aires where a tour guide took us to see the mortal remains of the late Eva Peron, and at a souvenir shop in the little French village of Caen near the hallowed beaches of Normandy. I've seen collaborating evidence of cat lady habitation by observing the large numbers of cats sunning themselves in the windows of a ground floor Park Avenue town house in New York City, on the second-story balcony of an apartment building in the North Beach section of San Francisco, as well as on the roof of a mansion on the shore of Lake Michigan in Chicago. I even know a cat lady at our local airport's US Airways ticket counter.

> The further I traveled through the town the better I liked it.
> Every step revealed a new contrast—disclosed something I was
> unaccustomed to ... I saw cottages surrounded by ample yards,
> ... I saw luxurious banks and thickets of flowers, fresh as a
> meadow after a rain, and glowing with the richest dyes ... I saw
> huge-bodied, wide-spreading forest streets ... I saw cats—Tom
> cats, Mary Ann cats, long-tailed cats, bobtail cats, blind cats,
> one-eyed cats, walleyed cats, cross-eyed cats, gray cats, black
> cats, white cats, yellow cats, striped cats, spotted cats, tame cats,
> wild cats, singed cats, individual cats, groups of cats, platoons of
> cats, companies of cats, regiments of cats, armies of cats, mul-
> titudes of cats, millions of cats, and all of them sleek, fat, lazy,
> and sound asleep ... I breathed the balmy fragrance of jasmine,
> oleander, and the Pride of India ... I moved in the midst of a
> summer calms as tranquil as dawn in the Garden of Eden.
>
> —MARK TWAIN ON HONOLULU

There is one problem, however, with the whole notion of cat ladies that needs to be addressed and that no one so far seems to have given much thought to: that is the problem of what to call men who love and hoard cats. A perfect example of this oversight I discovered during a weekend visit to Key West. For those who have never been there, Key West is at the southern end of a long chain of islands dangling off of the south coast of Florida. The highway leading to this two-mile- by- four-mile- square island is a marvel of civil engineering and the four-hour drive from Miami has to be among the top ten scenic roads in the world.

Besides all of the wild and hedonistic pleasures for which Key West is so famously—or infamously—noted, the island is also a serious destination of pilgrimage for all would-be writers and scholars of American literature. This is because from 1931 until the time of his death in the early 1960s, the island was the home of the great writer, Ernest Hemingway.

History has been very fickle with regards to how to deal with this great man's legacy, but with the exception of a few literary snobs most readers (myself included) agree that Mr. Hemingway's writing set a nearly impossible standard for the whole of twentieth-century authors to equal. For myself, whenever I find I'm in a slump, or I find that I cannot think of a single, solitary word to put to paper, I make it a point to stop right then and there and read the first fifty or so pages of his book, *A Movable Feast.* His advice to would-be writers in this story is priceless; but infinitely more important, the great man's prose, his cadence, and vivid clarity of description are a masterpiece to behold!

But beyond having the genuine thrill of standing in the very same secluded rooftop room where the author created many of his masterworks, you cannot help but notice as you stroll around the grounds all of the cats that now resolutely call his former home *their* home. It turns out that this verbose, macho, and occasional bully of a man was an absolute pushover when it came to his cats! When asked one time why it was that he loved cats so, he said that he admired their great spirits and independence. He was also quoted as saying, "A cat has absolute emotional honesty: human beings, for one reason or another, may hide their feelings, but a cat does not."

Most of the present-day cats scampering around the homestead are polydactyl (have extra toes). Legend says that all of the cats alive today descended from a single individual that Mr. Hemingway won in a poker game from a cantankerous and crusty old sea captain at his favorite watering hole, Sloppy Joe's bar. To this day, each cat at the Hemingway home is named after a famous movie star or writer.

As you walk around the garden behind the home, you can see that Hemingway went out of his way to spoil them all rotten. So that the poor creatures wouldn't ever want for fresh water to drink in the oppressive south Florida sun, he himself fashioned a huge drinking bowl in his backyard out of a discarded urinal. And the small cemetery in which he buried his beloved pets is a sincere and touching memorial to the love he had for these animals.

All of which leads up to the question of how to classify Mr. Hemingway with regards to the cat lady question. You cannot refer to him as a *cat man* because—at least for me—it just doesn't flow off of the tongue like *cat lady* does. And besides, if he were still alive, he would probably beat me up. I agonized over this quandary until I got the bright idea to check out possible solutions on Google.

And, sure enough, like there is for every other seemingly unanswerable question on earth, there were multiple web pages addressing the issue of cat ladies. One in particular caught my eye, mostly because of their solution to my Hemingway problem. On the *Crazy Cat Ladies Society* website, the society members manage to get around this problem of the naming guys who love to have lots of cats by referring to such men as Gentleman's Auxiliary. I think old Ernest would have liked that.

> The secluded anchorage into which we'd eased our sloop for the night looked like a photo right out of some ultimate South Sea Islands fantasy picture book. The unsullied water of the small cove, smooth as a baby's behind, varied in every nuanced shade of blue: from deep cobalt where we had just dropped our anchor to a delicate cornflower where the lagoon and the golden sandy beach touched on the near horizon. Farther west behind the beach, the gargantuan remnants of ancient volcanoes, birth mothers of these northern Tahitian islands, thrust skyward, their rocky slopes now covered in the raw greenness of primeval jungle. The setting sun somewhere behind the mountains saturated the sky with a warm orange glow. A sweet breeze blew in from the

sea, tempering the last of the day's oppressive equatorial heat
and helping, thankfully, as well to keep the voracious mosquitoes
inhabiting the island's ancient forests at bay. Paradise! We'd found
it at last! Later that evening, after a simple dinner of spaghetti
and canned meat sauce (topped off with a bottle of red wine that
I purchased a week before at a farm winery in Switzerland), we
went for a quick swim. Afterward, completely exhausted from our
day's open ocean crossing from Raiatea, with our bellies full and
our souls at peace, we slept a blessed and tranquil sleep. That is,
until about 4:30 A.M., when we were startled from our blissful
repose by a sound that I can only describe as all hell breaking
loose! Bursting forth from the darkened woods and shattering the
stillness of our serene sanctuary, shrieked a cacophony of crowing
roosters. We heard old baritone roosters, tenor roosters, young
soprano roosters, Pavarotti roosters, Dolly Parton roosters, Mick
Jagger roosters, Billy Idol roosters, squawking quartets of roosters … whole, haunting, disarticulated symphonies of roosters. It
was the Vienna Boys' Choir of roosters, the Mormon Tabernacle
Choir of roosters, with the Marine Corps band of roosters thrown
in for good measure; all seemingly jacked-up on steroids, and all
wailing in disjointed harmony as if God's judgment day itself had
finally arrived. When I look back on it all, I think we were lucky to
have escaped the carnage with our lives (and sanity) still intact!

–RICHARD ORZECK (IN A FEEBLE IMITATION OF MARK TWAIN'S *HONOLULU*),
RECALLING AN ACTUAL ANCHORAGE OFF OF THE ISLAND OF TAHAA.

Another universal phenomenon that travelers can expect to encounter would be the worldwide preponderance of chickens. Yes! Chickens!
Squawking roosters and cackling hens seem to be everywhere! You see
these creatures scratching through the garbage in the streets of Addis
Ababa in their never-ending missions to discover a tasty morsel of discarded food. They swarm the sides of back roads on every continent
(Antarctica may be an exception) in their relentless and unforgiving quest
for insects and little critters to devour. I've even seen them foraging on

the immaculately groomed lawns Aruba's Hyatt Regency hotel, the Ritz Carlton on Maui, and even on the grounds of the gorgeous Marriott Hotel in the center of downtown Bangkok.

Even if you don't actually see these elusive creatures, you'll still know they're there. It doesn't matter if you're sleeping in a jungle hut in Tanzania, a fancy bed-and-breakfast in Chamonix, France, or in the cabin of a sailboat anchored in a sheltered cove off the coast of the beautiful Tahitian island of Tahaa. As sure as a Timex alarm clock set for 4:30 in the morning, you can be guaranteed a merciless, chaotic chorus of crowing roosters and chattering hens to rouse you from your slumber. Sometimes they REALLY drive me crazy!

But as much as I might be making fun of these remarkable animals, it must be remembered that in many places on this earth, domestic poultry are people's only source of cheap and reliable protein. Chickens have the amazing ability to convert grass and insects and other waste products into meat, highly nutritious eggs, and beautiful feathers from which can be made bedding, insulation, and body adornments. Even their feces is important as a source of fertilizer. And, like most universally found animals, chickens and roosters have also spawned many myths and legends. One of my favorite legends of all times is the story we were told of how the roosters of the northern Tongan Island group of Vava'u helped save their highest mountain from being stolen by Samoan devils.

Sitting directly on the International Date Line in the middle of the Pacific Ocean lies the island nation of Tonga. Consisting of over 150 islands, Tonga today is the only surviving monarchy in the Pacific. The country also has the proud distinction of being the only Pacific Islands nation to have never been colonized by a foreign power. Beside my being astonished at the gigantic physical size of the Tongan people (the late king of Tonga, His Majesty Tupou IV, once had the distinction of being listed in the *Guinness Book of World Records* as the heaviest monarch in the world), one of my most vivid memories of our visit to the main island of Tongatapu was watching how, at low tide, the island's pigs would venture hundreds of yards out onto the exposed coral reefs that ring the island to forage for seafood.

In the Tonga Islands creation myth, an underworld spirit named Maui visited the Samoan island of Manu'a. It was here that he was given a magic fishhook by an old man named Tonga Fusifonua. As soon as Maui began to fish with his new gift, the hook became snagged on the coral-laden ocean bottom. Struggling with all of his strength, he managed to haul his new fishhook in, only to discover that he'd brought up the main Tongan island of Tongatapu. Pleased with what his wonderful magic fishhook could do, Maui continued his task as he sailed back northward to Samoa until the rest of the islands that make up the present nation of Tonga were pulled up as well.

The northernmost islands of Tonga, the Vava'u group, consists of some forty mixed volcanic and limestone islands, only half of which are inhabited. We spent five days sailing around the island chain in a chartered sailboat, the M/S *Melinda*, that came provided with a captain and two native crew members. Our days were spent sailing the pristine, azure blue waters around the outer islands, stopping wherever it pleased us to swim at a quiet, private, palm tree-lined, white sandy beach or to snorkel over an unchartered reef exploding with every species of fish and coral imaginable. Several times as we cruised the straits between various islands, we were blessed by seeing humpback whales as they passed us. At nights we'd feasted on fresh fish caught that day on our trolling line and on the tropical fruits and coconuts harvested by our boat's crew. The whole experience, I believe, was as close to a tropical island escape fantasy as a person can get in this modern day. It was fabulous.

On our last day at sea, as we sailed up the Ava Pulepulekai channel to return to our anchorage, the first thing I couldn't help but notice was what our captain told me was called Mount Talau. The huge, almost unnaturally flat-topped mountain dominated the harbor and its port city of Neiafu. What made the sight even stranger still was that sitting several hundred yards from the base of the mountain was the tiny triangular-shaped island of Lotuma. From at sea, the pair of mountain peaks looked as if someone had actually sliced the top off of Mount Talau, like it was a big birthday cake, and set its peak down into the harbor beside it. Noting my interest, our captain told us the following amazing story.

According to Polynesian mythology, in the days before time, Samoan tevolo (devil spirits), envious of their southern island cousins' great treasure, decided to steal Mount Talau's majestic peak and carry it back with them to Samoa. Because these devil spirits turn into stone in the naked light of day, the tevolo snuck over to Tonga under the cover of night and went immediately to work sawing off the top of the mountain. They wasted not a single second of time, because they knew they must complete their dastardly task before the sun rose.

Awakened by the noise of their sinister deed, the Tongan goddess Tafakula realized what was going on and decided that she must do something to stop the theft or else these Samoan devil spirits would be emboldened by their success to then steal all of the other many majestic mountains of Tonga. Greatly outnumbered by the Samoan tevolo, and with many more hours to go before sunrise, Tafakula thought up an ingenious plan. She called forth all of the roosters of the island and had them gather at the base of Mount Talau and wait for her signal. Tafakula then went over to the nearby mountainous island of 'Eua, located just east of Vava'u, and climbed to the top of the island's highest peak. When she and her roosters were at last all in place, she sent them the signal to begin. And it was none too soon!

Just as the mischievous devil spirits were beginning to lift the mountain peak from its base and were starting to haul it away to their island, the roosters—with all of their might—began a nonstop chorus of crowing. As they did, the goddess Tafakula turned away from Mount Talau, raised her ta'ovala (the traditional woven mat garment worn by Tongan men and women), and aimed her huge naked buttocks toward the Samoan devils.

Upon hearing the roosters crowing, and then looking over and seeing the reflected moonlight shining off of Tafakula's giant rear end, the tevolo were fooled into thinking that the sun was beginning to come up. Knowing that this would be sure death for them, they dropped the heavy mountain peak that they were carrying into the bay beside Mount Talau, where it resides today as tiny Lotuma island. The Samoan devil spirits then quickly flew back to their native island. Days later, when they discovered that they had been tricked by mere roosters and a single Tongan goddess, they were so embarrassed that they never again tried to steal another mountain from their island cousins in Tonga.

POSTSCRIPT

It sort of begs the question then, that, if I was so enchanted by the Catholic Mass in Tonga, was there ever one that I attended where I felt the exact opposite? The answer is, of course, yes, and it saddens me somewhat to say that, because it took place in my most favoritest city in the world, New York ... and more than just once.

Every time we drive to New York City for a weekend fling, we always make it a point to attend Mass at Saint Patrick's Cathedral. It's sort of the thing to do while visiting the Big Apple. But the irony is that while there in that mighty and magnificent house of worship, I have (so far) always felt about as far away from God as anywhere I have on earth. When pressed by my wife about why I feel so alienated, I find it difficult to nail down the precise reason.

The best answer I come up with is that His presence seems to me always just beyond my reach—sort of like He is there, but is somehow being obstructed. Maybe it's the overwhelming grandeur and ostentatiousness of it all. Perhaps the fault lies in the flawless—but rather passionless— choreography of the Mass and the precise harmonic precision of the choir. Or maybe it was just the cold and seemingly impersonal vastness of the place.

Holy Mass at Saint Peter's Cathedral in Rome runs a close second. A fellow traveler once told me the place reminded her more of a museum. And I sort of agree. And Wow! Talk about opulence: if the leaders of the Church ever decided to have a garage sale, they'd be able to feed the poor and clothe the naked of the world for the next one hundred years! The Vatican's saving grace, however, and what makes it exceptionally special for me, is that when you're in the basilica, you're in the physical presence of all the relics and bones of Christendom's numerous saints ... including, of course, the great "Fisher of Men," himself, Saint Peter.

ANOTHER POSTSCRIPT

On another recent trip to New York City, I had the chance to arrive a half-an-hour early for Mass at Saint Patrick's Cathedral. I took advantage of the quiet time to check out some of the church's side chapels dedicated to

Christianity's various holy saints. Because I'd been doing some research on mountain climbing for an upcoming trip to the French Alps and had seen his name mentioned a few times, I was surprised to discover that one of these chapels was dedicated to Saint Bernard.

I had read that Saint Bernard was the patron saint of mountaineers. Also, since I had been treating a dear client's Saint Bernard dog for cancer at the time, I briefly wondered if he was the same saint after whom the dog breed was named. And so, upon viewing my chance encounter with the Blessed Saint as a sign from God (as I am so predictably prone to do), I stopped, and meditated, and prayed for his intercession on behalf of Theresa and me during our upcoming trip to climb Mount Blanc that summer.

The only problem, however, (as future research pointed out to me) was that the Saint Bernard I encountered at Saint Patrick's Cathedral was not the Saint Bernard for either mountain climbers or the dog breed. The saint I prayed within that small chapel in that great house of God was Bernard of Clairvaux, who founded and led the monastery at Clairvaux, France in the eleventh century, and who later became the first Cistercian monk to be placed on the calendar of saints. This Saint Bernard is the Patron Saint of beekeepers, bees, candlemakers, wax-melters, wax refiners, and of all places, Gibraltar.

The Saint Bernard I was actually looking for was Bernard of Menthon, also known as Bernard of Montjoux. This Bernard was the Archdeacon of Aosta, Italy who spread the Word of God's love to the people of the Alps for over forty years. He started a patrol that cleared robbers from the Alps as well as established hospices (still there today) on the high mountain passes for travelers and pilgrims on their journeys from Western Europe to Rome. I was pleased to also learn that the large dogs trained to search for lost victims in the mountains, the Saint Bernard dog, with their iconic barrels of whiskey hanging around their neck and their propensity toward producing copious amounts of slobber, are named after him as well.

Although it has nothing directly to do with this story of mistaken identity, my investigation of Saint Bernard (the human, not the dog breed) turned uncovered some interesting information. There are at least eight other saints named Bernard. There was one named simply, Bernard, who was a Benedictine Cistercian monk martyred by the Moors in 1180. Another one is the Blessed Martyr, Bernard of Toulouse who was tortured and sawn in half in 1320 by Albigensians. There is a Bernard of Valdeiglesias, a Benedictine Cistercian monk who died in 1155. There is also Bernard of Vienne, a former military officer in King Charlemagne's army, who is the Patron Saint of agricultural workers, farm workers, farmers, field hands, husbandmen.

There is Bernard Due Van Vo, who was arrested in 1838 for the crime of priesthood, and became one of the 300,000(!) Martyrs of Vietnam. Another one is Bernard of Tolomeo, founder of the Benedictine congregation of the Blessed Virgin of Monte Oliveto. A final Saint Bernard, and one that's quite interesting as well, is Bernard of Corleone. Noted for his extreme austerity and self-imposed penances in an attempt to atone for his earlier life (he had killed a fellow Sicilian in a sword dual), he seemed to have had a strong gift of healing animals by prayer. Hmm!

All of which brings me back to the good Saint Bernard (of Clairvaux) that I met that Sunday morning in New York City. Even though I blew it with regards to the mountaineering and dog breed things, I did gleam one bit of information that he and I somewhat share in common. It turns out that every morning when this particular Saint Bernard awoke, he would always ask himself, "Why have I come here?" The answer he always divined: "To lead a Holy life." My answer every morning (when I'm not off on a journey somewhere) to the question would be: "To simply try and save the lives of a few cats and dogs and the occasional cow."

Falkland Island Minefield

CHAPTER 10

Good Morning Good People

⎯⎯∽∞∾⎯⎯

*A landmine is the most excellent of soldiers, for it is ever
courageous, never sleeps, and best of all, never misses.*

–ANONYMOUS KHMER ROUGE GENERAL

BRIGHT AND EARLY ON EVERY morning of our expedition the same cheery
voice boomed out over the ship's public address system: "Good morning,
good people!" It was the voice of our intrepid expedition leader, Mr. Don,
rousting us bleary-eyed passengers from our slumbers. After this hearty
greeting he would then announce the call to morning chow and fill us in
on the ever-dropping, Antarctic, outdoor temperature. One of the great
joys—and occasional frustration—of expedition travel is that you never
know for sure what great adventures might be in store for us, and Mr. Don
was a master in preparing us for these unpredictable events. He would
then conclude each of these dispatches by sharing with us an inspiring
quote of some great traveler or piece of profound wisdom about the nature of our world.

In our many ramblings around and about this incredible planet, both
my wife and I have been blessed more times than we can count with the
good fortune of meeting many dedicated and knowledgeable tour guides,
naturalists, and expedition leaders; Mr. Don was no exception. A native
of the great country of New Zealand, you knew the instant you met him

that he was a man who absolutely loved his job. His seemingly boundless enthusiasm for all things Antarctic was downright contagious!

But Mr. Don was not just an outstanding guide; he was also a benevolent and infinitely patient good shepherd to his frequently demanding—and sometimes, downright whiny—tour participants. He seemed to possess an innate sensitivity and insight into the needs and wants of his fellow humans and was a tireless advocate for all aspects of the natural world around us; he understood (but only grudgingly accepted) how the universe works. Because he pays attention and is willing to do battle on behalf of all that is good, Mr. Don is one of those rare individuals who makes it possible for the rest of us mere mortals to fall safely and soundly to sleep in our beds at night with complete confidence that the world as we know it will still be here when we wake up.

Every morning shortly after breakfast, Mr. Don would again brief us on our upcoming shore excursions. On this particular morning we had just spent the better part of two turbulent days steaming our way eastward from Cape Horn at the bottom point of South America across the cold and forbidding southern Atlantic Ocean. In a few hours we would be anchoring in Stanley Harbor, the capital of the Falkland Islands. Looking around at some of my fellow passengers, I could tell that several of them were still somewhat suffering from the effects of the open ocean crossing.

I had spent almost three and a half years in my fleeting youth sailing aboard a U.S. Navy aircraft carrier the Pacific Ocean, and with the exception of a few major typhoons, I had never seen the sea as rough and unrelentingly convulsive as what we had just endured. It bounced our two-hundred-foot-long converted Russian icebreaker up and down, up and down, up and down, like we were a wine bottle cork. Thank God I've been blessed with an iron stomach because —although I should know better than to tempt fate—I've never, ever been seasick. The majority of my forty fellow passengers, however, took it pretty rough. During those two days no more than fifteen or so made it to any of the meals. Some were retching so hard they needed the attention of the ship's doctor.

But soon we were safely within the bounds of the channel leading to Port Stanley, and the mighty *Polar Pioneer* glided along the still water as if it were on a millpond. After the usual detailed discussions about the history, culture, and wildlife we could expect to experience at our landing site, Mr. Don, for a brief moment before dismissing us, seemed stilled and reflective. He told us that if we had time, there was something he wanted us all to see. (He wouldn't tell us what it was.) He told us to walk up the hill behind the town as far as the road would take us. When we got to the top, we should then turn left onto the road headed down toward the sea. What we were looking for would be just off a side road to the right. "When you reach this spot," he said, "just take a moment and reflect on what it all means."

The Falkland Islands' capital city of Stanley is the quintessential little British town with its perfectly painted little houses, fire-engine red phone booths, well-tended flower gardens, and wide array of pubs. The place could have been lifted up in total from anywhere in Yorkshire or Swaledale and plopped down upon this barren, heath-covered group of rocks sitting in the middle of nowhere in the stormy South Atlantic.

After walking along the main road next to the sea and stopping by the post office to mail our postcards, we decided to check out what our expedition leader had asked us to visit. We found a street heading up the hill and then began the steep walk. When we got to where the town ended and the sheep pastures began, we turned left toward the sea. After about ten minutes, we saw off to our right what Mr. Don had wanted us to see. As it turned out, he and several of our fellow shipmates just happened to be there as well.

In front of us now, fenced off with rusted barbed wire that hung tightly on gray steel poles, and clearly posted with triangular-shaped, bright red skull and crossbones signs, was a minefield, a silent remnant of one of the most asinine armed conflicts of recent times, the Falkland War. For nearly all of the passengers standing there looking at this deadly little patch of land, this would be their first exposure to the diabolical horrors that these simple little devices can thrust upon a society.

For the last 150 years, the Falkland Islands territory has been a British colony. In 1982, for reasons that still to this very day no one quite completely understands, the government of Argentina decided to lay claim to the islands and began a full-scale land, air, and sea assault to capture them. A ten-week counterattack by the British government managed to retake the islands, but at a huge cost. Combat casualties were 250 British dead and 650 Argentines killed.

A legacy of that war now remained before our group. As of this writing, government authorities estimate there are about 25,000 antipersonnel and anti-vehicle mines distributed on 117 different minefields in the Falklands. Nearly all were placed by the Argentines around Stanley. Because of the high winds, large quantities of surface water, soft and boggy ground, and the use of plastic, poorly detectable devises, the removal of these weapons resulted in unusually high casualties for the demining units. Therefore, their removal efforts have ceased. Authorities instead rely now mostly on prevention and education.

As I briefly mentioned, the fact that land mines could be a problem in this peaceful, bucolic and isolated Western community, where the sheep outnumber people probably fifty- to- one was probably one of the last thoughts most anyone in our expedition gathering could ever have imagined. Everyone in the group had heard about, or was at least superficially aware of, the global curse of land mines and of the senseless devastation they inflict upon both combatants and innocent civilians. These cold and calculatingly cruel, insidious killers had been much in the news thanks to the efforts of the late Princess Diana, Angelina Jolie, and of several other celebrities. But most of the group felt that it was just a problem of war-ravaged, Third World nations; countries such as Cambodia, Vietnam, Bosnia, Afghanistan, and Angola.

And this lesson, I think, is what our expedition leader's purpose was in suggesting we all visit this lonely patch of wind-blown earth. He understood that for most of the people standing there on that hilltop, this would probably be the only exposure they would ever have of the horrible reality of land mines. He wanted to drive home to us the case that land mines are a real and horrifying fact of life in a lot of the world in which we live and that at least for those present, they would now know firsthand the tremendous potential suffering these wretched devices represent to all of life.

For Theresa and me (especially me), however, this firsthand witness to the brutal fact of land mines was not a new experience. We've seen the consequences of these barbarous devices several times before. I, personally, as a consequence of innocently stepping off into a cow pasture to take a pee while at a rest-stop in the middle of the Bosnian boonies, nearly became one of the 25,000 victims who are killed or maimed every year by land mines.

> Land-mines are uniquely savage in the history of
> modern conventional warfare not only because of
> their appalling individual impact, but also their
> long-term social and economic destruction

–Ms. GRAÇA MACHEL, UNITED NATIONS SECRETARY-GENERAL'S
EXPERT ON THE IMPACT OF ARMED CONFLICT ON CHILDREN

The United Nations estimates that there are more than 110 million land mines seeded in sixty-eight countries around the world. Children, they say (not surprisingly), turn out to be particularly susceptible to the lethal effects of these deadly devices, both unintentionally and on purpose. During the 1980s Iran/Iraq War, both sides of the conflict sent children ahead of soldiers into minefields with the righteous promise from their religious leaders that they would ascend directly to heaven if they died. It is said that the Russian army, during their deadly foray into Afghanistan, even designed a mine to look like a toy butterfly so that children would be more likely to pick one up.

And even when mine laying strategies tried to concentrate their lethal force on armed combatants, children are still a large percentage of their unintended casualties. Why this is so is quite obvious. Most of the child victims are illiterate or are simply too young to read or understand minefield warning signs. They have a natural curiosity and will pick up to explore all things different or interesting. But it is also because of their small physical size that they suffer most.

Before I go on, I must remind readers of one more layer of sinister intent that's often forgotten in the discussion of land mines: that not all mines are designed to kill. A great number of antipersonnel mines serve the psychological purpose of intentionally just maiming their victim. That is, they are designed to create hardship and angst by blowing away a foot or hand; some mines even specialize in blasting an enemy's testicles off! The lethal force needed to perform these dastardly deeds, however, is often more than enough to annihilate a small child. But even if the tragic young girl or boy just (I'm not sure the word *just* is appropriate in this context) has their leg or arm blown away, the difficulty and expense of properly fitting a prosthesis on their still-growing limb stumps is often insurmountable.

So far in my journeys, nowhere have I seen this horrifying reality of land mines more vividly demonstrated than in the war-ravaged nation of Cambodia. Depending on your source of information, the estimated numbers of the deadly devices seeded throughout the country range from six to ten million, making Cambodia one of the most heavily mined places on earth. Most of these are of Chinese and former Soviet Union manufacture and were laid down by Khmer Rouge communists during the country's civil war in the 1980s. And as if these land mines were not enough, it is estimated that there are over one-half million tons of unexploded ordnance left over from the American bombing campaigns during the Vietnam War. The end result of all this is that today, the nation of Cambodia has the highest percentage of amputees of any other nation on earth.

On a visit to the grand old ruins of the Khmer civilization at Angkor Wat and Angkor Thom, beginning with our arrival at the local airport in Siam Reap, and then continuing nonstop at every tourist site, restroom, or restaurant we came to, we were deluged by children of every age begging for food or money. Lovely children! Movie-star gorgeous young girls and boys! Kids you wished you could just pick up and bring home! The tragedy, of course, is that over half of these hapless children swarming around us were missing an arm from the elbow down or an entire leg.

Because of their inexorable persistence in harassing tourists for a handout, tour operators and guides often referred to these kids by the insensitive (but, sadly, very true) term of "land sharks." And if the truth were to be told—and it is with the greatest of shame that I say this—there were a couple of times that in moments of overwhelming frustration, these little darlings tried my patience as well. I recall vividly (for a reason I'll explain shortly) that one time, after enduring one these unrelenting feeding frenzies in which I actually felt my life was in danger, I just *could not* take these pestering little monsters any longer. Like I really meant it, I screamed at the top of my lungs for them to please, please, just leave me alone!

The children, of course, instantly scattered, not out of fear of some old verbose American hollering at them but rather because they knew that if they didn't back off, the hard-hearted local police, with their savage, ever-present nightsticks in hand, would soon move in. But my anger was to wane quickly, because from out of the dispersing horde, a little girl of about eight-years-old stepped forward directly in front of me and stopped. Without saying a word, she lovingly wrapped the tiny stumps of what were left of both her arms around my left leg and hugged me as hard as she could. Not quite knowing what else to do, I just stood there. After what seemed like an unbearable eternity, and without yet letting go, she looked up at me with her sad, SAD, little brown eyes and sobbingly pleaded with me to give her a dollar. She wanted just a single dollar!

An overwhelming feeling of sorrow—as well as a slight touch of shame—overtook my previously peevish anger, and at that moment I wished with every ounce of my being that I was God almighty, and that I could then give this child her precious little hands back. But I couldn't. And I didn't have a dollar either, having given them all away days ago.

But unable to resist this helpless child's obvious desperation, I reached my hand down toward my front blue jeans pant pocket. The little girl, who seemed to sense instantly what I was trying to do, then let go of her grip of my leg and backed a baby-step away from me. I reached into my pocket and pulled out the thin wad of money that I kept there for emergencies. I leafed through the bills and peeled out a ten-dollar bill. And no sooner than I did, the question instantly dawned on me of how I was going to give this little girl, who had no hands, the money. Not knowing what else to do, I folded the bill into quarters, with the intention of perhaps putting it into the upper pocket of her white cotton blouse.

But the little sweetheart had other ideas. As I started reaching my right hand toward her, she thrust her head forward, and with the precision of a brain surgeon—combined with the ruthlessness of a pit bull—she snatched the folded bill into her mouth. Looking quickly up at me with about a half inch of the ten-dollar bill still showing between her glistening white teeth, she smiled a quick smile of what I hope was of thanks, and in a flash, before the other kids could steal it away from her, she was gone.

> Mine removal is a lengthy and expensive business. Weapons that cost as little as $3 each to manufacture can cost up to $1,000 to remove. Land-mines can be blithely spread at rates of over 1,000 per minute, but it may take a skilled expert an entire day just to clear by hand 20–50 square meters of mine-contaminated land.

–Author Unknown

The Balkan Peninsula juts out under the central European continent like a giant upside down pitcher's mitt. At its western end the peninsula ends in the country of Greece. In the east, the southernmost tip ultimately joins Europe with the continent of Asia at the Great city of Istanbul. Bordered on the west by the Adriatic Sea and on the east by the Black Sea, this mountainous, relatively small piece of real estate is probably one of the most ethnically, religiously, and politically diverse territories on earth. Present-day ethnic groups include the Albanians, Bulgarians, Croats, Greeks, Hungarians, Italians, Macedonians, Maldivians, Montenegrins, Romanians, Russians, Serbs, Slovaks, Slovenes, Turks, and Ukrainians. Thrown into this mix are Roman Catholics, Muslims, Protestants, and several various forms of Christian Eastern Orthodox faiths.

The politicians have even come up with a word for this region's strict segregation and zealous maintenance of individual ethnic identity: Balkanization. And with very few exceptions, for more than two thousand years, these various confusions of faiths and ethnicity have been doing whatever they possibly can to destroy and obliterate each other. Sadly, to make matters even worse, this endless onslaught of war, the absolute lack of productive farmland, and its cultural isolation held in place by the region's nearly inaccessible and brutally mountainous terrain have all contributed to making the Balkan countries some of the poorest nations on the European continent.

We had come to this tormented, but beautiful land of endless contrasts, for two main reasons: to visit the World Heritage city of Dubrovnik in Croatia, and to do a pilgrimage to the Shrine of the Virgin Mary in the mountain village of Medjugorje, in the neighboring country of Bosnia/Herzegovina. One of my first memories of our visit to the region occurred during a short stopover on our flight from London to Dubrovnik in the little airport at the coastal Croatian city of Zadar. It was early morning, maybe around eight o'clock local time, and a cool, dreary mist hung over the airfield.

As soon as we landed, instead of taxiing directly to the airport's terminal, we rolled along in our giant Croatian Airlines Airbus 340 for a mile or more before reaching the gate area on what seemed to be a black-topped, back country road. Our jaunt through the hayfields and orchards came complete with crossing guards at all intersections holding back a line of donkey carts loaded with milk cans and bundles of corn stalks.

The contrasts continued as we explored the medieval city of Dubrovnik. This ancient, walled, seaside city of beautiful old churches, universities, and monasteries still had visible scars from artillery shelling during the recent Balkan Wars. In yet another example of mankind's seemingly ingrained jealously, avarice, downright stupidity, and incessant need for revenge, Serbian soldiers—for no strategic reason whatsoever!—for one hundred days rained down thousands of shells indiscriminately into the town.

Our car ride up the Adriatic coast to Medjugorje was no different. The stunning beauty of the sea contrasted sharply with the wanton destruction of every seaside town the entire length of our road trip. The carnage continued as we headed eastward from the sea across the Bosnian frontier into the countryside surrounding the village of Medjugorje. But here, the devastation seemed to stop. Perhaps it was through the miraculous intercession of the Virgin Mary, or perhaps the abject poverty of the region made the village just not that valuable as a target, but for whatever reason, this rural hamlet escaped the fate of most of the rest of the peninsula.

We spent three days in Medjugorje attending Mass, hiking and climbing the various pilgrim trails and mountains, and listening to the story about how the Blessed Mother appeared to five farm children. An air of profound holiness embraces the place, and all who make the journey to this little mountain village are blessed beyond all they could ever hope for. It's one of the few places on this earth that I sincerely hope to return to someday.

On our drive back to Dubrovnik, and just after we crossed the Bosnian frontier back into Croatia, our guide Anna asked our driver to stop at a small, mountaintop parking area that had a great view of the valley below. She told us it would be one of the most stunning sights we'd ever seen. And indeed it was. Stretching out in front of us like a giant sparkling blue topaz gemstone was the Adriatic Sea. In the far distance, I thought I could even make out the coast of Italy. Directly below us, dotting the Croatian coast up and down for as far as I could see, were hundreds of emerald green islands.

But like everything else in this land of great contrasts, the scenic beauty of the mountain pass upon which we now stood also harbored a sinister past. After allowing us a few moments to take some photographs, Anna pointed out to us two nearby mountaintop ridges. She told us that during the recent Balkan Wars, the Serbian army took full advantage of this strategic site to rain down artillery shells upon the Croatians below. When she was finished speaking, she excused herself and walked over to where our driver was standing to join him in having a cigarette. When she was somewhat out of sight, I stepped down the nearby embankment because I had to relieve my bladder. What happened next is still some-what of a blur.

I had gotten about fifteen feet down the hill and had just climbed over a four-foot-high barbed wire fence into what I thought was just an overgrown cow pasture when all of a sudden I heard a voice screaming at me from up on the parking area. It was our driver. Holding up both of his hands, his palms facing me in what looked like the universal gesture to halt, and hollering nonstop in what was probably Croatian, I—not know-ing what else to do—just stood still. A couple of seconds more passed, by which time Anna joined him. She shouted down to me to please stand perfectly still; I was in a minefield!

In utter disbelief, all I could think of in that moment was, "Jesus Christ, Richard, what in the heck (not the exact word I used) did you get yourself into this time?" I don't remember being scared; I didn't panic or anything, I just stood there slightly confused and not quite sure what to do next. And, to make matters worse, I still hadn't gotten a chance to go to the bathroom. But God must take pity on fools like me; there is no other way to explain my good fortune, because it turned out that Paval (our driver) was a mine removal expert. What were the chances of that ever happening to someone else?

I didn't know it at the time, but as a younger man and as a soldier for the Croatian army, Paval's job was to clear battlefields and strategic roadways of enemy land mines. Probably because his English was minimal, and my Croatian was none, during our whole three-day trip to Medjugorje, other than saying hello, good morning, etc., he only spoke with Anna or the other drivers we met along the way. He seemed, however, to enjoy the pilgrimage as much as we did, participating with us in all of the Masses, sacred walks, and Rosaries. Also, a fellow beer drinker like myself, we had treated each other to several rounds during our evening meals together.

But now Pavel was all that stood between me and the mess I'd now innocently gotten myself into. Anna stood, the terror of the who situation obvious in her eyes, right behind him. Theresa, not quite sure yet what was going on, looked anxiously down at the scene from the side of the parking lot. When Paval got to the barbed wire fence, he stopped and dropped to his knees and looked carefully at the twenty feet of ground that stood between us. With Anna interpreting, he asked me if I could see the footprints from where I had just walked. I told him I could see a few, but not all of them.

Since I was already facing them, and after what seemed an eternity, he said to step as gently and flatfooted as I could back toward him. For the first three steps I could make out my tracks and everything was fine. But then I was stuck; I couldn't make out a footprint to save my life! Pavel then stood up, walked a few steps to his right, and then back again to the left as if he was trying to catch a correct angle, a shadow, an indentation in the earth, or any other sign of where a mine might be.

With the intensity of a laser beam, he slowly scanned back and forth the grass and soil surface between us. After several minutes, he stopped and had a rather long discussion with Anna. Back and forth they went until finally, in what looked like a gesture of agreement, she finally spoke. "Richard," she said, the numbing sense of helplessness apparent in her voice, "Paval feels that the ground between where you are and the fence looks to be completely undisturbed. As slowly and as gently as you can, sir, walk back toward us." Then, after a few more words were spoken between them, Paval sent Anna back up the hill. Just in case.

I waited until I saw her reach the parking lot, and then without giving it another thought, I walked lightly but determinedly to where Paval was standing.

Thank God his professional assessment of the situation was correct! When at last I got to the fence, he helped me up and over to the other side. Obviously overjoyed and relieved at my safe return (and probably happy as well that he wouldn't have to explain to the police how he let this knucklehead American walk onto a minefield), he wrapped both his arms around me and in the Eastern European tradition, exuberantly kissed me on both cheeks. As he backed away from me and turned to go up the hill, I noticed something that I hadn't seen before. I saw that on the left side of his neck, just below his ear, was a giant scar. But either because I was elated that my ordeal was over or because I still had to pee—really badly—I gave the wound no more thought.

An hour or so later, after we had safely motored our way down the mountain to the coast, I mentioned my seeing Paval's scar to Anna. She and he then spoke there in the front seat back and forth for a bit. When they were finished talking, he shrugged his shoulders and returned his attention to his driving. Given his permission to do so, Anna turned around and told us the story. It turns out that what I saw of the scar on the left side of his neck was just a tiny bit of the total wound he'd received in the line of duty as a soldier.

Paval was wounded just after the Croatian army had regained control of the region we had just driven through. He had been part of the team of mine removal experts assigned to clearing the local roadways. Not far from where he had just probably saved my life, a land mine he was clearing exploded. The blast ripped a hole in his protective gear, allowing shrapnel to tear into his neck and left shoulder. He spent over six months in the hospital in Zagreb, the capital of Croatia, undergoing many reconstructive surgeries. Although he did a good job hiding it, he was deaf in his left ear as well.

When we got back down to the coast, we stopped for an afternoon snack. Paval and I, in rapid succession, belted back several bottles of beer together. He seemed to have taken the whole episode a little worse than me. But the delicious beer made us both feel better, the day was sunny and clear, and we both were still alive to enjoy it all. When it came time to pay the bar bill, I insisted on picking up the tab. And without argument, Paval let me.

Walking through the parking lot on our way back to the car, an old man approached us with a bunch of miscellaneous bullet and small artillery shell casings in a plastic grocery bag that he then tried to sell me. From the streets of New York City to a public park in St. Petersburg, Russia to a market stall in downtown Hanoi, I'd run into his kind many times before: brave, patriotic, former soldiers and sailors having to sell off their war mementos to buy food—or beer. And although interested, I knew there was no way I'd ever be able to get the pieces of disarmed (hopefully) ordnance onto an airplane.

Paval, somewhat now more relaxed, quietly spoke a few words to the old gentleman. As they both smiled at each other, the old man reached into his coat and pulled out a smallish seven-inch-by-ten-inch flat piece of slightly rusted metal. When he flipped it over, I could make out the universal skull and crossbones of a land mine field warning sign. It turns out that even though it is against the law to remove such signs, tourists like to buy—or steal—them for souvenirs.

I passed on the opportunity. I handed the old soldier the equivalent of ten dollars and then, raising my right hand up in the universal gesture of having a drink, asked him (via Pavel) to have a few beers on me.

Floating in the Indian Ocean below the subcontinent of India and looking like a large pear is the island nation of Sri Lanka. Formerly known as the

British colony of Ceylon, the island is famous for its coffee, tea, spices, and rubber. For three hundred years before the birth of Christ, Sri Lanka has had a continuous Buddhist religious tradition. To this day, over 70 percent of the island's inhabitants are still Buddhists.

As is frequently the case as I travel the highways and byways of this world (and often to the annoyance of my dear wife), I'm often confounded by the many contradictions that the creature called man is so capable of. Throughout the entire history of civilization, one of the greatest of these ironies is the seemingly endless propensity of our species to aggressively, and often without the slightest bit of mercy, slaughter one another in the name of religion. This is, of course, not the way it's supposed to happen. Be you a Christian, Muslim, Jew, Buddhist, Hindu, Rastafarian, Jain, or whatever, the basic tenet at the core of nearly all religious traditions is some variation of the Golden Rule: this is to love your fellow man. But somewhere along the line—and for reasons that are infinitely complex and not at all well understood—a vast majority of the human race has chosen to disregard this most basic of laws.

The wise men and women who inhabit the ivory towers of the world's great universities say that religion is rarely solely at fault. They say that if you scratch just below the surface of most "religious" wars, you will find that conflicting cultural, political, or socioeconomic issues are the actual driving forces responsible for the fighting. Religion, they conclude, is just a convenient way of keeping track of it all.

Far be it for me to question these distinguished scholars, but I think it all boils down to something more basic. I believe something resides in the very core of our human natures, our very DNA if you will, that makes it impossible for the vast majority of mankind to rise above the mayhem. I chose to blame it all on the avarice of a few, the need for revenge by the many, and the sheer lazy willingness of the majority to just mindlessly follow along for the ride.

A great example of this quandary is particularly obvious in Sri Lanka. Like far too many places on this planet, this island nation has been in the grips of a long civil war between the Sinhalese majority and the Tamil minority. What makes this bloody conflict somewhat unique is that the Sinhalese, who make up about 82 percent of the population of Sri Lanka, are mostly Buddhists, and their opponents, the Tamils, are nearly all Hindus. The demented irony, of course, is that both of these religious traditions, especially the Buddhists, zealously advocate their love and reverence for all sentient beings as the basic core of their religious beliefs. But here they are, for the entire world to see, blasting away at each other like warring, rabid dogs.

We were visiting this country for two reasons. The first was to do a trek to the top of Adam's Peak, the highest mountain in Sri Lanka. At the summit of the mountain is supposed to be a five-foot-long rock formation called the Sri Pada, which translated from Sanskrit means "the sacred foot." The creator of the footprint is a matter of some controversy. Buddhists believe it was made by the left foot of the Buddha (the right foot being somewhere in Thailand); the Brahmans believe it was laid down by the Hindu god Shiva; and Muslims and Christians believe that Adam made the print the first time he stepped upon the earth. Unfortunately, this trip had to be canceled at the last minute due to some terrorist activity in the region. We used the time instead to do a little local sightseeing and to catch up on some much needed rest.

Our second planned destination would be a road trip to the World Heritage city of Kandy, home of the Temple of the Tooth. Our driver/guide for our journey into the central highland city was a very handsome—and interminably talkative—older man named Joe. A native of the capital city of Colombo, other than his wont for strongly rolling the letter *R* in all his words, the gentleman spoke impeccable English. This was a good thing, because from the moment we left our hotel for the ten-hour round trip, he never stopped talking! As he navigated his way through the early morning rush hour city traffic, he began speaking by pointing out to us all of the spots where the Tamil "Tiger" terrorists had set off roadside and suicide bombs.

"Forty people were killed in the marketplace down this street when a car bomb exploded," he'd say. With his left hand on the steering wheel and the right hand pointing out the open right side window, and with the objectivity of a college calculus teacher, Joe told us of how eighteen men and women were massacred when a Hindu gunman stormed the government building we were passing. As we drove around a great traffic circle in the center of the city, he made sure to tell us the exact location of where a suicide bomber had blown up a city bus. Even though he said that it had happened a year before, I couldn't help but notice as we rode by that the asphalt and concrete highway barriers still were blackened from the deadly inferno. The explosion had to have been horrifying.

But not all of what Joe had to say was doom and gloom. At heart, he was a gifted tour guide who knew every type of fruit tree, local legend, which spices were for sale along the highway by local farmers, the breeds of cattle and water buffalo . . . everything! His life mission on that day was to make sure we learned every last detail about his country. "Have you ever tasted a mango?" He was pointing to a huge tree alongside the road. "Did you know that they originated in India? That one-half of all the fruit grown in the world are mangos? That there is a breed of mango called *huevos de toro* (a slang term for bull testicles)? Did you know that Sri Lanka has a long history of being visited by aliens? Yes, there are thousand-year-old cave paintings on our island that clearly show ancient men in space gear. Did you hear about the latest scandal in the office of our minister of agriculture?"

And on and on, nonstop, all the way to Kandy! But it was a pleasant drive otherwise, and even though it would have been nice to have enjoyed a peaceful moment, most of what he had to say was quite interesting. We'd lucked out again in finding a great guide.

The town of Kandy was quite a welcome change from the oppressive heat and humidity of the sea coast. For as long as civilization has existed on the island, political leaders, civil servants, government administrators, and their families came to this mountain oasis for relief from the extreme temperatures of the coastal lowlands and the pestilence and disease that would often follow. Joe drove us around a lake that was in the center of town pointing out a politician's house or some famous Indian actor's home. Again, his verbal assault was nonstop. But to this day, I'm still amazed at his encyclopedic knowledge of everything Sri Lankan!

After finding a parking place, we walked uphill to the entrance of the Temple of the Tooth. But before we could enter the temple grounds, we all had to be searched: men passing through one tent, women in another. Thinking this quite strange, and seeing that I was a little bit perplexed by it all, Joe told me as we waited our turns in line, that in 1998, suicide bombers had succeeded in sneaking into the temple and then detonated their deadly cargo. "Scores of people were killed," he said, "hence, the need for security." It turned out to be one of the most complete body searches I've ever had!

Legend has it that a tooth from the Buddha was removed from the ashes of his funeral pyre and then for the next eight hundred years followed the spread of Buddhism on the Indian subcontinent. The relic was brought to Sri Lanka in 313 AD. Supposedly this was at the request of the great Buddha himself because he felt that his religion would be safe in this country for 2,500 years. The sacred tooth traveled for centuries from one royal palace to another until the permanent temple complex in which we now stood could be built.

The altar upon which the tooth sits—that is, the multiple bejeweled caskets that contain the actual relic—is located in the center-most section of the sanctuary, down from the long hallway just recently blown up by the terrorists. (The tooth itself is only on view once a year.) From all over the world, devout Buddhists come to this very spot to venerate this tiny fragment of the mortal remains of the founder of their faith, the first human they believe to break free of the endless chain of death and rebirth.

Not wanting to interfere with their worship, we all stood quietly in the dim light of that inner sanctum back away from the altar and just took it all in. For me, all of the mysteries of the Orient that have seduced, marveled, and moved the hearts of Western travelers since the days of Marco Polo converged and were concentrated there at that precious moment in the temple's sanctum sanctorum. The thick, heady smell of thousands of sticks of incense wafting heavenward combined with the mesmerizing rhythmic and muffled mono-tonal voices of the priests and devoted pilgrims as they chanted their devotions to their bewildering pantheon of gods, making the experience for me truly otherworldly.

Even our guide was speechless! ... but for only a moment.

On our way back down out of the mountains, Joe asked us if we wanted to make one more stop at a place just off the highway called the Pinnewela Elephant Sanctuary. I remembered reading something about the place in the in-flight magazine on our Sri Lankan Airlines flight from Bangkok, and since both Theresa and I are great lovers of elephants, we readily agreed. He said that if we timed it right, we could see the elephants as they took their afternoon walk. And so about halfway back to Colombo, he turned right off of the main highway and drove us to the small village of Kegalle, home of the sanctuary. After finding a place to park, Joe showed us the dirt lane through the village where the elephants would be taking their afternoon stroll. Looking at his wristwatch, he said we had about fifteen minutes to find a good spot to see them go by.

The Pinnewela Elephant Sanctuary was founded in 1975 by the Sri Lankan government as an orphanage for the island's infant Asian elephants who lost their mothers either to hunting or to the war. Today, the Pinnewela Sanctuary has grown to contain the largest captive elephant herd in the world. Besides admission to the park itself, what makes the place so attractive to tourists is that twice a day, the whole herd is paraded down from the sanctuary grounds through the village to the Maha Oya River for their baths.

Theresa and I located ourselves a small area of elevated brick sidewalk next to the dirt lane the elephants would be walking up. After only a couple of minutes of waiting, we began to hear some distant shouting; this turned out to be the mahouts (elephant drivers) giving instructions to their charges to begin walking. Soon we could see the elephants themselves, led by one of the mahouts, ambling their way up the dusty alley. And what a magnificent sight it was to see these gigantic animals as they walked peacefully by.

But as is seemingly always the case with these blissful moments of discovery that make traveling such a joy for me, the malignant dark side of humanity manages to always slip itself into the scene. Looking down toward the river as the line of elephants passed by, I could see that one of them kept bobbing her head up and down quite violently as she approached where we were standing. As a veterinarian, one of the first things I thought of was that the elephant had a sore front foot and was hobbling along to take the pressure off it as she walked. When she got closer, I could see that it was more drastic than that.

Her right front foot, it turned out, was actually gone! In us humans, what would be our forearm just below our elbow was now on this elephant just a rounded-off stump. I would later find out that Sama, whose name in Sinhalese means "eternal peace," as a young elephant had become yet another victim of this island's asinine civil war by stepping on a land mine. Upon watching this magnificent beast as she awkwardly hobbled past us, doing her darnedest to keep up with her herd mates, I found my consciousness being subjected once again to the global tragedy, the vileness, the sheer evil of the legacy of mankind's use of land mines; never once had I ever thought of looking beyond the human toll of what these wretched implements of destruction were fully capable of inflicting upon all life.

Later on as I did further research on this issue, I realized that Sama was actually quite lucky. All throughout the civil war, and even now in peacetime, no less than ten elephants are killed every year in Sri Lanka by stepping on—or by sniffing with their trunks—land mines. The problem exists as well in several other countries plagued by these devices: Angola, Bangladesh, Mozambique, Nepal, Zimbabwe, and, of course, Cambodia. I read a report from a field veterinarian in Sri Lanka who described how elephants, due to their enormous weight and their total reliance on their trunks to survive, are particularly vulnerable to the maiming effects of land mines.

I'll spare the readers the details.

Back on the road home to Colombo, it wasn't long before Joe became reanimated. "Did you know that national bird is the Sri Lankan jungle fowl? (It looked like a chicken to me.) Sir, did you know that cinnamon is native to Sri Lanka? That the Hebrew God told your Prophet Moses to include sweet cinnamon in the holy oil of anointing? That Sri Lanka still produces 90 percent of the world's cinnamon? Did you know that in Hindu mythology there is a demon named Mahasona who rides on the back of a big black dog?"

And on and on and on

POSTSCRIPT

From the latest reports that I could find (2003) here are the annual land mine casualties for the following countries:
-   Cambodia: 834
-   Bosnia/Herzegovina: 72
-   Sri Lanka: 142
-   The Falkland Islands: 0

As I was putting the final touches on this story in preparation for sending it off to the proofreader, I got the idea to do one last Google search to find out just how the state of land mine removal is progressing in these five countries. And, of course, just as with every other aspect regarding life on this planet, it's as I expected: some news is good and a lot of it is still bad, world governments are still both enlightened and corrupt, and people continue to be both humanitarian and stupid.

Regarding Cambodia, I read a story of a man named Aki Ra that highlighted, once again, a phenomenon I've seen over and over in my life: the ability of a single determined individual to make a difference—both good and tragic—in this world. Mr. Ra was orphaned as a child when his parents were killed by Khmer Rouge soldiers during his country's civil war. At the age of ten (TEN!), the same Khmer Rouge conscripted him into their army. In 1983, he was captured by the Vietnamese and was forced to fight on their side until the war was over. Upon returning home, he got a job with the United Nations peacekeeping forces in his country where he learned how to be a land mine removal expert.

Discovering he had quite a talent for removing land mines, and with the only goal of making his country safe again, he decided to make it his full-time occupation. With no government sanction, and using only a knife, a stick, and his wits, he spent the next several years helping the peoples of hundreds of small villages throughout his country to live safely again. At first, he would pay for his activities by defusing and disarming the weapons and then selling the metal for scrap. But as word got out about his brave exploits, he began charging tourists a dollar to see his now somewhat substantial ordnance collection.

In his hometown of Siem Reap this collection ultimately became the Cambodian Landmine Museum. But something greater was about to happen. As Aki Ra worked to clear various villages, he began to bring home to his wife, Hourt, orphaned and abandoned children who had been mutilated by exploded land mines and other ordnance. According to the Wikipedia article that I used as the primary source for this story, today twenty-seven of these orphans call the Cambodia Land mine Museum their home. But there is a second part to Mr. Ra's story.

One of the gazillion things I've learned in my now many years of plodding along on this planet is that throughout the entirety of the history of the human race, the morons of this world, who seem to exist and find their greatest expression in the form of government bureaucrats, will always be lurking in the background waiting to justify their pathetic and paranoid existences. For reasons never made completely clear, the Cambodian government decided to close down Ra's museum in 2007. (They later did allow him to set the museum back up next to one of the Angkor temples some 25 miles from town.) But even more tragic, in their infinite wisdom—and again, for reasons that completely baffle any thinking person—as a trade-off to allow him to set up his museum again, they also ordered Ra to end his land mine removal activities.

A United Nations UNICEF report had the following data regarding the subject of land mines in Bosnia and Herzegovina. In spite of the decrease in the number of land mine fields due to ongoing demining activities, and in spite of the increased education of the dangers of land mines in general, there has actually been an increase of land mine related deaths! The deaths mostly occurred in adults who entered minefields while trying to provide for their families by collecting firewood, collecting iron, or harvesting fruits and mushrooms. And the biggest reason these otherwise intelligent people risked their lives (other than desperation and hunger) by entering these death traps? It's because of tourists and other mindless idiots stealing the land mine warning signs for souvenirs!

In Sri Lanka, the situation for the native elephants is good and bad. In the northern end of the island especially, fighting for the last thirty years between the government troops and the Tamil rebels caused tens of thousands of farmers and rural inhabitants to abandon their farms and villages and move to southern cities and refugee camps. This abandonment of thousands of acres of tilled and managed farmland, in turn, has led to a rapid return of native plants. And this combination of no people and a great abundance of a secure food source have led to a large rebound in the number of wild elephants.

However, now that a rather shaky peace has been agreed to by the former combatants, the citizens of these rural areas are beginning to return to their previous homes. This return back to the land has led to the increase in the number of fatal clashes (on both sides) between humans and the elephants. To their credit, however, the Sri Lankan government is taking a very proactive stand on the issue. They've set aside great plots of land to be spared as elephant sanctuaries, have built hundreds of kilometers of electrified fences to keep elephants out of select villages, and are creating habitat-enriched areas so that the elephants don't have to plunder the farmland. So it's not all bad news for the elephants.

In 2005, the citizens of the Falkland Islands petitioned the British government to forgo a planned mine removal scheduled for their island by 2009. The islanders felt very strongly that they would rather live with the mines than risk any fatalities to the army sappers. Instead, they requested that the government clear an equal number of square miles in countries such as Angola, Afghanistan, or Cambodia.

There has been one beneficial side effect to the land mine problem in the Falklands. In the areas where formerly public beaches have all been mined, the native bird life, especially penguins, has thrived beyond the imagination of all wildlife conservationists! With no human beachgoers to trample upon them, or livestock to graze them down, native vegetation has rebounded. And because they're too light to set off any of the thousands of land mines, this, in turn, has attracted penguins and other seabirds in great abundance to begin residing once again in their former breeding grounds.

Virgin Mary Tree

CHAPTER 11

Virgin Mary Tree

———⊗⊗⊗———

Man is a creature who walks in two worlds and traces
upon the walls of his cave the wonders and the
nightmare experiences of his spiritual pilgrimage.

-MORRIS WEST

FOR A MAJORITY OF THE world's Christians, the Basilica of the Holy Sepulcher located in Jerusalem's Old Quarter is believed to be the most sacred place on earth. Literally millions of pilgrims visit this church every year to see and to touch and to physically experience the two most important places associated with the Passion of Jesus Christ: The hill of Calvary (Golgotha) where He suffered His death upon the cross and the tomb of His resurrection.

With God-awful difficulty and a lot of frustrating confusion, we had just completed the labyrinth of what we hoped were the first nine stations of the Stations of the Cross as the path threaded its way along the Via Dolorosa (Jesus' Way of Suffering) through Jerusalem's Old City. We now stood in the courtyard of the Holy Sepulcher Church figuring out what to do next. Inside the church, the guide book said, we would find the last five of the fourteen Stations.

I remember saying to my wife as we stood there hot and sweaty and worn out from our journey through the narrow alleyways, crowded coffee and tea shops and merciless gauntlet of holy relic hawkers and religious souvenir shops that line the Via Dolorosa, that for something as spiritually obligatory to the Christian pilgrim's Holy Land experience as the chance to retrace the steps Jesus took on the way to his crucifixion, it sure was a real pain in the neck to find.

But there is a phenomena that we've noticed occurs, especially throughout our travels of the Middle East, that always manages to rescue independent travelers like my wife and I from our despair. As it nearly always is in these cases, we were approached by a very well dressed, middle-aged, Palestinian man named Hamad who courteously presented us with his business card, and asked us if he could be of any assistance. When I looked at the card I saw that he was a licensed tour guide specializing in Jerusalem's Old City, the Temple Mount, and Bethlehem—exactly all of the places we planned on visiting. We were game for just about anything to make it easier; and so to see just how knowledgeable Hamad actually was, we hired him to show us around the inside of the church in front of which we now stood.

He would turn out to be a genuine gift from God.

The immeasurable benefits of Hamad's great skill as a private tour guide began right off the bat. Like it was the most natural thing in the world to do, and like we were a couple of diplomats, he very efficiently shepherded us to the head of the long line of tour groups waiting in the scorching-hot courtyard to get into the church, and with a knowing nod to the doorman, eased us inside past the chaos. Once inside the gigantic structure, he lead us around and explained to us the various minor chapels associated with Jesus Christ's Crucifixion and resurrection scattered throughout the building, allowing us time to stop and reflect upon these sacred spots, and saving the two most important ones (Calvary and Christ's Tomb) till last.

The Chapel of Altar of the Crucifixion is built over the traditional site of the top of the hill of Calvary. The main altar of the chapel is under the control of the Greek Orthodox Church and seemed to me the most adorned and opulent spot in the whole building. There is a glass window to the side of the altar where you can look down at the actual limestone outcropping upon which the Cross of Jesus was set. Hamad pointed out to us that there is also a small space under the altar where you can kneel down, stick your hand through an opening in a silver shield, and actually touch the hole in the rock into which the Cross was placed!

When my turn in the short line came around—and with some difficulty because of my large bulk—I knelt down upon the white and grey-streaked marble floor, scooched myself forward under the altar, and slid my right hand and arm into the opening of the plating. Then, and with a bit more effort (because the hole was quite small) I managed to reach far enough down the hole and lie my hand upon the holy ground. Wow! Talk about authenticity of place! If I had died right there and then (which now, of course, I'm glad I didn't) I know with absolute certainty that I would have passed beyond this veil of tears in a pure and ecstatic spiritual bliss. It was really overwhelming!

The ethereal spell, however, was quickly broken when the time came for me to pull my arm back up out of the hole. Because my upper arm is so big, it got stuck in the hole of the silver plate covering over the rock below, and when I went to pull it out all the way, the whole thing came with me. This caused quite a stir among the Greek priests in charge of maintaining their vigil. Holy cow! Pure pandemonium reigned as I now found myself still scrunched under the alter half kneeling and half sitting with a twenty pound bracelet of what looked like pure silver, not quite knowing what to do as a now large crowd of pious (?) holy men started hollering at me in what was probably Greek, Russian, Arabic, and perhaps even Syrian. Although I had no idea what they were saying, it probably was something to the effect of "You gosh-darned Americans! You're always screwing things up!"

With a great bit of exertion, I managed to drag myself backwards from underneath the altar, silver plating and all, and stood up. With the help of Hamad and a dozen priests, they pinched and squeezed and compressed my upper arm and managed to remove the metal plate intact. One of the younger monks then (with much mumbling and gnashing of teeth) slid the covering back up under the altar, and with some pounding in its corners with his bare fists, set the silver plate back in its place

All the while, poor Theresa, as she so often has to do in situations like this, could only stand back and shake her head in disbelief as her blundering old husband gets himself in trouble for trying to trash the second most holy place in Christendom. Hamad, in that way Middle Eastern men have of using gentle understatement, then said to us, "Sir Richard, this would be a good time to move on to the Lord's tomb."

> In the end of the Sabbath, as it began to dawn toward the first
> day of the week, came Mary Magdalene and the other Mary to
> see the sepulcher. And, behold, there was a great earthquake:
> for the angel of the Lord descended from heaven, and came and
> rolled back the stone from the door, and sat upon it. His countenance was like lightning, and his raiment white as snow

–MATTHEW 28:1-3. KJV

The Tomb of Jesus is in the very center of the church inside of a large stone chapel called the Edicule. It was here, again, that Hamad's skill as a guide came in really handy. As one can probably imagine, the waiting line to get in to this ultimate Holy of Holy Christian sites was quite long. But Hamad, in the self-assured, confident—and quite audacious—manner he demonstrated to us at the entrance to the church, gently grabbed a hold of my right elbow, and with Theresa crowding close behind me, ushered us to the head of the line. There, again with the slightest of nods to the priest/guard, he shoved us into the first of two portals we needed to pass through in order to enter the tomb. And just like that, there we were.

There are two parts to the Tomb of Jesus. The first is a small room called the Chapel of the Angel and it features a two-foot-square chunk of the stone the Jerusalem Temple guards had used to seal Jesus' tomb and which the angel of the Lord had pushed aside. Hamad waited in this chamber (probably because he was a Muslim, or because he just wanted to chat with his friend the priest/guard) while Theresa and I bent far down and continued through the small opening into the actual tomb.

The burial chamber itself was very small, probably six feet long by four feet wide. The original living rock of the tomb's ceiling had been long ago removed by Emperor Constantine's workers in order to build the burial chamber in which we now stood. In front of us, covered over (unfortunately) by a thick white marble slab, was the most holy spot in all of Christianity: The tragic place where the disciples, Joseph of Arimathaea and Nicodemis laid the broken, crucified body of Jesus Christ.

Kneeling down as billions have done in solemn veneration before me, I laid my hands upon the stone, bent over and kissed the marble, said a few prayers, and then kissed the marble once again. But although my spirit was filled with overwhelming awe and reverence at being in the physical presence of this holiest of holy places, I felt a surprising disconnect. The feeling of "oneness" that I will bend heaven and earth to achieve didn't happen. And I didn't quite know why until several minutes later.

Upon exiting Jesus' tomb, we were met by Hamad who told us he had one more place to take us in the church. He said it was a special place that no public tours ever visits, and that now, because we were his friends, he could arrange for us to get into it.

Unknown to most visitors to the Church of the Holy Sepulcher is that directly behind the Tomb of Jesus sets a little obscure chapel that is under the jurisdiction of the Egyptian Coptic Church. Because we were now his special clients, and (of course) because he just happened to be good friends with the priest on duty, he assured us we would get to do something very few people who visit the church ever get to do.

> In that day shall there be an altar to the Lord in the midst of the land of Egypt, and a pillar at the border thereof to the Lord.. And it shall be for a sign and for a witness unto the Lord of hosts in the land of Egypt: for they shall cry unto the Lord because of the oppressors, and he shall send them a savior, and a great one, and he shall deliver them. And the Lord shall be known to Egypt, and the Egyptians shall know the Lord in that day, and shall do sacrifice and oblation; yea, they shall vow a vow unto the Lord, and perform it.
>
> –Isaiah 19:21.

The Coptic Church, along with the Syrian Orthodox Church, are the "little guys on the block" when it comes to spaces to call their own in the massive church. The Greek Orthodox Church controls the majority of the basilica's chapels followed by the Armenia Church and the Roman Catholics. The Copts control only the tiny chapel in front of where we now stood as well as a few hermit huts on the roof of the building.

The Egyptian Coptic Church is relatively unknown to most westerners. This Christian Sect traces its Apostolic foundation back to Saint Mark, the author of the Gospel of Mark, who preached—and was ultimately martyred— in the city of Alexandria during the reign of Emperor Nero. It is believed by many religious scholars that the Coptic Church with its mysterious Eastern rituals is one of the most ancient forms of Christianity practiced today; a case can be made as well for the Egyptian Copts being the only "Church" mentioned in the Old Testament.

There are believed to be 18 million Coptic Christians in the world today with an estimated 14 million of these living in Egypt. The newest spiritual leader, who has the rather long and formal title of Coptic Pope of Alexandria and Patriarch of All Africa on the Holy See of Saint Mark is the 118th pope on a direct line from Saint Mark. The Coptic Christians see themselves as both the fulfillment of Old Testament prophecy and as the guardians of the holy sites associated with the Holy Family's exile into Egypt.

As we entered into the tiny chapel we were greeted by a short and very stout, older, priest with a thick salt and pepper colored beard exhibiting upon his weathered face a very serious countenance. Covering his entire head was a thin black skull cap adorned with a ring of embroidered golden crosses extending from ear to ear. He wore a plain, slightly threadbare, black, pullover-type, monk's robe; a large, ornate, silver cross on a long silver chain dangled down the front of him almost all the way down to his belly. He had been sitting reading what looked like a Bible, but rose quickly when we entered his chapel and seemed genuinely pleased both to see Mr. Hamad and, as likely as not, to have some visitors.

Obviously good friends, the priest and Hamad spoke for a couple of minutes together in Egyptian, and as they did I took the opportunity to look around the small room. The subdued level of light in the chapel made it hard to see. I could just make out on either side wall what looked like golden Persian rugs with very simple representations of Joseph, Mary and the infant Jesus. In front of the chapel, on what would actually be the back wall of the Edicule containing Jesus' tomb, was a marble altar. Over this altar was hung a magnificent icon of the Virgin Mary holding baby Jesus.

After they finished their conversation, Hamad introduced us to the priest. Shaking my hand only, he asked us in broken English where we were from. "Ah, New York," he said, again, obviously pleased. He and Hamad then said a few more words together in Egyptian, at which time the priest bent down, and after lifting up the lid from a small wooden box (that had also served as a small table) next to his chair, removed several small packages, a couple of which were wrapped in linen cloths.

He stood back up, and as he held them in a little better light, I could see that they were little boxes containing Holy Land souvenirs. Each box contained an olivewood cross and four small bottles, each of which held a small sample of Holy Land soil, a few crystals of frankincense, oil, and holy water from the River Jordan. In one of the linen bundles were several crude, handmade, crucifixes; in the other several small candles.

Needing to buy some gifts for family and friends at home anyway, I told him I'd take one of the sample boxes, and three each of the crucifixes and candles. He then placed all of my newly acquired treasures into a plastic bag and handed them to me. When I asked him how much I owed him, he just stood there smiling. Hamad broke in saying: "Mr. Richard, he just wants you to give him what you wish to pay."

Until I became accustomed to it, I always got a little nervous when put on the spot like this. I was always afraid of offending people. But what I've discovered over the years, however, is that most of the time the people you're dealing with have a ball park figure in their minds of what they expect. If what you offer them is too high, they'll humbly accept it; if you don't offer enough, they'll be sure to tell you. Most importantly, when dealing with enhanced museum access, private behind the scene tours, or any religious sights— especially really holy sites of any denomination or sect—it is better to err on the side of being over generous.

And that was the case during our visit to this humble chapel. I don't remember what the exact amount was that I paid (probably the equivalent in Israelis Shekels of forty dollars) but the little priest seemed obviously pleased with my offer because he and Hamad spoke a few quick words together, after which Hamad said (with an uncharacteristic seriousness), "Mr. Richard and Madam, the holy father says that you are exceedingly generous and kind-hearted people and he wants to show you something very special."

The priest then walked over to the left side of the altar, slowly dropped down to his knees, and pushed aside a small curtain. After moving away a bronze-colored shield that lie behind it he stood up and motioned to me with his right hand to join him. A little confused by it all, I looked toward Hamad, who looked (again, very seriously) back at me and then said, "Mr. Richard, as a special gift to you and your wife, the holy father is going to allow you both to set your hand on the actual living rock upon which Jesus was placed after His death on the Cross."

I was speechless! What a blessing we'd been given! I never in a million years thought such a thing could be possible! But after a couple of seconds passed to let it all sink in, the priest helped me to my knees, and still holding the plastic bag full of relics, I crawled forward about three feet under yet another alter. With a bit of contortion, I then reached my right hand up into the dark space and set my it down upon the cold and surprisingly smooth, bare limestone bed, the exact surface upon which the crucified Christ had lain. This time no manmade marble slabs, no golden plates, no anything inauthentic got in the way between me this most Holy of Holy of experiences. Whew! I tremble still as I write these words years later.

I lingered there, *one* with that consecrated and sacred mass of mother earth for several minutes. When I was finished, I set the plastic bag up against the tomb so I'd be able to tell the intended recipients that these relics had been where very few had ever been before. I then eased my way backwards from under the altar, and let Theresa share the experience. I remember as I stood there waiting for her to finish, that my hand smelled of fresh baked sugar cookies

After we were done we walked over to thank the priest for his exceptional act of Grace. But before he said good bye, he placed one hand onto each of Theresa and my shoulders and recited what sounded like a prayer. When he finished, he made a sweeping sign of the cross before each of us as a final blessing. He then smiled, shook my hand gently, and gave Theresa a slight bow. I genuinely liked that little man of God.

After a long exuberant good bye ceremony with Hamad, we walked back into reality

Cairo! Just the very name of this timeless and eternal capital city of Egypt conjures up visions of ancient pharaohs and their awe-inspiring pyramids, sensuous belly dancers, and the alien aroma of exotic spices. Chaos! Absolute, unabashed chaos could just as well be another name for this crowded urban sprawl of eighteen million people.

I've never seen a more disorganized city, especially its roadways: beaten up old Russian Yugo taxis, Mercedes-Benz limousines, an endless armada of army trucks and jeeps, black smoke-spewing public buses, trolley cars overflowing with humanity that insist upon mysteriously appearing out of nowhere, and rickety, wooden-wheeled donkey carts overloaded with every commodity on earth that you can imagine; all hurrying and scurrying along the dusty, poorly marked city boulevards. Crosswalks, stop signs, traffic lights (when they are working) and highway dividing lines are all in place, just like in any other city, but these public safety contrivances seem to be regarded by most of the city's unceasingly jabbering pedestrians as something to be willfully ignored. Likewise, nearly all of the maniacally aggressive, horn-honking, motorists seem to view the same assorted traffic control devices as just mere suggestions of how they should get from here to there.

It was into this pandemonium that my wife, our driver, Mr. Samahy, and I now found ourselves. Having spent the biggest part of the day at the Cairo Museum with all of the Pharaoh mummies, King Tut's treasure, and artifacts older than the memory of man, we were now driving toward Cairo's northern suburb to what was once the tiny desert village of El Matariya. We were hoping to visit the much revered and ancient

Virgin Mary Tree. Long a destination of pilgrimage for Coptic Christians, this two-thousand-year-old relic is (sadly) so seldom visited by westerners, that Mr. Samahy told us that we were the first American, Australian, or European tourists he recalled ever taking to the sight.

In the New Testament (Matthew 2:13) an angel of the Lord appeared to Joseph in a dream and told him, "Get up, take the child [Jesus] and his mother and escape to Egypt. Stay there until I tell you, for Herod is going to search for the child to kill him." Forever obedient to the will of the Lord, the Holy Family left Bethlehem that very night. The Egyptian Coptic Church, which is Christendom's primary guardian of the traditions of the Holy Family's sojourn in Egypt, believes their journey through Egypt took three years. (Muslim tradition believes Jesus, Mary, and Joseph spent seven years wandering Egypt.)

Avoiding the main roads wherever possible, the Holy Family journeyed south from Israel, down through the Gaza Strip, across the Sinai, and entered Egypt through the modern-day border town of Rafah. From there they continued westward along the Mediterranean coastline until they reached the Nile delta. Here they traveled southward, passing through ancient Heliopolis, Old Cairo, Memphis, and twenty-five or so other small villages before ultimately ending up in the central Egyptian city of Mount Qussqam. It was here that the tradition says (Matthew 2:15) the Holy Family remained until the death of Herod "that it might be fulfilled which was spoken of the Lord by the prophet, saying, 'Out of Egypt have I called my son.' "

One of the places where the baby Jesus and his parents sojourned was El Matariya, our destination. In those days, El Matariya was just one of hundreds of small and inconsequential desert villages that dotted the Nile River valley. Today the old village is a noisy, crushed-together conglomerate of houses, market stalls, and garbage-strewn alleyways that otherwise unaware travelers must pass through on their way to Cairo's airport. After miraculously maneuvering our Mercedes sedan through a jumble of confusion, Mr. Samahy parked our car directly in front of a small concrete-walled compound. At a tiny wooden desk in front of the enclosure under the shade of a tree sat a much bored-looking uniformed guard/

ticket agent; reclining on a wide straw mat a few steps away from him was a young man. As we got out of the car, both men arose with an obviously great joy at seeing Mr. Samahy.

Looking back on that day—and all of the other days we spent driving around the greater Cairo area with him—I came to the inescapable conclusion that Mr. Samahy must have known, or was related to, everyone in Egypt! It didn't matter if we were at the pyramids of Giza, the temples at Karnack, or at one of the hundreds of papyrus shops, onyx markets, or carpet dealers we visited; they and every ticket agent, tour guide, camel-mounted policeman, and store clerk seemed genuinely pleased to see our driver. The same was true here. Mr. Samahy and these men spent the better part of five minutes shaking hands and hugging and carrying out a very lively conversation. When they were done, he introduced Theresa and me, and the whole process began all over again. And when we were finished, I felt genuinely welcome.

After our introductions, we paid our entrance fee and were then led into the compound by the young man. Whether we thought we needed one or not, he was to be our guide. Mr. Samahy stayed with the gate attendant. No sooner had we all walked through the gate than we found ourselves standing face-to-face with the object of our afternoon's quest. Walking closer to the ancient relic, we all stopped for a few seconds in order to consume the sanctity of this holy place into our consciousness. After a minute or so of reverent silence, our young guide told us the history of the Virgin's Tree.

According to him, there were actually two legends involving the Virgin Mary Tree. The first one was rather mundane; the second one—and the more likely true of the two stories—was quite an amazing tale. The first story simply had the Holy Family stopping for some much-needed rest and repose under the cool, refreshing shade of this once-giant sycamore tree. After setting the baby Jesus on the ground, a spring of water miraculously gushed forth from the earth to provide them and their donkey with God-sent relief from their burning thirsts. In honor and thanks for its aid and solace in their time of need, the Lord granted this humble tree eternal life.

The second legend is a little more astonishing. According to Coptic tradition, Jesus, Mary, and Joseph were on the run once again. This time, however, they were fleeing the temple guards and priests from the ancient Egyptian city of Heliopolis. It was said that for thousands of years, the city of Heliopolis existed as cultic center dedicated to the worship of the gods and goddesses of ancient Egypt. But as the Holy family made their way through this great city, the granite and alabaster statues of its silent gods and goddesses ingloriously crumbled to dust; her venerated golden idols of half men/half beasts burst into flames on their alters; all of this in a solemn recognition of the Son of the True God. The priests and scribes, seeing that their life's work was all in vain, became furious and sought, once again, to try to kill the baby Jesus.

As the Holy Family fled southward from this raging band of zealous, bloodthirsty murderers, they came upon a solitary, tall and noble sycamore tree. Huddling for just a short few seconds of rest in the cool, refreshing shade of this magnificent tree, terrified, they came to the realization that it would be just a matter of time before the angry mob would be upon them. They prayed and prayed and prayed, and just when all was thought lost, a miracle happened. The mighty tree under which they had settled began to crack and creak and scrunch itself up; and in doing so, it had lowered its majestic full canopy of leaves gently downward, thus hiding the Holy Family and their donkey from their pursuers. Within the bosom of that great tree, they anxiously waited for the end, which we all know today never came.

After several hours, when the danger had finally passed, they crawled out from under their hiding place. The once lofty and proud sycamore that had so valiantly protected them from certain death was now just a doubled-over, misshapen trunk, and a mass of twisted branches and leaves. The Holy Family rested for a few more days near the tree until the Angel of the Lord told them it was safe to continue their journey. But just before they were about to depart, as Mary held Him in her arms, the baby Jesus reached out His sacred little hand and in grateful thanks, touched the trunk of this humble tree gracing it with the blessed gift of eternal life.

It was now in front of this very tree that Jesus touched and upon the very ground that the Holy Family stood that we all stood as well. The gnarled and ancient trunk of the original tree that provided sanctuary to Him and His family is propped up on several wooden blocks. According to our young guide, the tree actually almost died in the early seventeen hundreds. However, before it chose to give up its life force, Church officials and botanists managed to propagate several living branches from it. These new growths, now several hundred years old themselves, continue to graciously provide pilgrims and visitors like us cooling shade and protection from the unforgiving Egyptian desert sun.

As we stood there within the confines of this tiny courtyard, the relentless noise and confusion of the surrounding city vanished, and at least for those few minutes, I actually felt I'd been transported back in time. A light and refreshingly cool breeze blew through the courtyard gate, and a great peace overcame me. It was amazing!

We spent the next several minutes taking it all in before starting to walk around the jumbled cluster of old- and new-growth sycamore trees to explore the rest of the small courtyard. On the backside against the whitewashed wall, we found the water well that had miraculously sprung from the earth that had given the Holy Family sustenance. It still bubbled up from the ground, filling a stone basin that had been placed there to collect the water. Our guide said that Christian and Moslem women alike came from all over the north of Africa to step over the water to insure their ability to have children. (Being not the family-oriented type, we made sure Theresa kept her distance.)

Working our way back around to the front gate, we all stopped once again to take in the experience of this sacred place one last time. By now, Mr. Samahy had finished his conversation with the gate attendant and was waiting with the patience of a saint for us to finish our visit. We shook hands with our young guide and thanked him immensely for his excellent tour. Then, after the mandatory rituals of him pretending to not want to accept payment for his work and me insisting that he please accept the token amount of money for his great service to us (which he did, indeed, earn and which he finally accepted), we started to walk away.

But before we could get too far, Mr. Samahy walked toward him and the two of them spoke a few words together in their Egyptian Arabic that I couldn't quite make out. Our young guide kind of smiled and laughed a bit, and then he walked over to us and said that Mr. Samahy reminded him a another tradition involving the Virgin Mary Tree that he had forgotten. If we could wait just one more minute, he would demonstrate it for us. We agreed. He then went over to the original old sycamore and looking around at the base of the old tree, he picked up a small half-inch-square piece of bark that had fallen off to the ground. He walked over to where the basin was that had been collecting the miracle spring water, and he wet the piece of bark in it.

He returned over to where we were standing and asked Theresa to hold up her arm. He then gently rubbed the wet piece of bark on the skin of her forearm. As he did so, he said that if the sap turned her skin red, then she had special favor with the Virgin Mary; if it turned brown or black, then she needed to pray more. As expected, her spot did turn a beautiful rose petal–colored red. He then asked for my forearm. I raised it, and he rubbed the bark on my skin.

I'm not going to tell anyone what color it turned!

My First Betel Nut

CHAPTER 12

No Such Thing as Bad Beer

———⊶∞⊷———

Myth facilitates [man's] attempts to probe into the mysteries
of existence, to explore the apparent limitlessness of the
psyche, and to endow individuals with a sense of awe
and wonder as they gaze upon, and ultimately embrace,
the incomprehensible marvels and horrors of life.

–Dr. Carl Jung

While sailing the seas around the northern islands of the Tongan archipelago, Philip, the captain of our chartered sailboat, told us the following bizarre legend concerning the discovery of a popular intoxicating beverage that's drunk throughout the whole of the South Pacific known as kava. I warn you in advance that Philip's story is a sad and not a very pleasant tale.

He told us of a time of great famine on the islands, and of how the mighty king of Tonga set off one day from his home island of Tongatapu in enormous oceangoing canoes with a large group of men in a co-operative effort to try to catch fish and to find other foodstuffs that they could bring home to their starving countrymen. But no great quantity of fish was to be had and, for reasons unknown, the otherwise always-dependable coconut trees failed to produce their nourishing bounty. Tired and hungry, the king and his men landed on what they thought was a deserted island in one last ditch attempt to find something—anything—to eat. The island, however, turned out to be not completely uninhabited.

There lived on this island a husband and his wife and their beloved daughter, Kava. The family had been forced by local taboo to live there in isolation from the rest of Tongan society because sadly their twenty-five-year-old daughter was a leper. But upon hearing of their all-powerful monarch being desperately hungry, the parents—being the loyal and devoted subjects that they were—did what all butt-kissing cannibals did back in those days: they sacrificed sweet and innocent little Kava in order to feed the young girl to the king. As she was cooking in the 'umu (an underground type of oven), word reached the king as to what the sycophantic parents had done. Grief-stricken at their overzealous effort on his behalf (or, perhaps, he was just fearful to consume her because she was a leper), he ordered the wicked couple to forever leave the body of Kava undisturbed in the ground where she now lay roasting. The king and his men then left the island.

It wasn't long, however, just a couple of weeks after poor Kava had been placed into the fertile earth, that her parents began to notice two plants growing from the ground above her grave. One grew from the head end of the body and the other one grew up from the foot. And as time went on and the plants grew bigger and bigger, they further observed that whenever a stray mouse ate of the stalk and roots that grew from the head end of Kava's grave, the critter became very shaky and erratic in its walk, almost like it was drunk. When the same mouse next ate of the plant growing from the foot end of her grave, its walk seemed to straighten back out again.

The befuddled parents sent word of their discovery to the king, who then made a second voyage to their island. Greatly touched by what he saw, he named the sweet plant growing from the foot of the grave *sugarcane*. And to honor her tragic death, he named the narcotic plant that grew from the head end of the young girl's tomb *Kava*.

In every culture I study and make the effort to spend time with, I've noticed that besides mother's love, the universal need to find a safe place to live, or mankind's ceaselessly driving urge to find mates, there is yet one additional universal human desire: the want by many to alter their states of consciousness.

From the exhausted Irish day laborer who stops off at the corner pub for a pint of Guinness on the his way home from work, to the Ethiopian highland hermits who literally starved themselves into enlightenment, and to the learned and pious Native American shamans who consumed peyote to summon up the ancient spirits; from the former old hippie seeking to reconnect with their long lost youth who smokes a little pot at a Grateful Dead concert to the Tibetan Buddhist monks who chant themselves into ecstasy, and all the way to the extremes of the Aztec priests of old who pierced their tongues with stingray tails and gave themselves cocoa enemas in order to communicate with their bloodthirsty gods, all of these people have one thing in common: they are all trying to change their mental state from what it presently is to a higher (or lower), enlightened (or duller), transcendent (or debased) state of being.

And if the truth is to be told, on almost a daily basis I'm guilty as well of this most human of transgressions. My most favorite portal into a more subdued state of consciousness is the consumption of beer. I love beer! Sure, I'll drink the occasional dram of a good single-malt scotch, or a glass of dry red wine or a vintage ruby port, and even the occasional Bloody Mary, but my true love is beer, all of the beers on this planet! Bira (Turkish), cerveza (Spanish), chang (Tibetan), piwo (Polish), or pombe (Swahili); stouts, pale ales, pilsners, porters, or lagers, it doesn't matter to me in the slightest, I enjoy them all.

A scuba diving buddy on a diving boat anchored off of the Caribbean island of Saba once told me this saying about beer that I believe says it all: he said that as long as you don't assume the ambient sea temperature—that is, you don't drown—then there is no such thing as a bad scuba dive or a bad beer. He added, however, that there is such a thing as bad wine; also, if you were to ask his mother, she'd say there are a few bad women out there as well.

But having just rambled on and on about this true elixir of the gods, I am not averse to trying other legal or culturally accepted, mind-altering substances that I've encountered in my travels ... and I have shamelessly done so many times.

One of these experiences involved drinking kava. While sailing with Captain Philip on a chartered ketch among the islands of the northern Tongan island group of Vavau, a broadcast announcement came across the ship's radio inviting everyone sailing in the vicinity to attend a traditional Tongan feast later that evening that was being put on by one of the local chiefs' family. We instantly decided to do so.

And what a feast it would turn out to be! The central table in the village's meeting hall groaned under the weight of an entire roasted suckling pig, barbecued chicken, delicious sweet corn, mashed breadfruit, yams, and fresh tropical island fruits. All the while we ate we were entertained by beautiful women and children dancing their native dances and singing their local songs. Outside the building sitting in a circle on the ground on a woven coconut frond mat were six men. In front of one of the men was a hand carved wooden bowl about two feet in diameter. In the bowl was a large quantity of a muddy brown looking liquid that this headman was ladling out to the other men in the circle, as well as to the occasional visitor who temporarily wished to join them. Our sailboat's skipper told me the liquid was kava.

The beverage that the people of Tonga call kava is well-known throughout Polynesia and the entire western Pacific Ocean basin. The drink is derived from the roots of a species of the black pepper plant that botanists feel originated on the island of Vanuatu. Up until the very recent past, these tough plant roots would be ground up by teenage girls who chewed them into a fine mash and then spit the psychoactive liquid into a large wooden bowl. Philip said they used the young native girls to chew the kava root because their teeth had not yet rotted away. Today, and quite fortunately for adventurous travelers like me, the kava is extracted from a mixture of pounded roots and cold water.

From Hawaii to New Guinea and all the way down to Australia, kava has played an important role in the social lives of the Polynesian people. Traditionally, the ceremonial drinking of kava has been used from everything to the confirmation of the higher social status of chiefs, to the celebration of weddings and the birth of children, to the simple alleviation of sickness and stress. The wide range of rituals involved in the consumption of the drink throughout all of Oceania is similar in social function to the formal tea ceremonies of Japan, the smoking of tobacco by several of the Native American tribes, the drinking of potent coffees in Ethiopia and Turkey, as well as the male bonding beer keg party rituals celebrated at college fraternity houses all over America.

The kava ceremony I participated in was a semiformal get-together by friends for the benefit of the tourists attending the banquet. Per Philip's instruction, I waited until an empty spot to the right of the headman became available, at which time I sat down onto the mat next to him. Without saying a word he dipped a hollowed-out coconut shell into the large four-legged bowl in front of him, filled it about three-quarters full, and then handed it to me. I thanked him for sharing his kava with me, turned around and poured just a small amount of the thin, brownish liquid onto the ground, turned back around and, facing the group, I drank the remaining contents of the coconut shell in one smooth gulp as Philip told me was the custom. The flavor, as best as I can recall, was a cross between that of dirt and walnuts; it was not unpleasant. I then handed the shell back to the headman, and he filled it several more times giving each of the Tongan men in the circle another round.

Almost instantly, I felt a weird numbing of my lips and tongue like I had just been given a shot of Novocain by my dentist. That was all. Hoping for a bit more of the expected intoxication, when the coconut shell got back around to me, I drank it down again in one swallow. (You only have to pour out an offering to the earth on the first drink.) Feeling only what I thought was a mild sense of well-being, and seeing that there was another brave soul waiting patiently for his turn at the bowl, I tried to stand up. However, much to the amusement of the men in the circle, my legs didn't seem to want to listen. After much effort—and with the help of Theresa and Philip—I managed to shakily stand up.

But once I was on my feet, everything seemed to be fine. That is, unless I closed my eyes! When I did it was like someone had turned on a light switch that ignited an immediate rushing sensation through my brain of raging, rolling, white waves of cosmic energy that were a little too hard for me to handle standing up. However, if I kept my eyes open, all I felt was a warm sense of calmness and well-being. As I sit here at my desk in upstate New York I vividly still remember—with an absolute certainty—thinking to myself then that if only every man and woman on the planet could have sat in that circle with those wise men of Tonga on that glorious beach on that sultry South Pacific night and drunk with us a couple of shells of kava each, that all would be right with creation, and the world would be at a perpetual state of sheer unadulterated bliss and peace.

Afterward we returned to the food table and pigged out some more on the fabulous banquet that the gracious and lovely ladies of Vavau prepared for us. The euphoria I experienced at the kava ceremony stayed with me as a mild buzz for about another hour. But while we were at the feast the tide had gone out, stranding our dinghy high and dry on the beach. My last memory of the evening, therefore, was of Philip, Theresa, and me having to push the dinghy out across the now partially exposed reef into water deep enough to float it back out to the sailboat. But all was still right with the universe—at least in MY mind—and I don't think I even worked up a sweat. Back on the boat, whether it was the glut of food in my belly, the gentle lulling of the ocean, or the lingering effects of the kava, I slept like a baby.

Another one of the many things that I find especially interesting about this enthralling and infinitely enchanting planet is how all societies everywhere share a fascination with telling and listening to stories. It is the one absolute behavior (in my humble opinion) that makes us all "human." Be they legends, parables, myths, yarns, songs, or a lengthy epic, everyone loves a good story. And we use these stories not only for entertainment and respite from a hard day of dodging saber-toothed tigers and hunting woolly mammoths, but also to teach each other where we came from, where we are going, and how to behave and to fit into society (or not). The greater of these sagas try to answer the BIG questions: How should we treat our fellow human and all other sentient life? Why there is both good and evil in the world? What is the nature of the Divine? And, ultimately, what is the meaning and purpose of it all?

> *Bloody Mary is the girl I love.*
> *Bloody Mary is the girl I love.*
> *Bloody Mary is the girl I love.*
> *Now ain't that too damn bad!*

> *Bloody Mary's chewin' betel nuts.*
> *She is always chewin' betel nuts.*
> *Bloody Mary's chewin' betel nuts.*
> *And she don't use Pepsodent!*
> *Now ain't that too damn bad!*

–FROM THE ROGERS AND HAMMERSTEIN'S MUSICAL, SOUTH PACIFIC

An old South Asian legend from time immemorial tells the story of two brothers, both of whom were in love with the same woman. Even though she loved them both equally, because it was the custom, the older brother wound up actually marrying the young girl; this, in turn, broke the younger brother's heart. Forlorn and unable to live with the pain of having to see his beloved sister-in-law, to be near her nearly every hour of every waking day, the younger brother made the decision to run away from home.

The older brother, who loved his little brother with all his heart, soon missed him so badly that he left his wife and home to search the world for him. Years later, in a distant land of what would someday be known as the nation of Vietnam, a farmer tells the still searching older brother that, tragically, the younger brother had drowned just six months before while trying to cross a rain-swollen river. The farmer further said that where the young man had died, a large white rock now stood on the river's bank. Upon seeing his little brother's memorial, the older brother was so overtaken by grief that he died instantly on the very spot. Shortly afterwards, a tall palm-like tree grew from the rich, well watered, soil next to the white rock.

Longing for the return of her husband and missing both him and her brother-in-law, the young bride decided to set out on a quest of her own to bring them both back home. Like her husband before her, she followed whatever leads she could regarding the brothers' whereabouts and her journey ultimately brought her to the same farmer both men had met before. The farmer, a bit reluctant at first to break the news of the tragedy to this lovely brave girl, eventually agreed to tell her the bad news that had taken place down by the river.

He told her about how the younger brother, inpatient for even a day to escape the romantic pangs that so plagued him, ignored his warnings about the river's strong currents and decided to risk it all to escape further despair. He told the woman about how her husband who, after seeing the white boulder that had mysteriously appeared along the river bank after his brother's death, fell dead upon the very spot, and of how a palm tree now grew from where the older brother had fallen. Finally, not able to put the moment off any longer—and fearing the worse for her life—he took the young bride down to the river bank to see the sacred spot for herself.

And, of course, as these Polynesian myths always seem to go, the farmer's worse fears were indeed realized. Upon seeing the white boulder on the riverbank and the tree that miraculously grew out of the ground from near its base, she too became over come with grief and collapsed to the ground in utter heart-broken despair. But she did not die, at least not immediately. Instead, after several minutes of uncontrollable weeping, she picked herself up off of the ground, collected her emotions as well as she could, and walked towards the tree and the rock.

When the farmer—still fearing for her life—asked her what she was going to do, she told him that she believed in her heart that it was because of her and her confused passions for the brothers that she felt responsible for their deaths. Knowing there was nothing that could humanly be done to resolve the tragedy she decided to make amends by forever uniting all three of them together for all of time. She then climbed up upon the rock that was the younger brother and reaching as high as she could, embraced her beloved husband's tree.

And there the young wife/loving sister-in-law stood until eventually she was transformed into a vine that unites the three of them together to this very day in a magical (and actual) sort of way. It turns out that the story of the lovers spread throughout the entire kingdom and on one day a few years later the king himself made a pilgrimage to the now sacred site. Wanting in some mystical way to become *one* with the family, he plucked a nut from the palm tree, split it open, sprinkled some fine scrapings from the white stone, and wrapping the two brothers' essences in a leaf from the vine, then put it in his mouth and chewed it. From then on, the chewing of betel nuts has gone on to become a much loved wedding tradition throughout all of south Asia, Southeast Asia, and all the islands of the Pacific Ocean basin.

> Myth, because of its indistinct, metaphoric, poetic nature offers
> a more discriminating and more personally relevant explanation
> of the world to individuals than does the language of ... science.

–Dr. Brad Olson, *The Truth of Myth*

Continental Airlines has a series of flights to several islands of the central Pacific Ocean that its pilots call "the milk run." Beginning in Hawaii and ending most of the time in the Philippines, each flight, literally island-hops the thousand-mile-wide expanse of the Marshalls and Micronesia island groups taking off, and landing in places with exotic sounding names like Majuro, Kwajalein, Truk, Kosrae, Pohnpei, Guam, Yap, and Palau. If travelers manage to time it right, they can luck out and just hit a couple of stops. Even though we have landed during our various trips in all of the above places at one time or another, on our trip to the island of Yap, we managed to schedule our flight from Honolulu only having to spend a long day and a relaxing overnight on Guam.

We had come to Yap on a scuba diving jaunt that was to also include a trip to the island nation of Palau. As part of the Federated States of Micronesia, Yap is considered by the anthropologists who study this stuff to be the most "traditional" of the Polynesian cultures that still dominate a huge portion of the central and South Pacific Ocean. Even though the people of Yap are politically considered one of the four states of the nation of Micronesia, their local governance is still strongly influenced by strict divisions of tribal chiefs, nobles, and commoners. Yap is also unique throughout the world as well for its continued use of big stone disks that the islanders use as a form of currency.

Although the habit is little known to the majority of Westerners, the chewing of betel nuts is one of the major forms of intoxication common throughout all of tropical south Asia, the Far East, and Oceania. With the exception of those who have traveled to these parts of the world, most of the people who live in the West who have any familiarity at all with the chewing of betel nuts acquired their knowledge by either reading the late James Michener's book, *Tales of the South Pacific*, or by watching the Broadway musical based on it.

Like most plays or movies that take their inspiration from a novel, there is a wide gulf between the two genres with regards to their content, which I personally—as a former U.S. Navy man—find quite disappointing. The actual book (in my humble opinion) is second to none in its depictions of men at war, both on the front lines of battle and of those who had to endure the monotony and the tyranny of routine in the rear echelons. The novel was years ahead of its time in its graphic discussions of race relations in the United States military, its straightforward explorations of the then-delicate concept of mixed marriages, and in its depictions and exposures of the wide range of native societies and cultural behaviors found in the South Pacific that were completely unknown to the world of that day.

But all of this having been said, regardless of which commercial form the story line ultimately took, one of the most colorful characters of modern literature always manages to dominate the show: good ol' Bloody Mary. In the book she was the enterprising, brusque, slightly repulsive but otherwise compassionate mother of Liat. In the musical, she was the lovable grand old dame who sold grass skirts to the sailors. For those who never read or saw anything regarding *Tales of the South Pacific*, Ms. Bloody Mary got her name because she was constantly spitting out the blood red juice that results from chewing betel nuts.

There is an especially strong tradition of the chewing of betel nuts on Yap. The palm tree from which the nut grows thrives well on the island. Quite interestingly, the betel nut is Yap's number one export. In 2004, which is the last year I could find these statistics, the island's seven thousand inhabitants exported over 211 tons of the intoxicant.

My first memorable close encounter with the habit of betel nut chewing occurred as we checked in to our hotel in Yap. Having just arrived after the flight from Guam, we were greeted at the front desk by three young and stunningly beautiful teenage girls. As one of these young ladies processed my hotel booking and credit card information, I couldn't stop thinking to myself as I stood there and waited in the refreshingly cool tropical sea breeze that gently wafted through the hotel lobby that it was this arresting beauty of the Polynesian Island races that had conspired over the centuries to entice sailors throughout all of recorded maritime history to jump the safety and security of their ships; that lured Western businessmen fed up with the rat race of modern life to up and abandon their lucrative careers in order to go native; or that even to this very day still inspires innumerably famous—and some not-so-famous—artists and writers and poets who long to try (mostly in vain) to capture in words or on canvas the allure of these sybaritic, brown-skinned island girls that stood before me now.

In this present case, however, this spell was quickly broken when this young lady smiled at me as she handed back my credit card. I couldn't believe my eyes! The poor girl looked like she had just finished chewing on a chunk of raw red meat! Her inner lips and teeth were stained a grotesque, nasty-looking, bright bloody red! It was like something out of a vampire movie! I pretended really hard not to notice, but it was a struggle not to look away in revulsion. She, it turned out, like most of the people we would meet on Yap, was a betel nut chewer!

But putting betel nut chewing aside for a bit, Yap turned out to be an enchanting place. The scuba diving in my opinion rated among the top three places we've ever dived: pristine reefs; abundant varieties of corals and fish, sharks, and rays; bright blue sky; clear, calm, seas—bathtub warm—with infinite visibility. It was a diver's paradise. Because it is a rule in scuba diving that you can't fly within twenty-four hours of your last dive, on our next-to-the-last day on Yap, we hired a guide to give us a tour of the island.

Our driver/guide Wendell had also been one of our diving assistants. Yap was his home, and with the exception of having served four years in the U.S. Army, he'd never left the island. He took us to mudflats, beaches, and mangrove habitats where we could look for seabirds. He showed us many relics of the Japanese occupation during World War Two, including several crashed bombers and fighter planes. He took us to several villages where, prominently displayed for all to see, were the world-famous stone money disks.

The stone disks he told us are still being used today in major financial transactions such as land purchases, payment of penalties in law disputes between villages, and for major wedding ceremonies among the royal families. Most stones are about three feet in diameter with some as large as seven feet around. Each has a hole in the center to allow them to be carried from place to place on large wooden poles. There were hundreds of them all over the place. And even though to us they seemed rather random and casual in their display, Wendell assured us that each one is completely accounted for. The history of each disk is known by all, as is its intrinsic value in the monetary scheme of things. There are many legends attached to some of the more famous disks, and several even have their own names.

As our long morning together exploring the island was coming to an end, it was at one of these villages that Wendell offered to share with me another island tradition: he asked me if I would share a betel nut chew with him, and I eagerly accepted. We then sat down together outside of the village's men's house and he (rather formally) prepared my chew.

He first reached into his fanny pack–like woven basket that each man on Yap seemed to carry and selected for me a perfect-looking betel nut; it was about the size of a large, lime green grape. He then cut the nut in half and from what looked like an old baby's bottle, sprinkled onto it a specially ground coral. This limestone, he told me, helps the body better absorb the effects of the betel nut. When he was all finished, he put the two pieces of the nut back together and wrapped them in a pepper leaf. This was for flavor, he said. He then handed it to me. I waited until he prepared a nut for himself before beginning my chew. I noticed that he also incorporated a one-inch piece of tobacco cigarette into his chew. Without me even asking, he kind of smiled a bit and said that it was just a bad habit of his.

The flavor of the chew was not unpleasant, sort of a peppery, spearmint taste. The nut, however, must have had some direct effect on my salivary glands because I quickly found myself needing to spit out large amounts of the famous betel nut blood red spit. Though quite pleasant, the narcotic sensation was a bit overwhelming at first, and I soon found myself needing to sit down for a few minutes to let the dizziness pass. When the initial sensation mellowed out after a few minutes, I discovered that an incredible energy and clarity of perception had taken the place of my dizziness. Everything, from the infinite spectrum of the island's lush green and sumptuous vegetation, to the stunningly blue sky of that crystal clear, cloudless day, to the primal smell of damp, dank forest earth and campfire smoke, all had co-mingled in my head and blared through my senses as if the whole world was once again all new to me. I liked it, but as quick as it came on, it was gone.

Or so I thought.

After dropping us back off at the hotel, I thanked Wendell for the excellent tour of his home island and for sharing a betel nut with me. He complimented me on my ability to handle the effects of the nut and sort of jokingly offered me another one in parting. Still not quite sure the effects of the first chew had worn off yet, I politely declined. Theresa and I then had an excellent lunch of fish and chips at the hotel's bar. I ate with great gusto and remember vividly how exquisitely delicious the French-fried potatoes tasted.

After lunch, as is my wont while on holiday, I laid down to take a nap. Being as there was not too much to do for the rest of the afternoon, and wanting to be better prepared for our trip to the island of Palau the next day, Theresa decided to do some laundry. The girls at the hotel's front desk had told her about a place just about a half mile walking distance away. She packed up two pillowcases full of dirty clothes and then left me to my slumber.

However, try as I might, I could not sleep. Even though I was a bit tired, my whole body buzzed with an energy that I wasn't used to. And so I got up, got my camera, and started walking to the Laundromat to see if I could help Theresa, and maybe take a few pictures of the seabirds along the way. Feeling quite light on my feet, I covered the half mile in about five minutes. As I got closer to the building where the laundry was, Theresa saw me coming and met me partway to tell me she needed some more quarters to finish drying the clothes. No problem, I said.

Still quite pumped up, I think I walked that half mile and back again in record time. I must admit that I was still feeling pretty good. That is, until I walked into the Laundromat to give Theresa the hand full of quarters. Just by chance as I walked through the door of the building, I looked over to my right and saw a sight that at first glance—probably because I was still under the effects of the betel nut—scared the poop out of me.

Standing there around a low table, laughing and jabbering and appearing quite sinister (at least according to my distorted senses) were eight or nine, older women; each one buck-naked from their belly buttons up! All were chomping away on betel nuts, with a couple of them having the blood red juice running down the corners of their toothless mouths. In my drug-induced state, all I could think of as I stood there in horror was that I had stumbled upon a covey of topless grandmother vampires and that if I didn't get out of there quickly, I might turn out to be their next sacrificial victim.

Seeing me standing there in some kind of trance, Theresa walked over and asked me what in the heck I was doing. Stepping cautiously outside the front door with her, I quietly told her that those old ladies standing around the table looked to be up to no good and that we'd better run for our lives. Not quite sure of exactly of what I was talking about, but knowing me well enough to realize that on occasion my imagination has a tendency to get carried away, she led me back into the building and walked me over to the table where the ladies were standing. It turned out that they, indeed, were just a group of sweet and delightful grandmas, albeit topless; all chewing betel nuts and were just out on a lovely afternoon folding their family's freshly laundered clothes.

For the next couple of hours—and even to this very day as I write this chapter—I kept thinking to myself: "Now there's something you don't see every day!"

In Ancient Greek mythology, the title of the god of beer, wine, and all other intoxicants seems to be shared by two men. Most famous is Dionysus. This god is known also as the Liberator, the idea being that strong intoxicating drinks liberate the drinker from the shackles of his/her inhibitions. Lesser known, however, is the god Silenus. He actually was the stepfather and mentor/tutor of Dionysus. Therefore, because he taught young Dionysus everything he knew, Silenus, in my humble opinion, is the more worthy of the title. I also like the fact that in Greek art and sculpture, he is always depicted as a slightly balding, fat man with a huge beer belly, and with (or without) the ears, horn, and legs of a goat. He reminds me of myself, only without the ears, horns, and legs of a goat!

Several summers ago, Theresa and I had the opportunity to accompany our friend Richie to attend the wedding of his cousin on the Greek island of Nisyros. And what a fantastically incredible event—a genuine blessing!—the whole trip turned out to be. In my charmed life I've been graced by many, many wonderful experiences, but this wedding, and all of the customs and rituals and pageantry that were associated with it, will forever be right up there in the top ten great moments of my life.

Because the tiny island of Nisyros doesn't have much of a tourist infrastructure, until the day of the wedding, we all stayed at a hotel just across a small stretch of the Mediterranean on the nearby, much larger island of Kos. This turned out be quite an additional treat as well, because the island of Kos is the birthplace and home of the great Hippocrates, the "father of medicine." So besides the honored gift we'd been given to attend the wedding of his cousin, the trip for Richie and me, as men of medicine ourselves, turned out to be a pilgrimage of sorts as well.

Born in 460 BC, Hippocrates is best known as the founder of modern western medicine. He was the first doctor in recorded history who firmly rejected the superstitious views of his time which held that illness was caused by possession of evil spirits or the disfavor of the gods. Hippocrates based his medical diagnosis on the careful observation and study of living animals and humans and on the systematic dissection and autopsy of those who died of disease. He was a strong believer in the "holistic" theory of wellness (lots of rest, a good diet, maintaining personal cleanliness, and moderation in all things) and would not be too far out of place in the more enlightened medical centers we have in our world of today. Hippocrates is also credited with stating the foundation principle by which most (human abortionists are the one vile exception) men and women in medicine, both veterinary and human, try our best to live up to: *Primum non nocere*, "First, do no harm."

But before I say more about dear Hippocrates, I'd like to share a story about one of the pre-wedding rituals I was honored to attend. Two nights before the wedding, the bride's parents threw a dinner party near our hotel on Kos for members and close friends of the immediate family. And what a feast it was: fresh fish, clams, and mussels caught from the sea just hours before, fresh lamb and beef and sweet tomatoes and cucumbers and zucchinis all grown on the rich volcanic soil of that island paradise. And wine. Oh yes, I can't forget the wine! An endless supply of local red and white wines; wines grown in a country that has been making and drinking the fermented juice of the grape all the way back through thousands of years in history to the time of mighty Achilles and Hercules.

My friend Richie doesn't drink, and so it fell upon me (sort of) to not only consume my share but a good part of his as well. (It was a tough job, but somebody had to do it!) His uncle, who I got along with like he was one of my own dear uncles, and who also shared my love for this local "nectar of the gods," insisted on making sure I sampled every single bottle of the various wines the restaurant had in their cellar. When all was said and done, in the couple of hours it took us to eat, he and I probably polished off ten bottles between us.

We then retired to a beautiful patio at a tavern next door to the restaurant that overlooked the sea and the distant island of Nisyros. We would all sail over to that island in a couple of days. As we sat there on that spectacular evening, Richie's uncle had me sample a popular Greek liquor called *ouzo*. Carefully taking a sip of the unfamiliar liquid first, I discovered that it was quite good. The liquor had the strong smell and mild flavor of licorice, but with the throat-burning sensation of whiskey. I found the combination quite pleasing.

As the evening stretched into early morning, and after a consuming an unremembered quantity of ouzo, I was beginning to get a little bit tipsy and felt it would be best to gracefully slip out with Theresa and head back to the hotel. Also, or so I thought, it would be a polite way for us to depart so that Richie and his cousins could catch up on any private family gossip. But my new and dear friend wasn't quite finished with me just yet.

Having found a fellow lover of all things intoxicating who, at least so far, could match his ample consumption drink for drink, and as a gracious host wanting to make sure I got the maximum opportunity to sample all of the alcoholic blessings the fertile Greek earth could bring forth, he had our waiter bring us two small cylindrical shot glasses of something called *raki*. The liquor, he told us, was a potent spirit made out of fermented grape seeds. Although the raki was crystal clear when brought to us, when you added the traditional little bit of water to it, it turned milky white, similar to a drink I'd once had in France called absinthe. The drink had a very strong alcohol content that bordered on the narcotic; it tasted like formaldehyde. I limited myself to two small glasses before insisting on stumbling off to bed.

[In my later researches for this story, I found out that in the country of Turkey, which lies just forty miles to the east of Kos, the white color that appears in raki when you add water to it, is referred to reverently as *aslan sütü*, "lion's milk." The reference is directed to any strong or courageous man who would dare drink such a strong intoxicant.]

The next day Theresa, Richie, and I all went sightseeing. Our primary quest on that bright and stunningly beautiful morning was the famous Hippocrates's Tree located in the island's capital city. Richie drove; which was a good thing. As I sat there in the front passenger's seat, my head felt as if my dentist back home, Dr. Regnier, had taken the biggest hypodermic needle he had, shoved it deep into my left ear, and then injected 100 milliliters of Novocain directly into the center of my brain. I wasn't at all nauseous or sick in any way, just completely and utterly benumbed. I literally had trouble putting two words together in a sentence. However, and almost as if by miracle, this was soon to change.

When we finally got in to town, we immediately sought out the famous Hippocrates Tree. And as we found ourselves in the presence of that tree, THE VERY TREE that Hippocrates himself had planted (and under which it is said the Apostle Paul also preached the Gospel of Jesus), an amazing healing happened. As we all walked around marveling at that ancient tree, I got the uncontrollable notion (as is my wont in these situations) to become *one* with our father of medicine.

Stopping under the lowest overhanging branch I could find—and much to the embarrassment of both Theresa and Richie—I very shakily climbed up an iron fence that surrounds the tree and reached up and touched a gnarled limb of this sacred 2,500-year-old patriarch. It was at the instant that my hand rubbed the bark of that special tree that the cloud of my previous evening's drunken oblivion was mercifully lifted from my brain, enabling me to rejoin the world.

And to have the fortitude to start all over again that same evening.

> Do we really want to travel in hermetically sealed popemobiles through the rural provinces of France, Mexico and the Far East, eating only in Hard Rock Cafes and McDonalds? Or do we want to eat without fear, tearing into the local stew, the humble taqueria's mystery meat, the sincerely offered gift of a lightly grilled fish head? I know what I want. I want it all. I want to try everything once.
>
> –Anthony Bourdain, *Kitchen Confidential: Adventures in the Culinary Underbelly*

POSTSCRIPT

MAYBE THERE IS SUCH A THING AS BAD BEER

As it is with everything else in this world of ours, there are exceptions to nearly all of the rules our fellow man has ever tried to lay down. So it is with my scuba diving buddy's quote about there being "no such thing as a bad beer." My one-time exception to his rule took place during our visit to the Ethiopian Highland city of Axum.

We'd had a full day of taking in the sights of the now long gone and almost completely forgotten capital city of the Axumite kingdom, an empire that in its prime rivaled Persia, Rome, and China. We visited what tradition says is the palace of the Queen of Sheba, the biblical consort of King Solomon. We explored the World Heritage Axum Stelae Field that contains many of the world's largest stone obelisks, the biggest of which—though now toppled over—legend says covers the grave of the Queen of Sheba. Another stop we made was at the ruins of what Ethiopian tradition says is the home of Balthazar, one of the three wise men who brought gifts to the baby Jesus at His birth. (Balthazar brought frankincense, the production and distribution of which the Axumite kingdom forcefully controlled at the time.)

The highlight of the day for me was our pilgrimage to the Church of Our Lady Mary of Zion. The present-day modern church building, which was built by the late Emperor Haile Selassie is the most important church in Ethiopia. But more importantly, just adjacent to the modern building are the ruins of the original church upon which is a fortified stone chapel that today houses the original Ark of the Covenant. It was quite a thrill, at least for me, to be within such a close proximity to such a famous holy—very holy—relic. (I say it was a thrill for me because sadly for Theresa, women are not allowed on the ancient church's grounds, so she had to view the chapel from a distance.)

Driving back to our hotel that afternoon, I happened to mention to our guide Samuel that in my travels, I always like to try a sampling of the local beers. (Local beers and wines, with their intimate connection to our dear earth, are a great way of helping me become *one* with local environments.) He told me he knew just the place where I could do this. Thinking that he would take me to a pub or some other type of barroom where I could open up a bottle or two of local brew, I told him it would be fine with me.

About five minutes later, after driving down a maze of bumpy dirt roads and back alleys, he pulled up in front of what I can only describe as the most sinister-looking dive I'd ever seen. But I had no real fear because Samuel seemed like a good man who, like most tour leaders or guides, only wanted to please his customers. Theresa (always very prudent in these situations that I so blithely put us into) said she'd wait in the car. He and I then walked through a door into a small courtyard. To the left of the entrance was a barroom with about ten men sitting at small tables, talking and enjoying each others' company ... just like any other bar on earth. But Samuel had something more special in mind for me.

Continuing another thirty feet ahead, he took me into this darkened, three-sided shed. Barely visible in the subdued light of the building were what looked to me like three big fifty-five-gallon oil drums. Directly behind them stood an older, somewhat gaunt, and very tired-looking woman. Samuel spoke to her in his language and her face immediately beamed a bright smile. In marginal English, she looked at me and said, "OK, yes sir. OK sir, no problem."

This nice lady then lifted the cover off of one of the barrels, and as she did a million flies came swarming out from under the lid. I saw that the barrel was full to near the top with some sort of liquid, upon which a layer of nasty looking scum floated. I immediately had a bad feeling about the whole situation. As I stood there in absolute dread, she grabbed a home-made ladle hanging on the wall behind her (made out of a stick with a pork and bean can lashed to the end of it) and, after swirling it around in the layer of gunk, she thrust it down into the heart of the barrel.

She then pulled the ladle back up, picked up a tall glass from the chair right next to her, and in one effortless, quick motion, poured the dark, molasses-colored liquid into the cup. Then, with a proud smile the size of all of the horn of East Africa, handed it to me. As I stood there in that hot dark shed, in that ancient and exotic Ethiopian highland city, on that glorious afternoon, I wondered for a brief moment (as I'm often prone to doing) just how in the heck did I get myself into this mess. For I now came to the unsettling realization that I had only two choices: the first would be to as graciously as possible turn down this nice lady's gift of which she seemed so very proud. This would have been the safer and more discerning thing to do, but it would have made me look like a pompous, portentous, ass. And somewhat of a coward as well!

The other would be to suck it up, stand up to the plate, stiff upper lip, win one for the Gipper, and all of those other American colloquialisms that frequently get our nation into hopeless 'poop' storms all over the world, and to just drink it; knowing full well that if I did so, I would very likely die, or at least never have normal digestion again. And that's what I did.

Without any more thought, I held the glass of liquid up to the light as I would have done with any other new beer I'm sampling, and seeing that it was surprisingly clean looking, brought it to my lips and chugged it down to about half a glass. Despite my worst fears, however, it wasn't bad. Once I got past the fact that it was flat and pee-warm, I discovered that the liquid had the pleasantly bitter taste of draft Guinness beer. But having now done my patriotic duty, I decided to not press my luck any further. Under the pretense of wanting to share the bounty, I gave the half-full glass to Samuel, who downed it with great gusto. Handing the empty glass back to the lady, he asked me if I wanted some more. I delicately declined.

[Without going into too much detail, the answer to everyone's question is: no, it didn't kill me, but within a few hours later that night, I thought for sure that my consuming that glass of beer was going to do so. And as I recall, it took almost a month before things were right (digestion-wise) again.]

Yangtze River

CHAPTER 13

On a Chinese Screen or A Cruise Down the Yangtze River

If all else perish, there will remain a story-teller's world
from Singapore to the Marquesas that is exclusively and
forever Maugham, a world of verandah and prahu which
we enter, as we do that of Conan Doyle's Baker Street,
with a sense of happy and eternal homecoming.

–Cyril Connolly, *Sunday Times*, 19 December 1965

Warning! In this chapter, I am going to talk about our visit to Communist mainland China, and I'm sad to say that it is my least favorite of the book. This is because as I wrote these little stories—and no matter how hard I tried not to do so—I couldn't get over the unsettling notion that I was China bashing. And as much as it pains me to say that, I will, however, make no apologies to anyone, except perhaps to **all** of the other non-communist Chinese people, both in mainland China and to all those around the world, who have rejected the maniacal Marxist leadership of their tragic, ancestral homeland. If my haranguing on the concepts of freedom and the rights of the individual to life, liberty, and the pursuit of happiness makes me sound too much like an ideologist or a hopelessly American romantic, that's too bad.

I would tell you that if you think I'm some kind of a pro-democracy, propagandist nutcase, then just travel to mainland China and visit Tiananmen

Square yourself. Here, if you look hard enough, you still can see blood stains on the concrete of thousands of massacred freedom protesters; or try to visit (or even worse, try to openly worship at) an authentic, cultural religious site or shrine that has not been destroyed or desecrated by the mad dog atheist followers of the late Chairman Mao; or (the worst of all) visit Tibet, where the madness and the conscious annihilation of the Tibetan culture continues to this very day. Actually, I will consider my entire point made if a loyal reader reads only the Tibetan story postscript at the end of this chapter.

I believe that one of the greatest writers of all time is the English writer William Somerset Maugham. Trained in his youth as a doctor at London's Saint Thomas Medical School, Mr. Maugham put all of his surgical and diagnostic training aside after the publication of his first book (a novel based on his student obstetric experiences in London's Lambeth slums) and never practiced professionally. At a very early age, his firsthand experiences with suffering and illness and death, combined with the methodical, objective, and nonjudgmental skills of observation that he learned as a physician, are what made Maugham such a genius at chronicling the human condition in his books and stories. He was an ambulance driver in France during World War I, a spy for the British government who tried to derail the Russian Revolution, an Impressionist art collector, a propagandist for the British cause during World War II, and, with regards to my personal interests, an accomplished world traveler.

When a person walks into a Chinese home, restaurant, or Oriental museum, they're very likely to see one or more examples of Chinese screens. As their name implies, they are screens used to divide a room, set off a corner for a token amount of individual privacy, or to just be used to decorate a space. They are often painted with collected scenes of everyday Chinese life: a farmer tending his cows, women planting rice shoots in a flooded paddy, or scholars studying in a temple. When viewed as a whole—that is, if the artist is successful—the viewer is rewarded with a holistic snapshot of what it is like to live in China.

On a Chinese Screen was one of two books that Mr. Maugham wrote with the nation of China as its main theme. Published in1922, the book consists of fifty-eight very short stories and vignettes in which he details his impressions and observations of his travels throughout that vast nation. Like those who came before him—and those travelers and writers who have come along since—he found it frustratingly impossible to do justice to a culture that has been around at least since the time of the pyramids of ancient Egypt. All he could do for his readers was to offer little glances, little insights of the nation of China, like those painted upon a Chinese screen, and then hope that his readers could put them all together in their minds and come away from his book just a bit more enlightened.

And I'm struggling to share my vision of China as well.

> Heaven knows from what mysterious distance he had come. He rode down the winding pathway from the high Mongolian plateau with the mountains, barren, stony, and inaccessible, stretching on all sides, an impenetrable barrier ... He held himself erect, riding a little ahead of his followers, proudly, and as he rode, his head held high and his eyes steady, you wondered if he thought that down this pass in days gone by his ancestors had ridden, ridden down upon the fertile plain of China where rich cities lay ready to their looting.

–"THE MONGOL CHIEF," *ON A CHINESE SCREEN*

Mainland China is the birthplace of the concept of Yin and Yang, the philosophical notion that sums up the nature of existence as being that of polar opposites that are constantly at work, both with and against each other, to shape the world that we all perceive: darkness versus light, good versus evil, love versus hate.

These opposing forces of yin and yang are at work within me as I sit at my desk trying to make some sense of my feelings about this ancient and enterprising and still most populated nation on earth. Like Maugham, for as long as I can remember, I, too have loved all things China: her unique writing system, her philosophers, her scientific achievements, and the way her artists depict her rural character and architecture. I recall as a U.S. Navy sailor in the early 1970s standing on the boundary line of the then-isolationist country of Red China on the Hong Kong side of the border looking out over the frontier with a fascination that always accompanies the forbidden. And my notions of all things Cathay (the old cartographical term for mainland China) would have remained a warm and fuzzy romantic illusion had I not visited the country. Unlike Mr. Maugham, who left China with his positive perceptions of the overwhelming grandeur of the nation still intact, I, unfortunately, did not.

In all fairness, however, I need to emphatically point out that the China I experienced was not the same one that Maugham did. Even though China found itself being pulled kicking and screaming into the 20th century, for Mr. Maugham it was still the old nation of rickshaws, imperial warlords, mysterious Taoist temples, and a forbidding vastness. The China I saw in 2000 was a struggling modern nation that had been ravished and raped by the Japanese during World War II, ripped apart by a brutal and bloody civil war, and stripped naked of her artistic, religious, and intellectual heritage in the rabid frenzy of Chairman Mao's several Communist Cultural Revolutions. To this day, her fretful citizens live in perpetual fear and paranoia of being tattled upon or ratted out by their neighbors, teachers, parents, and even their sons and daughters for criticizing their corrupt government or for something so basic as worshiping the god(s) of their choice.

It's always risky to attempt to paint with a broad brush any nation or culture or people. I need, therefore, to once again make my intentions perfectly clear before going any further: All of the references I make to China or the Chinese people in this chapter refer strictly to that behemoth of a country known to most westerners as Communist mainland China, Red China, or, if you prefer to be politically correct, the People's Republic of China, and exclusively to those citizens of that country who still insist on embracing the failed belief systems of the Communist ideology. I deliberately omit the brave people of the various administrative regions such as Tibet, Hong Kong, and Macau, and I particularly exclude the free nation of Taiwan. Also, with great admiration and profound respect, I especially do not include the millions of my fellow Chinese American citizens and their fellow compatriots all over the world who soundly reject the culture-bashing, paranoid, and spiritually dead, communist political cancer that infects the vast majority of their mainland China brothers and sisters.

And as he went along quickly, for the Consular's bearers were fine
fellows, his mind was distracted a little by their constant shouts to
make way ... The human race [the Consular thought] has existed
so long and each one of us is here as the result of an infinite series
of miraculous events. But at the same time, puzzling him, he had
a sense of the triviality of life. One more or less mattered so little.

—"THE VICE-CONSUL," *ON A CHINESE SCREEN*

Our tour guide and his driver picked us up from our Holiday Inn hotel around ten o'clock in order to begin our whirlwind day tour of the
capital city of Beijing. We had newly arrived the night before and had
allocated only two days of sightseeing around the city before flying out
to our ultimate destination in the southwest region of the country, the
city of Chongqing. Tomorrow we would go to see the Great Wall. Besides
the requisite visits to the Forbidden City and the infamous Tiananmen
Square, the highlight of the day was going to be the Emperor's Summer
Palace and its famous marble boat. There, at this ancient relic to the
nation's dynastic past, in order to honor and to share in yet another
connection with her late grandfather, we were going to take my wife's
photograph.

On one of our many visits to her grandparents' home, her grandfather showed us an old sepia-tinted snapshot from his days with the China
Marines taken in the early 1930s. It was quite a fascinating thing to see:
There he was, a handsome young marine, his cap poised in a confident,
jaunty angle, standing alone next to the famous Chinese landmark we would
see later that day.

[In spite of extensive searches through all of my wife's family's photo
collections, we could not find the photo of her grandfather standing next
to the monument.]

This "boat," in its modern-day incarnation nick-named the Boat of
Clearness and Comfort, was the idea of Empress Dowager Cixi. In the
1890s—because she could—the empress embezzled much-needed funds
from the building of a real navy in order to finance the project of building

this boat (whose base is actually made of marble) and enlarging the huge man-made lake it sits in. Her sole purpose in building the faux boat was for

decoration and to entertain guests. Later historians would claim that this act of royal self-indulgence helped the Imperial Japanese forces in their victory over the Chinese mainland prior to World War II. And as I was to discover really soon, the empress dowager's selfish behavior seems to have set the tone for her present-day, fellow-mainland countrymen.

Driving along the jammed, bumper-to-bumper, six-lane expressway on that morning, one of my first recollections of Beijing was that if it wasn't for the highway billboard signs being written in Chinese, we could have been in any overcrowded, polluted city in the world. What a mess it was. On this drive I also got my first insight into the personal philosophy of the modern-day mainland Chinese Communist citizen: that of a self-centered, seemingly borderline selfish attitude with absolute zero regards to everyone who wasn't their individual selves. From not holding doors open for others to not assisting the elderly, all the way to the complete disregard for their laborers, I would witness this total non-concern for the welfare of their fellow men and women over and over again during our whole three weeks in the country.

We were crawling along at about fifteen miles per hour when from an on-ramp to our right an ambulance in full siren entered the expressway and was now behind us. Five minutes, maybe more, went by, and our driver—in spite of having plenty of opportunities—had not yet pulled over to let the emergency vehicle pass. When I mentioned something to our guide, he looked at me as if I was crazy. He said, "Sir, if he pulls over, the only thing that will happen is that another car will steal our place." And so for the next thirty minutes until we exited the ramp to the Forbidden City, like it was the most natural thing in the world to do, we listened to the shrill of the siren and hoped that whoever the poor slob was that was being transported to the hospital would make out OK.

> She was an old woman, and her face was wizened and deeply lined ... It was plain that she was very poor ... She came down to the harbor; it was crowded with painted junks; her eyes rested for a moment curiously on a man who stood on a bamboo raft, fishing with cormorants; and then she set about her business. She put down her basket on the stone of the quay, at the water's edge, and took from it a red candle. This she lit and fixed in a chink of the stones ... She bowed herself three times and muttered certain words ... Then without further ado, she took up her basket, and with a leisurely, rather heavy tread, walked away. The gods were duly propitiated.
>
> –"A Libation to the Gods," *On a Chinese Screen*

Although it's often easier said than done, when journeying about on this amazing planet it is imperative that travelers occasionally must leave their cultural prejudices and social notions back home, especially when they're visiting exotic, remote, off-the-beaten-path locations. This doesn't, of course, mean you necessarily have to acknowledge, accept, or participate in these disagreeable and sometimes repulsive norms, but as a visitor to their world, you sometimes just have to let them pass.

First, and most important, there is no way that one can ever, as an outsider just passing through, completely understand the immeasurably complex set of social, environmental, ethnic, or ideological factors that lead up to how a culture functions or behaves. Secondly, it's you who have chosen to visit them; this is their home. If you want to get all self-righteous and indignant about having to view this or being offended by eating that, it's best to either partake or just politely pass and keep your opinions about the matter to yourself until. Elitist, judgmental, self-righteous attitudes are just plain rude and do nothing but piss people off.

You don't like seeing the bloody skin of a freshly killed polar bear drying on a shed during your walk through a Greenland village? Then you shouldn't be there. If the thought of children working away with their nimble little fingers knotting rugs in the basement of a carpet store near the pyramids breaks your heart—as it did mine—then don't walk into the showroom, or even worse, don't buy a rug! Or, if you don't like seeing whale meat on the menu in a restaurant in Norway—even though you and the whole world know that many whale species are at great risk of extinction—then don't buy it; order the reindeer steak instead.

[I actually tried to do this once at a restaurant in Bergen, Norway, just so I could say I ate whale meat; I figured that since the poor beast was already dead, there would be no point in it going to waste. Rest assured, my dear wife quickly put a stop to that notion, as a matter of fact, I'm thankful there were only butter knives on the table! Otherwise, my speaking voice would be an octave or two higher.]

During our visit to Mainland China, besides being enthralled by the history and overwhelming flow of humanity in that immense and unfathomable country, I also learned that the Chinese people really love their dogs. This love had two distinct forms. The first kind of love was the same as that of the rest of the world, that is, dogs as personal pets. Everywhere we traveled, be it in the big cities—and these are some really big cities—or countryside, you see people and their dogs. As one might expect, mostly what you see are little dogs: Pekingese, Shih tus, Tibetan spaniels, etc. Never once did I see a dog owner with a Rottweiler, Labrador, German shepherd, or even my beloved basset hound. The other form of "love" for their dogs, because it might upset many Western readers' sensibilities, I will tastefully (maybe that's the wrong word to use) explain later.

Located 1,400 miles inland from where the Yangtze River finally emp-ties into the East China Sea is the port city of Chongqing. Even way up here, this far inland, the Yangtze is already one of the world's mightiest riv-ers, having been birthed and sustained by the meltwater of the Himalayan glaciers in the lofty heights of the distant Tibetan plateau some 2,600 miles to the west. Standing on the city docks as we waited to board our small river boat, the Yangtze was an formidable sight to behold as her swift, sediment-laden waters roiled and churned angry red as she flowed past us. It was a bit poignant as well to stand there and realize that because a new dam—the world's largest—was being built two hundred miles downriver, this wild and only minimally tamed aspect of the river would someday be the western end of one big lake.

We were in Chongqing to board a river boat for a ten-day cruise. Known to locals as the Mountain City, for over three thousand years this inland port has served as southwest China's commercial, cultural, and, for a short while during the Chinese/Japanese War, its political center as well. My first impression upon our drive into the city from the airport was that of the sweltering heat. The humidity can only be described as oppressive. An English-language guidebook in our hotel room referred to Chongqing as one of the "three furnaces" of the Yangtze River Valley. My next impres-sion of the city was of how steep the streets were; you either had to go up or down, which also explained the lack of any great quantity of bicycles, which you see in most other mainland Chinese cities.

Being a veterinarian, another thing I noticed as we were being driven to our hotel from the airport was that right up until we reached the city limits, there were many small, fenced-in pens, each about twenty-five or thirty feet square, and each of which contained several dogs. Most of them looked like large, reddish brown chow mixes, some were Rottweiler-like, and a few looked like oversized black Labradors. When I asked our young guide about this large number of dogs, he confirmed (without the slightest hesitation) what I had already suspected. And it turned out that the question I asked must have touched upon a subject quite close to his heart because, for the first—and only—time during our visit to China, he turned out to be a tour guide that was self-motivated enough to actually engage us in a conversation.

Evidently a bachelor—or at least I hope he wasn't married—this question seemed to provide him an opportunity to ramble on for the next fifteen minutes on a topic that he seemed very excited to share with us. He began by telling us in great detail about a local method of food preparation in Chongqing called hot pot, and that dog meat was a common ingredient. And without actually coming out and saying so, he made a rather disconcerting implication.

He told us an old Chinese saying that went something like this: Married men who visit Chongqing soon realize they married too early. "This," he said, "is because the women of Chongqing are reputed to be the most beautiful and most fiery-natured in all of China." He then explained how the strong spiciness of the local cuisine kept the women healthy and clear of mind.

He spoke on and on, in an almost dreamlike trance, about how their having to walk up and down the mountainous topography of the city helps the local girls stay slim and fit and have beautiful legs. And with extreme reverence, as if he was sharing with us alone some great cosmic secret, he told of how the perpetually foggy, humid, and nearly windless weather pampers and softens their skin, keeping the Chongqing girls looking young well beyond their actual age. When I asked him about their fiery temperament, he smiled, and with just the slightest wink of his eye, said just three words: "Chongqing hot pot."

Another example of love for one's dog—though somewhat extreme example—was one I learned about during a port-of-call our riverboat made at the central China city of Wuhan. A huge, very modern city of over ten million people, Wuhan, because of its importance as a transportation hub, is often referred to as "the Chicago of China." It was here in the early 1970s that, while on military maneuvers just outside the then city limits, a group of soldiers noticed that the soil upon which they were camped was a different color from the brick-red clay they were used to seeing. When archeologists arrived to investigate, they discovered that the soldiers had actually stumbled upon a huge, perfectly undisturbed, 2,400-year-old tomb.

The tomb was that of a minor government official named Marquis Yi of Zeng. Although he was of no great consequence to the history of China, his tomb turned out to be an invaluable, well-preserved treasure trove of common, day to day, 4th-century BC relics: ancient manuscripts written in the calligraphic style of the day, rare examples of glass making, and hundreds of instruments of war. The most famous (and valuable) of these finds, at least for the average visitor, is a massive set of sixty-four bronze bells. The Chinese government has thoroughly excavated the site, collected all of the hundreds of thousands of artifacts, and built the Hubei Provincial Museum in which to display and preserve them.

The museum collection also includes the coffin and remains of Marquis Yi, the coffins and remains of his eight concubines (quite a horny guy, the old marquis), as well as the bodies of his thirteen servants, all of whom had the dubious honor of being buried with their master. But what piqued my interest the most was that in addition to the marquis and his postmortem entourage, there was one additional small coffin located in the position of highest honor at his feet. Was it that of his beloved wife? Nope. [And as an aside, with eight concubines, I personally don't see how the old marquis could have had time for a wife.] It turns out the coffin contained the remains of his most-treasured little Pekingese dog, probably placed there to protect him in his eternal afterlife.

He was junior partner in a well-known and respectable firm, and one of the peculiarities of China is that your position excuses your idiosyncrasies. It may be notorious that you beat your wife, but if you are manager of a well-established bank the world will be civil to you and ask you to dinner. So when Henderson announced his socialistic opinions they merely laughed. When he first came to Shanghai he refused to use the rickshaw. It revolted his sense of personal dignity that a man, a human being no different from himself, should drag him hither and thither. So he walked. He swore it was good exercise and it kept him fit; besides, it gave him a thirst he wouldn't sell for twenty dollars, and he drank his beer with gusto. But Shanghai is very hot and sometimes he was

in a hurry so now and again he was obliged to use the degrad-
ing vehicle. It made him feel uncomfortable, but it was certainly
convenient. Presently he came to use it frequently, but he always
thought of the boy between the shafts as a man and a brother.

–"Henderson,." *On a Chinese Screen*

The old guy's name was Herbert. He was an absolutely insufferable little
man, maybe around sixty-five years old, and part of a larger group of otherwise delightful Canadian tourists sailing with us on board our Yangtze
River boat. What struck me the most about Herbert was that he spent
the first three days of the cruise complaining to anyone who would listen
about how rotten and no good all Americans were.

At each meal, this virulent little creep, knowing full well that about
twenty of his other fellow passengers were American citizens, would blather
on and on and on about the corruption of the United States' political
system, the country's bloodthirsty military/industrial complex's intent on
world domination, and, especially, the overall, unabashed rudeness and
arrogance of the nation's citizens. All of the passengers, especially his
fellow Canadians, not wanting to cause a scene, chose to just ignore his
rants as that of an angry, possibly senile old man; and after two days on the
river, no one except his wife, Ruth, would intentionally sit next to him. But
even then, as he dumped his anti-American venom out upon his obviously
nervous wife, his whiny voice managed to rise above the din of the general
conversation taking place in the dining room and act as a cancer to any
congenial conversation.

Being as there were only so many tables in the dining room, and being
as all the other passengers went out of their way to avoid him, it inevita-
bly was only a matter of time before we would get stuck with the dubious
honor of being seated next to him. For the first two full days we lucked
out; however, because we were a bit late getting to breakfast on the morning of the third day, we were forced to take our turn. And sure enough,
no sooner had I wished him and Ruth a good morning, and even before I
could pour the cream into my waiting coffee, he started in on us. Looking

over the top of his little round gold-rimmed glasses, and in a dismissive tone of voice he might have used to describe a venomous snake, he said, "You both must be Americans."

It was at this moment that I had three choices. The first was that I could tell him to please keep his opinions to himself or I would knock him unconscious. This option, of course, would solve the problem, but I'd probably end up in a Chinese prison. Not that great an idea. Or I could just dismiss him as an angry man who obviously had an ax to grind with all things American and like everyone else, be as civil as I humanly able and just tolerate the slings and arrows he was about to fling at us. Or, I could fulfill his expectations and give the little bully a whopping dose of good old American ball-busting. And being my dear departed father's son, I decided on this last option.

"Yes," I said. And with the complete intent of at least starting out civil, I stood up and offered my hand for him to shake. I then introduced my wife and myself and said we were from New York. But rather than having the decency of politely returning my courtesy, I was met instead with a glaring, doltish look; a look like, "How dare I speak to me, you little American worm!" Sitting back down, and still wanting to win the guy over—or at least to antagonize him a bit further—I said, "Sir, from the accent in your voice, it sounds like you're from Canada, our great and honorable neighbor to the north."

With those words, the entire dining room went silent.

Now, over the years I have known many, many Canadians, and every last single one of them has been the most friendly, outgoing, and talkative person to be found anywhere on the planet. I even have a dear aunt who hailed from Newfoundland. Deciding to play upon his possible patriotism a bit further, I said (with all sincerity), "And you great folks from Canada, throughout our long and peaceful history together, have been true friends and a trusty ally, fighting right beside us in the world's times of need." This seemed to piss him off immensely, which sort of pleased me, but surprised me nonetheless.

"And much to our damn government's shame," he scowled, "murderous thugs you all are, and I'm embarrassed and saddened every time a Canadian boy picks up a rifle to die for an American cause." He then proceeded to spew out a litany of transgressions perpetrated by the American military's quest (his words) for world domination, beginning with the First Gulf War to Vietnam and Korea and all the way back to World War I. When I gently reminded him about the Gulf War and Korea being the work of the United Nations, and that World War I was a response to *his* commonwealth's mother country's call to arms, he started on another rant that lasted a good five minutes about how that formerly revered world body (the UN) was now fouled (his exact words) with the fetid corruption of America's money-grubbing global corporations, especially those located in New York, and this led to another ten nonstop minutes of his literally spitting and sputtering on the violence, moral decay, and overall decadence of how we Americans live.

"And your damned music!" I wasn't sure why he singled out this aspect of American culture, but he was on a roll, and even though Theresa seemed a bit nervous from it all, I calmly smiled the whole time and held his gaze, all the while thinking to myself that this creep must see himself as some kind of elitist. My not backing down, combined with my placid countenance and willingness to let him babble on served to fuel his rage even more. It was also about this time that I had an insight.

Probably expecting us both to come to blows, I looked around once again to see that all eyes in the room gazed anxiously toward our table, and a frigid silence still prevailed. Knowing in advance that I had nothing at all to lose—and beginning to have a bit of fun with this moron as well—I next asked him if he and his wife were enjoying China. Relaxing some, he said, "Absolutely! This renowned nation is one of the best-run countries on earth." This opened him up to then give a highly complementary—almost gushing—lecture on the merits of Chinese governmental policies and how this exceptional form of governance, with its universal health care, land reforms, and wage equality should be a model to which the whole world should strive. When I pointed out China's abysmal human rights record, its ruthless suppression of religious freedoms, and the government's almost manic need to dictate and control its citizens' most basic forms of personal expression, he dismissed my rebuttals with a wave of his hand, saying that it was all just the result of my being brainwashed by the anti-Chinese bias of our American media. I thought to myself, "Hmm, our little Canadian bully is a friggin' Communist as well as a moron."I recalled—but kept to myself—that Soviet President Vladimir Lenin even had a name for pitiful little propagandists like Herbert: Useful Idiots.

Expecting another five minutes of American-bashing diatribe, I was then surprised by his sudden silence. Maybe he'd already used up all of his anti-American rhetoric. Perhaps he (smugly) convinced himself that my attentive silence was a sign of my acceptance of the validity of his silly arguments. Or perhaps he was just worn out. Whatever the reason for his verbal hiatus, I chose that moment to let him have it. Looking him squarely in the eye, which I knew just irritated the hell out of him, I asked him, with perhaps just a touch of condescension, "Herbert … what's the matter?" Momentarily confused, either by the fact that I'd known his name all along or by my audacity to ask such a question, he mumbled something to the effect of "Huh?"

Again I asked, "What's the matter, Herbert; why do you hate us Americans so much?" Not knowing quite what else to say (and just wanting to break his balls a bit more), I then casually asked, "Did your little daughter run off with some American rock-and-roll drummer or something nifty like that?"

Whew! Before I even got that last word out, he became downright apoplectic! He started huffing and puffing and turning red, and I thought for a second he was having a coronary. Herbert had so worked himself up that for the first time his wife actually spoke a few words (to no avail) to try and get him to calm down. Agitated almost to the point of insanity, he forcefully stood up, thrust his chair back from the table, and hollered to no one in particular, "You damned Americans think you know everything! Well I'll have you know, sir, that he was a jazz musician! Not a drummer!" And having gotten that off his chest, he yelled at his wife to leave with him "Now!" and they both stormed out of the room.

So Little Herbie turned out to be not just a moron and a Communist, but the creep was a racist as well. But that was OK. With this one little— though somewhat heated— exchange between Herbert and me, peace at mealtime returned for the duration of the cruise. We would all see him and Ruth on the occasions of various shore excursions, but from then on the two of them took their meals in their stateroom.

> In China it is man that is the beast of burden. "To be harassed by
> the wear and tear of life, and to pass rapidly through it without
> the possibility of arresting one's course—is not this pitiful indeed?
> To labor without ceasing, and then, without living to enjoy the
> fruit, worn out, to depart, suddenly, one knows not whither—
> is that a just cause for grief?" So wrote the Chinese mystic.

–"THE BEAST OF BURDEN," *ON A CHINESE SCREEN*

The Zhang Fei Temple was built by grateful subjects in remembrance of—who else?—Zhang Fei, a famous general of China's Three Kingdom Period (220–280 AD). Legend says that the general was beheaded by a pair of enemy assassins, and his head thrown into the Yangtze. A local fisherman of the County of Yunyang was told in a dream to net the head as it bobbed its way downstream in order to prevent it from falling into the hands of the region's enemy. The fisherman did what his dream told him, and at the same time he retrieved the general's head, he fished in a large quantity of gold. In remembrance of their fallen leader, the citizens of Yunyang built a temple in his honor beneath the Phoenix Mountain. And here, for 1,700 years, the head of the good General Zhang Fei rested in peace; that is until his temple will need to be moved to higher ground in order to prevent being submerged in rising waters behind the Three Gorges Dam.

Two hundred miles downriver from Chongqing, our cruise boat stopped at a rather small—at least by mainland China standards—dumpy town so that we could make a visit to the soon-to-be moved Zhang Fei Temple. The visit was interesting in that the temple complex, perhaps because it had no overt religious context, still had a sense of authenticity about it. By this, I mean the buildings and their contents seemed to have mostly escaped Chairman Mao's mindless destruction by his antireligious, half-crazed followers that literally gutted their nation's collective soul during their Cultural Revolution.

Preparing to set sail that evening, I stood with Theresa on the uppermost deck of the boat (as we are prone to doing on trips like these) and watched the activities of the crew as they made ready for our departure. On shore behind the docks the land rose upward about five hundred feet to the actual location of the town. A hard-packed, gravel access road, which we all drove up earlier that morning in air-conditioned minibuses, switch-backed its way up the hill.

It was at this time that I caught sight of a man who earlier been sitting at the foot of the pier begging for alms. He was a young man, twenty-five or so years old, who was missing both legs halfway between his hips and knees. His earnings from our group could not have been that great as I'd seen only one couple other than us drop money into his begging bowl. The young man was now about to be loaded into a small cart by a much older man, obviously debilitated by arthritis, who himself didn't seem all that able to walk.

As we watched the old-timer painstakingly but gently pick up the young man and set him into the small two-wheeled cart, we speculated as to whether or not they were father and son, and we decided that it was most likely the case. After helping him settle into the cart as comfortably as he could, the old man picked up the wagon's handles and, like he was a beast of burden, began what looked to us the seemingly insurmountable task of hauling his son up the hill. Watching him slowly—agonizingly slowly—pull that cart upward along the gravel road, we speculated on the cause of the son's legless condition. Because of the symmetry of the amputations, I was sure the disability had to be the result of an industrial accident. For the last couple of hundred miles, we could see the entrances to several coal mines with their thousands of workers unloading by hand hundreds of small railroad cars of coal into waiting barges tied up along the banks of the river.

When the old man reached the first of about eight switchbacks, he set down the handles, put his hands upon the front of the cart, and rested for about two minutes. We had just begun to pull away from the pier as we saw him gaze up the hill to the next switchback. The old man then carefully picked up the wagon's handles, resigned himself to the task at hand, and with great resolve began the long trudge to the top. In no time, our river boat found herself caught up in the currents of that mighty and—for the moment anyway—eternal river, and we were out of sight just before they had reached the second switchback. During the whole of the twenty minutes we watched this drama, I would estimate no less than fifty men passed the father and son team as they, too, headed uphill to the village. As likely as not the majority of them had to be strong men: able-bodied seamen, stevedores, and other ancillary dockworkers. But whoever they were or whatever their occupation, these men all had one thing in common with what I observed to be the vast majority of their countrymen: not one of them lifted a finger to help ease the father's burden.

> It was a stumpy little tower, ten feet high perhaps, made of rough-hewn blocks of stone. At its foot were a number of baskets thrown about in disorder. I walked round and on one side saw an oblong hole, eighteen inches by eight perhaps, from which hung a stout string. From the hole there came a very strange, a nauseating odor. Suddenly I understood what the queer little building was. It was a baby tower ... and while I stood there [a young boy] made me understand that four babes had been brought to the tower that morning.
>
> –"The Sights of the Town," *On a Chinese Screen*

In Mainland China, they call the phenomenon, the Little Emperor syndrome, and everywhere we traveled in the country we saw (and heard and had to endure) the results of this warped social experiment: on the airplanes, in the passenger terminals, on the streets, in the restaurants, all around us all of the time! Little whining, brats—exclusively young men and boys—screaming constantly for attention, being spoiled rotten by their parents and grandparents; their highly pampered, narcissistic behavior shamelessly on view for the whole world to see. We were told by our fellow passengers that these little beasts were one of several unintended side effects of China's one-child-only birth policy. And it was on an excursion to the Huangshan Mountains that the poignancy of this government-imposed—and rigidly enforced—mandate became apparent to me.

Known to westerners as the Yellow Mountains, the awe-inspiring granite peaks of the Huangshan Range are one of China's major vacation/honeymoon destinations. The mountains are not named as they are because they're yellow, but rather they're named in honor of Emperor Huang Di, the Yellow Emperor and founder of the Han Dynasty, who legend says ascended into heaven from one of the range's summits. As we walked around the miles of trails, many of which were literally carved into the cliff's sides, we stopped for a few minutes at the high point of one of them to watch several newlywed couples perform a rather charming local tradition.

At several of the scenic overlook sites, there are chain-link safety fences. Locked onto the wires that make up the fence are thousands of brass padlocks. It turns out that the thing to do is to walk over to a nearby vendor and buy a lock with two keys. The vendors will then engrave the couple's names onto the lock, which they together, in turn, will fasten to the fence. They then complete the ritual by each throwing the keys away into the forested canyon below. For fun, and even though we'd been married for over twenty wonderful years, Theresa and I also bought a lock, had it engraved with Chinese characters that represented our names, and secured it to the fence.

After this, we rested for several minutes at a nearby café, enjoying an ice cream and a bottle of delicious jasmine iced tea and watched as one after the other of the young (mostly) couples symbolically solidified their lifetime bond. It really was heart-warming watching them, all beaming with happiness and joyful expectation of their future lives together. But it was at that moment that I came to realize yet another potentially even darker and repugnant side effect of China's one-child policy, a consequence that many of these elated new mothers and fathers would have to soon confront.

Sadly, as it still is in the vast majority of the world, there exists a strong traditional cultural bias toward having male children. In this preference for sons lies a problem that parents in these societies must deal with: what to do with their little girl babies. Before the advent of diagnostic ultrasound and its ability to determine an unborn child's sex, this "problem" was solved mostly by a couple just having more babies until the desired number of boy children was achieved. However, with their government's strictly enforced one-child-only policy, Chinese parents are now forced to make a bitter choice. And, from the number of male little emperors that are out there, it's easy to guess which sex ends up paying the ultimate price.

Historically, before the one-child policy, more times than not—and this is just speculation on my part—parents probably accepted whatever newborn blessing came along. Those who did succumb to their personal preferences or cultural, economic, or family peer pressure solved their little baby girl problem, as Mr. Maugham witnessed on his trip to China over one hundred years ago, by selective infanticide or abandonment. Today, again with the facilitation of prenatal ultrasound, the gender-cide continues, but under the more socially acceptable (but equally deadly for the innocent unborn little girls) practice of elective abortion. (In my follow-up research for this chapter I found out that human rights' groups actually have a name for this phenomenon as well: China's Lost Girls, and it's estimated that there are over five million new victims every year.)

> Outside the walls bedraggled houses are built on piles, and
> here, when the river is low, a hazardous population lives on
> the needs of the watermen; for at the foot of the rock a thou-
> sand junks are moored, wedged in with one another tightly,
> and men's lives there have all the turbulence of the river.

> –"A City Built on a Rock," *On a Chinese Screen*

Beginning about forty-eight miles upstream from the city of Yichang, our Yangtze River boat entered a section of the waterway known as the Xiling Gorge. As the last in a series of river channels known collectively as the Three Gorges, the Xiling Gorge throughout history was considered by the sailors who dared risk her whirlpools, submerged reefs, and merciless shoals as the most deadly of the group. A tourist pamphlet I read on board our boat quoted an unknown river man as saying that "Xiling's shoals are as dense as a bamboo thicket and that even ghosts as they pass by look at them in disquieting dread!" And of all the navigational hazards in the gorge, the most feared of all was the Kongling Shoal.

Known infamously as the *Gate of Hell*, Kongling Shoal was home to the notorious Come to Me stone. Due to the turbulence of the water flow and the location of as many as twenty-four submerged reefs, navigators learned early on that the only way to safely make their way through the hazards was to steer directly toward a giant stone in the narrow channel that legend says had the Chinese characters meaning "come to me" carved into it. As they drifted toward the rock, the helmsman had to keep a steady and courageous hand on the rudder, and at just the right time, turn starboard into the rushing current; if he turned too soon, his ship would be grounded on the nearby submerged reef; too late, his boat would be dashed upon the Come to Me stone.

The Come to Me stone now, of course, is gone, as are the swirling eddies and twenty-four killer reefs. When we sailed through on our Victoria Cruise Line ship, those navigation hazards had long been blasted away and dredged clean by the government. And today, as I write this story from my jumble of notes I made during our visit, everything—including the entirety of the Three Gorges themselves—is now submerged in over three hundred feet of water in the lake that has formed upriver from Xiling's most recent man-made addition, the giant Three Gorges Dam. Ironically, our captain's most dangerous navigational challenge was piloting our ship around (which as an old sailor myself, I can say was no small feat) the still-uncompleted end of the dam's southern end.

Our visit to the Three Gorges Dam construction site turned out to be quite an educational experience. To me the project seemed a genuine marvel of engineering, from the excavation of the five sets of gigantic locks being blasted into living rock, to its hydroelectric generating plant and to the 594-feet-high behemoth wall of concrete and steel itself. When it is completed, the 1.4-mile-long structure will be the largest of its kind in the world. But like everything else mankind contrives on this planet—especially appropriate for the land of the yin and the yang—the benefits of this great structure come at a great price.

Although the secretive Communist government never really has given any exact figures, at the height of its building, an estimated one-quarter of a million laborers (40 percent of whom were women) worked on the project. Our guide told us that worker turnover was so great that a million other job seekers waited in the wings to take their place. (She didn't say why, although after watching the various methods of construction, the reasons most likely were due to worker injuries and death.) As the water level in the lake formed behind the dam will rise over 300 feet from its current level, an estimated 1.5 million residents will be relocated to higher ground and over 1,000 cultural sites and artifacts will suffer inundation. The Three Gorges section of the river, so popular with centuries of Chinese screen artists and poets and adventurers, along with their 149 major shoals and rapids, will be gone.

The island of Taiwan lies one hundred miles off the east coast of mainland China. It was to here that the Nationalist Chinese government fled after their defeat by the Communists. Known officially today as the Republic of China, the country is home to nearly twenty-five million people. Although she is not recognized as a sovereign nation by the majority of the world's governments—mostly because they (the world) don't want to upset the Chinese Communists—Taiwan has her own military, her own constitution, and a vibrant free-market economy.

A few years after our mainland China visit, while returning from a scuba diving jaunt to Indonesia, I arranged a three day layover on Taiwan to break up the long journey home. Much to my surprise and delight, it would be here on this island that I would discover the bona fide China of my youthful expectations. Gone were people's paranoid self-centeredness and their nearly total lack of regard for anyone but themselves that rule personal behavior in such totalitarian societies as mainland Communist China. Whether in the train stations, on the city streets, or in the museums, the people of Taiwan that we encountered demonstrated a free people's decency and humane respect for their fellows. Rather than incessantly having to look back over their shoulders in constant fear of displeasing their government or having to consider everyone they meet a potential adversary, they could be kind to strangers.

Unlike their Communist counterparts on the mainland, the founding government of Taiwan made it a matter of policy to preserve (rather than senselessly destroy) their authentic Chinese heritage. By *authentic* I mean the heritage of old China's thousands of years of cultural tradition, not the faux architecture and mind-numbed theatrics one sees today when you visit mainland China.

The arts, such as opera, literature, calligraphy, and Chinese paintings, were made a matter of cultural priority as soon as Taiwan was founded. When the Nationalists escaped their former homeland after their defeat by the Communists, they also rescued and brought with them hundreds of thousands irreplaceable cultural artifacts that would have otherwise been consumed by the conflagrations set ablaze by Chairman Mao's Cultural Revolution and lost for eternity. These treasures, most of which can be seen in their original glory at the National Palace Museum, are safe.

So long as the citizens of Taiwan are allowed to remain free!

But for me, the most life-affirming aspect of Chinese life today in Taiwan is their religious zeal: the Taiwanese—unlike their spiritually dead, mainland, Communist cousins— exercise their God-given human right to worship the god(s) of their choice to a degree seldom seen in that part of the world. There are an astounding 18,255 temples and churches on the island with Buddhism and Taoism being the most common sects. The capital city of Taipei has over 5,000 temples alone!

One of the great things I noticed about the Taiwan government's policy of allowing its citizens unconditional freedom to worship is the high level of religious tolerance that seems to exist in that country. It's almost hard to believe, but on that small island there are twenty-six officially recognized religious sects. Many exist side by side as neighbors; some exist side by side under the same roof. One Buddhist temple we visited had chapels dedicated to not only the gods of Buddhism, but also Taoism, Hinduism, Confucianism, and even Christianity.

Postscript

> In the early 70s one pushed the boundaries by lighting up
> a joint and engaging at a sit-in in Berkeley. For the Red
> Guards of the Cultural Revolution a good night be spent
> destroying a Ming temple or torturing the teachers and
> intellectuals accused of possessing revanchist tendencies.

> *–Lost On Planet China*, J Maarten Troost

No discussion of modern-day Communist China could be complete without confronting the issue of Tibet and the plight of the Tibetan Buddhist people and culture ... an issue that (it seems to me) the vast majority of the rest of the world has chosen to turn their backs upon. Oh yes, the cultural and politically privileged of the Western world may do lip service to the problem with their rock concerts and black tie benefits; and yes, braver politicians who are not worried about offending the Chinese Communist government bureaucrats (and their deep financial pockets), will grant the occasional token audiences with His Holiness the Dali Lama, but that's where it all ends. As I write these words in the fall of 2014, the wanton brutality and the heartless, systematic cultural and human genocide of Tibet and the Tibetan people still continues in full, unabashed—and unrepentant!—view for everyone on the planet to see.

A question to ask at this time is: Why? Why, as with the case of Tibet, does the world continue to turn a blind eye on the millions of slaughtered civilians in Rwanda and the Congo, or the selling of young girls into the sex slave industry in South and Southeast Asia, or the rape and pillage of Darfur? The answer, at least in these sorts of cases, both in our present day and in past history, is that the concept of this savagery occurring is so completely foreign to the vast majority of people that we find ourselves emotionally numbed into complacency and helplessness.

This may, indeed, be the case with Tibet, but it's only a partial answer. Since Karl Marx first penned his *Communist Manifesto* over one hundred years ago, leaders like Joseph Stalin in Russia and Fidel Castro in Cuba and Mao Tse-tung of Red China have all been the darlings of the academic elites on university campuses all over the world. Especially Chairman Mao! And therein lies the quandary of Tibet: Educated men and women who have based their political and social ideology on the Communist model, especially as it was personified by the "good" Chairman, cannot ethically support the cause of Tibet without violating everything they've believed their whole lives.

And so I'll close this sad chapter with the following story. My truest wish is if the reader—who has so patiently stuck with me until now—gets no other lesson from reading this humble book it is that this true account of our visit to Tibet would be what he/she remembers the most.

We had flown from Kathmandu, the capital of Nepal, over the Himalayas, to the city of Lhasa, the capital of the tragic and wondrous nation of Tibet. (The Chinese occupiers prefer the territory to be referred to as the Tibet Autonomous Region.) We spent four days exploring that ancient city and all of the sights of the surrounding countryside. After this, we spent the next eight days traveling overland by Land Rover jeeps across the Tibetan Plateau and then over the top of the Roof of the World back to Nepal.

Breathtaking, awesome, and *spectacular* are just a few of the words I can think of to describe our Tibetan journey. However, on the other side of this same coin, words like *bittersweet, defeated, oppressed*, and *poignant*, also portray what we saw. Everywhere we traveled in Tibet, side by side with the beautiful scenery and in full shameless view for the world to see, exists the brutal evidence of the mass destruction and conscious effort by the Chinese Communists to annihilate the Tibetan culture. Hundreds of ancient monasteries and centers of learning have been demolished and millions of innocent people killed. Every town, village, and city still has the ruins to prove it. As I mentioned earlier, this cultural and human genocide continues to this very day. While touring with our group (there were nine of us in the group; my wife and I were the only Americans) at one of the few remaining monasteries still left standing after the Chinese Communists savaged the country, I stopped for a long moment to look around the inside of one of the monastery's many chapels. The darkened room was lit only by the burning flames of hundreds of butter lamps. The ancient tapestries, golden statues, mysterious old Tibetan inscriptions, humble offerings of fruit, and the pungent smell of incense all added to the delight and wonder and otherworldly enchantment I felt in that sacred place.

Sitting at the exit to the room was an elderly Buddhist monk. Because I had lingered so long and the group had moved on without me, this holy man and I were all alone. As I walked by him to exit the chapel, he looked at me and I looked at him; we both smiled at each other, and I said hello. Still smiling, he, too, said hello. Then (in very broken English) he asked me where I was from. I told him I was from New York. Unexpectedly, he reached out and grabbed my right hand with both of his hands, and as he did so, the sweet smile left his face, and he lowered his eyes in what seemed to me to be pure anguish. All the while, for what seemed an eternity, he held our grasp. The dear man was holding on to me so hard that his ancient hands were trembling. When at last he looked back up at me, I saw in his eyes the look of a thousand of years of pain and sorrow. Then, in a voice charged with a heart-wrenching, emotionally gripping reverence, he spoke just two words: "America!" Tears were now running down his face. "Freedom!" And then he lovingly let go of my hand, gave me what I believed was a blessing, and reassumed his peaceful countenance and said no more.

Sligachan Glen With Her Sligachan River
Photograph by: Leigh Woolford

CHAPTER 14

Scotland

—∞∞∞—

All the pathos and irony of leaving one's youth behind is thus
implicit in every joyous moment of travel: one knows that the
first joy can never be recovered, and the wise traveler learns
not to repeat successes but tries new places all the time.

—PAUL FUSSELL

ABOUT FIVE YEARS AGO, I took time off from my practice to attend the World
Congress of Veterinary Dermatology, being held that year in Edinburgh,
Scotland. I like to go to these conferences to see what's new in the world
of veterinary medicine and to attempt to keep up on my mandated con-
tinuing medical education. However, I didn't spend the whole of time in
Scotland looking at nasty, rotten dog and kitty skin.

Before the last speaker of the last scientific session asked if there were
any questions, I was flying out the door to do some sightseeing in one of
my most favorite places on earth. Right off the bat, we made a day-trip was
to the ancient town of Stirling. The visit to this sacred realm of William
Wallace would turn out to be particularly thrilling from both an historical
and a scenery perspective—and as things turned out, quite risky as well!

Stirling has been traditionally known as the Gateway to the Scottish
Highlands. More importantly, as we all know from watching the movie,
Braveheart, the town is quite famous in Scottish history as the spot where
the Scottish patriot, William Wallace, fought the battle of Stirling Bridge.

Also, the town borders on the battle site of Bannockburn, where the future king Robert the Bruce won his country's independence from England. Overlooking all this neat historical stuff is ancient Stirling Castle.

We visited the castle on an absolutely gorgeous Indian summer (they don't call it Indian summer over there, however) day. After a guided tour to get a better feel for the place, we set off on our own, exploring. We marveled at the grandeur of the Great Hall where for seven-hundred years, Scottish royalty have feasted. We viewed with some sadness the ancient and humble chapel where the hapless Mary, Queen of Scots, was crowned and where her son, James, the first king of both Scotland and England, was baptized. We visited the museum and former army headquarters of the Argyll and Sutherland Highland Regiments and got a quite different perspective on our own American Revolution from the British point of view.

We closed out our visit to Stirling Castle by walking the complete circumference of her famous wall walk. From this vantage point the glory of Scotland can be seen for hundreds of miles around. And this all would have been an almost perfect Kodak Moment had it not been for one fairly major complication—at least for me! Our walk ended on the north side of the castle, and after taking one last look at the foothills of the distant Scottish Highlands, we began our climb down from the battlements. It was during this time that I caught my first fearful glimpse of them scampering across Queen Margaret's Garden.

No, they weren't savage looking, blue-painted-faced, half-naked Scottish infantrymen loyal to Mel Gibson storming the castle keep. No, they weren't Jacobite army forces loyal to Bonnie Prince Charles that were charging the ramparts. Oh, how I wished at the time that it was one of these two groups of warriors; at least then I'd have had a fighting chance. But it was not to be! I barely managed to escape with my life. The problem, which is the same problem that I have to contend with every year around autumn time … yes, you probably guessed it: The squirrels were out gathering nuts.

> No sooner had the warm liquid mixed with the crumbs touched
> my palate than a shudder ran through me and I stopped, in-
> tent upon the extraordinary thing that was happening to me.

An exquisite pleasure had invaded my senses, something isolated, detached, with no suggestion of its origin. And at once
the hardships of life had become indifferent to me, its disas-
ters innocuous, its brevity illusory—this new sensation having
had on me the effect which love has of filling me with a precious essence; or rather this essence was not in me: it was me
... Whence did it come? What did it mean? How could I seize
and apprehend it? ... And suddenly the memory revealed itself.
The taste was that of the little piece of madeleine. [A madeleine is small, lemony-flavored, shell-shaped, sponge cake.]

–Marcel Proust, from *Remembrance of Things Past*

One of the real pleasures of living in a small town like Trumansburg,
New York, and of owning a one-doctor professional practice, is that
when I have time—and I always *try* my best to make the time—I can really get to know my clients: not only as pet owners but as good neighbors and friends. I try to learn about their occupations, their personal
skills, their hobbies, their hopes and dreams. My veterinary practice
provides me not only a source of income but also a venue for my personal and spiritual development; it's sort of my own personal life's university. Getting to know a bit more about my fellow sojourners on this
sacred journey we all call *living* means they get to know a little bit more
about me as well.

A few years ago, just about a week
before Christmas, two of my clients,
Andy and Kim, brought in their golden
retriever, Hobbs, for his annual physical
exam and vaccinations. Andy and Kim
have been with my practice since I first
hung up my shingle over twenty years
ago. Kim is an entrepreneur and business manager, and Andy is a city policeman and former Army Ranger. Both of

them are fellow travelers. Andy is also a connoisseur, as am I, of single malt Scotch whiskey. It was their unexpected generosity that inspired this story.

After we all had finished our work on Ol' Hobbs, and had filled out all of the paperwork, Andy reached into his coat and gave me a gift bag containing a bottle. When I pulled the bottle from the bag, I was delighted almost beyond words to see that it was a bottle of Scotch whiskey. But it wasn't just any old Scotch, it was a bottle of ten-year-old Talisker Single Malt from the enchanting and mysterious Isle of Skye! Out of the hundreds of single malt whiskies there are out there, he picked out my most favorite brand. And no sooner had I recognized the label on the bottle than a sweet ecstasy overcame me, and for several seconds I was speechless.

I think my exaggerated response to his generous gift on that cold winter's evening surprised them somewhat. So much so that Andy, maybe thinking that my heart had stopped, asked me if I was all right. Shaking my head and returning to the here and now I stood up from my desk, reached across it, and gratefully shook both their hands, thanking them profusely for the whiskey and told them not to worry, that everything was wonderful.

Later that evening as I sat in our outdoor hot tub and soaked away the day's cares and aggravations, I made the evening extra special by pouring myself three (maybe four) fingers' worth of Andy's special gift. The night was freezing cold, with just the slightest hint of a breeze. A gentle snow of big puffy flakes silently fell upon the world, the ones that landed on my bare shoulders giving me a bit of relief from the heat of the hot water in the tub.

In this inexorably complicated, multitasking, modern workaday life with which people in the Western world have voluntarily saddled themselves with, there is something so refreshingly simple, maybe even primal, about nursing a wee dram of an adult beverage in the fresh cold air of the great outdoors. For me, the greatest blessing of my middle age is always the amplification of my sense of taste and smell—particularly my sense of smell.

In the case of single malt Scotch whiskey, especially those produced in the Western Isles, like Talisker, the peaty smell becomes exceptionally vivid.

Scholars who study these things say that the word *whiskey* originates from the Gaelic term *uisge breatha* (or *aqua vitae* in Latin) both of which mean "the water of life." And I agree! But for me, just like the young man in Marcel Proust's long and almost unreadable book, *Remembrance of Things Past*,** whose small bite of a piece of madeleine unlocked in his mind a bittersweet involuntary memory, so it is that at rare treasured moments—like that night in the hot tub—all it takes for me is just one deep whiff of Talisker's pungently sweet, peat-smoke aroma for it all to transpire within me: then, like a sweet dream or a ride on a magical Arabian carpet, I'm transported in my fondest of memories back home to the loving bosom of the mystical magical, bonnie Isle of Skye.

**As an aside, I don't want to give any false impressions regarding my literary prowess in tackling such a monumental piece of literature. I've attempted Mr. Proust's *Remembrance of Things Past* no less than three times, but I just can't stay with it. Between the occasional moments of literary transcendence that very few authors can match, there are, unfortunately, interminably wide expanses of sheer boredom.

> Speed, bonnie boat, like a bird on the wing,
> Onward! the sailors cry;
> Carry the lad that's born to be King
> Over the sea to Skye.

> –Sir Harold Boulton, "*The Skye Boat Song*"

In all of my assorted wanderings over the years, there have been only two times in two very different areas of the world that I've felt certain—certainty to the very marrow of my bones—that I'd been there once before. I mean this quite literally! I'm not talking about the safe and sound familiarity of home sweet home. I'm not talking about those déja vu experiences I get occasionally where things seemed somewhat familiar, either because of something I've seen in a book or a movie, or because of something that someone in the past might have shared with me. Nor am I referring to a familiarity with regards to an ancestral or family heritage.

Being part Polish, I can be quite stubborn and literally very hard-headed. Being partly Russian, I also have the Russian emotional propensity to arrive at a conclusion first, and then—if I so choose—to amuse myself with rationalization and logic. But I'm sorry to say that in my trips to either Poland or to Russia, never once did I get that warm and fuzzy feeling that these lands were ever a part of the earth from which I was formed.

Sure, some of the long strings of consonants that make the Slavic languages so tongue-twistingly difficult to speak sounded vaguely familiar to my ear. And yes, the buttery onion smell of pierogies frying on farmers' market day in the city square in Krakow, and the rich, earthy flavor of a bowl of borsht at the Grand Hotel Europe in downtown St. Petersburg both served to warm my soul with memories of my dear, departed grandmothers; likewise, the omnipresent icons of our Lady of Częstochowa and the long and wonderful Polish Catholic tradition of pilgrimage I witnessed while in that country gave me a great joy and peace in their intimacy. But one would think that within the borders of both these countries that something, somehow, on the level of my primordial genetics would have touched a nerve of familiarity somewhere. Sadly, it never happened.

Once again, without trying to sound too New Age-like (or crazy), the specific feeling I'm trying to express is that of a genuine and overwhelming conviction of not only having been there before, but that the place was, at one time in history, my (or some other essence of myself) former home! And this is the exact feeling I had both times!

The first time that this phenomenon happened, I wasn't quite sure what to make of it all, and if the truth were to be told, I was as frightened as much as I was bewildered. It took place at night. I was then a nineteen-year-old sailor standing on the deck of an aircraft carrier as we steamed westward through the San Bernardino Straits, the passage of water that separates the main Philippine island of Luzon from Leyte Island and her more southern neighbors.

I had stepped up onto flight deck to catch a little bit of fresh air before heading back down into the sweltering, dank, stifling dungeon, better known as our sleeping quarters. All the lights on deck had been darkened to help the helmsman better navigate his way through the maze of narrow passages and hundreds of small islands through which we now sailed.

Being only about ten degrees north of the equator, the breeze that blew up and over the ship's massive bow was hot and sultry. And because all around me was totally devoid of any man-made light, the stars above shone with a vivid luminosity that I'd never seen—or at least I never appreciated—before. A thin sliver of a waning moon shed just enough light upon the world to define the huge mountains to the right of our north-by north-western course that formed the section of Luzon Island that we were now passing by. Some distance to the south, rising up from the sea like the enormous breasts of naked blackish-green women, were the perfectly formed cones of countless extinct volcanoes. I found myself spellbound, almost in a trance at the exoticness, the newness, the unfathomably beauty, and the sheer wonder of it all.

For at least an hour, I just stood there, taking it all in. When finally I found myself being overcome by tiredness (the crew and I, after all, just had a long, hard Pacific Ocean crossing), I walked across the flight deck toward the hatchway leading down to my bunk. As I gave one last look to the north, I noticed that our course through the strait had brought us to within about a half mile of the shore of Luzon. It was at this time that I noticed a large cluster of lights from a lonely village. At about the same time, I caught just the smallest whiff of the aroma of campfires. And then, bam ... it hit me! I had the overwhelming absolute certain sensation that I'd been there before!

Suddenly, in vivid detail, I saw in my mind's eye the straw-covered wooden huts lining the main, pothole-strewn, dirt road that wound its way through the center of the village, their bamboo-floored front porches loaded with chatting people as they tried to cool themselves in the languid heat of the late tropical evening before going to bed. I felt that if I was to suddenly materialize upon the scene, I would know every single person by name. And they would know me! I literally smelled the sweet aroma of their banana wood cooking fires as they still smoldered from their evening meal. On the mountainside rising up behind the village, like some sur-real Tarzan movie soundtrack on steroids, I heard the endless symphony of roosters crowing, of babbling monkeys, and of buzzing jungle critters. Somewhere on the outskirts of the village a dog barked incessantly.

Then, as now, there was no way I could have known any this stuff; I was just a young farm boy from upstate New York. My meager worldly experiences and collective memory of only nineteen years could in no way explain my insight. I had been to the Philippines just a year before on my first Vietnam cruise, but I had flown into the country landing at the old air force base at Clark Field. When we departed Subic Bay on the western coast of Luzon Island, we'd headed directly north to Japan for a bit of R & R, and had not passed through the straits we now sailed. No, this awareness of my having been here before originated from some-place far deeper, emanating forth from something at the very core of my DNA.

The second—and only other time—I experienced this absolute cer-tainty happened on my first overseas trip with my wife to England, Wales, and Scotland. We were visiting these countries with the intention of learning about the wide variety of sheep that are found in the British Isles. The trip had the distinction of being not only our first major trip together as husband and wife, it was the only organized bus tour we've ever done since. (I'll allude to the reason why we've never purposely taken this sort of tour again later.) A one-night side trip to Scotland's Isle of Skye was included in the tour.

> The King O' drinks as I conceive it, Talisker, Isla, or Glenlivet.
>
> –ROBERT LEWIS STEVENSON

The Isle of Skye! The mystical, magical, perpetually mist-enshroud-ed Isle of Skye! In the mind's eye her sweet name conjures up visions of all that is old and ancient: dark mountains, deep forbidden glens, Viking marauders, Bonnie Prince Charlie and long-ago battles between the clans Macleod and MacDonald. Lying just off the western coast of Scotland, the island takes its name from the ancient Norse word *Skýey* meaning—as would soon become obvious to us—isle of clouds. At the time of our visit, the journey across to Skye could only be accomplished by ferryboat. And not having been on a boat of any kind since my discharge from the U.S. Navy, it was this part of the journey I was most looking forward to.

My feeling of familiarity and having been there before happened on the afternoon of our first day on the island. We had just sailed "over the sea to Skye" earlier in the morning, crossing the half-mile-wide Kylerhea Narrows that separate the island from the Scottish mainland on the Glenelg Car Ferry.

The ocean current flowing through the narrows is one of the strongest in the British Isles and made for quite an exciting ride! After we docked, our bus driver, George, headed northward along the coast road toward our destination, a little spot on the map called Sligachan. It was raining, of course, a light, but cold, bone-chilling rain! But one good thing about when it's lightly raining on Skye is that the mist goes away and it gives you the chance to see her beautiful scenery. And the ride to Sligachan has got to be one of the most scenic drives on the planet.

After making a stop at one of the island's crofts (a small farm) to look at its Highland sheep and cattle, we arrived in time for lunch at Sligachan. Not much more than a fork in the road on the way to the island's northern port city of Portee, the whole of the community of Sligachan consisted of one hotel, aptly named the Sligachan Hotel, and a small campground. The hotel would be our home for that night and the next day.

As I waited for George to unload the luggage from under the coach, I walked over to a small knoll next to the parking lot to take it all in. Considering that the place warranted no more than the tiniest of dots on the map, what a spectacularly beautiful spot it turned out to be! To the east was the tip of a long and narrow finger of the sea called Loch Sligachan; behind the hotel toward the north and west were the rounded domes of the Red Cuillin Mountains; and to the south and west, thrusting upward like some kind of a devil's buzz saw, were the rocky crags and hulking summits of the forbidden Black Cuillins. In the gap that formed between the two mountain ranges was Sligachan Glen, down whose center flowed—you guessed it—the Sligachan River.

In all of those forbidden hills and freezing cold waters of her countless lochs lie the tragic essence of Skye as well: in the landscape before me I could see vivid evidence of the islanders' constant battle with the brutal, unforgiving weather and their never-ending struggle to eke out an existence on the island's rock-strewn marginal soils; of her centuries of conquests and plundering by the Vikings and other seafaring marauders; of the endless Highland clan wars and family feuds; the oppression by the English; the Scottish potato famine; and, of course, the final blow to whoever and whatever had managed to survive it all, the great purges by the landlords who believed that sheep were more valuable on the land than the peasant farmers. This, too, was Skye: hard, uncontrollably wild, and intoxicatingly beautiful almost beyond words—all at the same time

> I will make mountains which shall be the essence of all that can
> be terrible in mountains. I will pack into them all the fearful
> shapes. Their scarred ravines, on which nothing shall grow, shall
> lead up to towering spires of rock, sharp splinters shall strike the
> sky along their mighty summits, and they shall be formed of rock
> unlike any other rock so that they will never look the same for
> very long, now blue, now grey, now silver, sometimes seeming to
> retreat or to advance, but always drenched in mystery and terrors.
>
> –H. V. MORTON, REFERRING TO THE BLACK CUILLINS.
> FROM THE SLIGACHAN HOTEL WEBSITE

The tour's plan was to have our lunch in the hotel's dining room, to rest for a couple of hours, and then head off to see the Clan Donald Center and some more of the island's crofts and more sheep. Being not all that tired, after finishing lunch Theresa and I decided to take advantage of a much welcomed break in the rain—a relentless cold drizzle that had dogged our group since our arrival into the highlands three days before—and go for a walk. (We were also thankful for the opportunity to get away from the rest of the group, who were driving us crazy.)

After notifying the front desk of our plans, we stepped outside into a rare early afternoon sunshine. For no good reason, we walked south down the highway for a couple of hundred yards, crossed the bridge over the tannin-rich, brown water of the Sligachan River (it was more like a big stream) and turned right onto a well-worn trail that headed westward for a short distance along her south bank. Our original intention was to walk down the trail for a short distance and climb up the slope of one of the nearby Black Cuillin peaks to see if we could get a few photos of our hotel and the nearby loch. We only had two hours, so we debated as to whether or not it would be worth the effort.

But as we stood there trying to decide, something strange happened. From seemingly out of nowhere there wafted the pungent, but not un-pleasant, odor of burning peat. The smell lasted for just the smallest of a moment, but it stopped me dead in my tracks. Upon seeing this, Theresa walked up beside me, quite worried (I guessed), and asked me what was wrong. But for several more seconds I just stood there quietly looking around. The only sound that could be heard was that of the roiling water of the rain-swollen river beside us as it flowed without repose on its eternal journey from the mountains to the sea. It was as if I had just awakened from a dream. When I finally spoke, all I could say to her was, "Theresa, I know this place; I've been here before!"

As I said earlier, this tour we were on was our first major overseas trip together. Although we'd known each other, and had been married for about seven years, Theresa still had not completely gotten used to my many personal reactions and spontaneous reflections of this world—as well as my various other eccentricities—and I think that for just a moment, she was a bit freaked out by the situation. But being the calm, open-minded person that she is, this uncertainty of my mental status at that moment quickly turned into curiosity, and she encouraged me to tell my story.

As we stood there in that ancient glen under a now clouding-up sky, I told her that at that very moment in time I had the absolute certainty that I'd stood once before in this very spot, that I'd breathed in this pristine mountain air laden with the sweet-smelling essence of the heather flower, that I'd imbibed of the refreshingly cold brown waters of this creek, and that at some time in the past I'd been "one" with this rocky, savage, hardscrabble earth. I couldn't say when it all took place, but I was sure that it was long, long ago.

[Many years later, a movie titled *Braveheart* came out which stared the actor Mel Gibson. The film's storyline was based loosely on a Scottish freedom fighter and national hero named William Wallace, and it featured several gruesome battle scenes fought by Wallace's animal skin–clad, blue face-painted, ancient Scots warriors. In moments of quiet reflection—and wishful thinking—this would have been the time frame of my Scottish Highlands past life that I think I would have personally preferred to have lived in.]

I knew, in my heart of hearts, that at that moment, if we were to continue walking up that trail to where it passed beyond the distant horizon between the two Cuillin ranges, that I would know every bend in the creek, every bolder, and every ruined, abandoned farmstead along the path. Theresa, with one of those loving expressions of skepticism on her face, combined with her "Oh well. My husband just sees-the-world-a-bit-differently-than-most" sort of looks that are now an all-too-common occurrence during our worldly travels, just stood there patiently listening. After a few more moments she just nodded her head and said, "All right then, let's get going; I'm starting to get a chill standing here."

But Theresa and I never got the chance to test my vision, because time had soon run out, and we had to get back to the hotel to rejoin the tour. That afternoon we visited the Clan Donald Center, the ancestral home of all of the McDonalds (the family, not the hamburger restaurant chain) of the world and had a private tour of their Highland sheep. It would have been nice to linger for a while and explore some of the center's Armadale Castle and its walking trails, but we had the all-important tour schedule to keep. We visited a woolen mill and killed an hour looking at the store's overly priced hats and gloves and sweaters. Near the village of Portee we visited a sheep farm and Gaelic College. I remember thinking to myself as we breezed through the village that it would have been kind of nice to have stopped at a pub for a pint or two. But no, we had to rush back to the hotel in time for the evening meal. Overall, both Theresa and I were a bit let down by the day's events.

Upon our arrival back at Sligachan, as we were washing up for dinner, we decided then and there that if we could afford it in the future we would never again be part of an organized economy bus tour. It wasn't so much having to put up with the old jerk who whistled constantly; who was there only because his wife forced him to come along on the trip. Nor was it having to wait on every single day of the trip, at every single stop we made, for the two elderly maiden sisters who had the annoying habit of never being on time for the bus's departure.

The biggest problem with the trip was the absolute lack of individual freedoms: the freedom to climb those mountains, to stop on a whim at a roadside vista along the way, or to explore those off-the-itinerary trails whenever or wherever we wanted to. Even something as mundane as being able to go to the bathroom whenever you had to is just not possible on a tour bus. And so far, as I write these stories one hundred–plus countries later, we've still managed to avoid them.

But our day was not to be a complete loss. After a long and soothing hot soak in our room's oversized bathtub helped quell the chill that had settled into our bones, we headed downstairs to the hotel's restaurant. And what a beautiful dining room it was. The preserved heads of multiple Scottish stags hung on the walls as did several large paintings, all of which reflected the hotel's original purpose for being built: to be a lodge and sanctuary for aristocratic game hunters and fishermen. A large fire burned in the hearth and the sweet smell of peat—the very same smell that earlier that afternoon had so aroused my deep former Scottish memories—delicately scented the air. It was all posh and warm and very comfortable. George, our coach driver, sat with us at our table.

We knew from previous conversations with George that his occasional trips to Scotland as a tour bus driver ranked among his favorite of all the places in the British Isles he had to work; the journey over the sea to Skye was his most favorite. Having eaten at this hotel countless times before, he made a couple of suggestions on how to improve the meal. As people who travel on these types of bus tours know all too well, you usually have two dining options: You can chose the restaurant's fixed tourist-fare meal, which is usually included in the price of the tour. This option, which, of course, most travelers choose, is normally quite ample and tasty, but the choices of what you're able to eat are limited to just a few entrées. The other option is a la carte. This choice lets you chose your meal from the regular restaurant's menu, but for travelers on a budget (which we were at the time) it can be cost prohibitive.

George suggested that we have the regular tourist menu as it was really very good, but to also have as a paid appetizer the hotel's smoked Scottish salmon. I said that I'd try it (Theresa passed), and he ordered some for himself as well. I'd had raw salmon many times before in my youth. In New York, the fish was called lox and it was often eaten with bagels. The flesh was always a bit greasy, and for most people, lox was an acquired taste. But the Scottish salmon that we ate that evening was different. First off, the meat had a drier, firmer texture that was meant to be eaten without any sort of adornment. It also had a pleasant hint of the taste of peat smoke.

George spent the next ten minutes expounding on the various qualities of smoked salmon I could encounter in Scotland. He told me that nearly every restaurant, pub, and bed-and-breakfast in the country had their own special technique for smoking—or not smoking—the raw fish; some, he said (with slight disdain), even marinated the fish in various herbs to produce a lighter-flavored taste. He concluded my education of all the intricate nuances in the world of smoked salmon by telling me how lucky I was at that moment. Given the absolute freshness of the fish (many were landed from the nearby river), the genuineness of the peat used to smoke it, and the special preparation given to the meat by the hotel's chef, this (with the possible exception of the Hotel George in Edinburgh) would be the finest smoked salmon I'd ever eat anywhere on the planet. Although I'd never tried it before, after that moment I agreed with every word he said.

He advised me to skip the Guinness beer that I was considering and have a pint instead of the McEwen's Scottish Ale that the bar had on tap. Not as precise as he was of his knowledge of Scottish smoked salmon, all he could say was that for some reason, perhaps the salt sea air, this particular lager just seemed to taste better. Thinking to myself that I might be stretching the budget a bit, but wanting to show my appreciation for sharing with us the gift of his various culinary insights, I offered to buy him a pint as well. Without hesitation, he said he wouldn't mind it a bit! And again, he was right about the McEwen's.

The dinner was excellent—as George had predicted. Served family style, it consisted of split pea soup and a big platter of boiled beef, all accompanied by endless bowls of root vegetables and homemade bread. It was a feast fit for a Scottish nobleman. Dessert for me was another first: a yellow custard-like dish covered with a strong burnt sugar liquid called flan. I wasn't crazy over it at first, but like a lot of things in life, once you acquire a taste for it, you'll never settle again for Jell-o. After we finished eating, and the waitresses had cleared the table, George invited us to the bar for a nightcap. He said he had one more thing to teach me. Theresa, worn out by the day's travels and because we had an early start scheduled for our trip back to the mainland, stood up and quietly said she wanted to turn in for the evening. Like the English gentleman George truly was, he stood up as she rose from the table and wished her a pleasant evening.

George asked me as we walked me to the bar if I'd ever had a single malt Scotch before. Not quite knowing at the time what he was talking about, I said that I'd had Scotch before, that my father liked to drink something called Chivas Regal (a blended Scotch whiskey as I was soon to learn), and that I'd tried it and that I thought it was OK. A dear uncle of mine from California had let me sample a brand of Scotch called Glenlivet, and it wasn't too bad either. With the look of someone who had a great secret he was just dying to share, he then said I was in for a real treat. Pulling up a couple of stools near the center of the highly ornate, old-style wooden bar, George began yet another teaching session on the fine qualities of single malt Scotch whiskey, one that would give me great pleasure to this very day. He ordered two glasses of Talisker.

He said that Chivas Regal was a blended whiskey. That meant that a professional taster/blend master would co-mingle together Scotches from several different distilleries to accomplish his brand's classic flavor. Because it was affordable, the drink was good for parties and for making highballs (mixed drinks). The Glenlivet, he continued, was a fine example of a single malt Scotch.

He then said nothing for a few seconds as the bartender poured a wee dram of the Talisker into the two glasses that sat before us on the bar. (When the Scottish drinker says "wee dram" they're not kidding! The whiskey he poured into the glass barely came to a finger's width in height!) George then showed me how to swirl the liquid around in the glass, to appreciate its rich golden color and to see how well it coated the glass. After he finished, he lifted his glass upward toward me and proposed a toast that went something like, "Here's to those who loves us or lends us a lift!" Then, raising the glass to his lips, he took a sip. I, too, then took a drink; however, instead of a sip I took a good old all-American gulp. Instantly, both my sensations of taste and smell were overwhelmed by the heavy flavor and overwhelming aroma of smoke! It was a bit too much to bear at first, and even though I could drink American whiskey by the cupful, I coughed and gagged like a schoolboy.

George—and the bartender—got quite a big laugh out of it all. He asked me if I could taste the peat. "Taste it?" I said, still reeling from the sensory overload, "George, it feels like I just stuck my tongue down into a coal fire chimney!"

"Give it time he said," and, of course, he was right. Within half a minute, the flavor sort of mellowed out into a mildly sweet, slightly briny, almost seaweed-like aftertaste. I didn't know it at the time, but it would be love at first taste!

He continued on to say that you must slowly savor the sensation of a good single malt whiskey. "Always be gentle," he said. "You must cradle it, caress it, and appreciate its qualities like you would that of a beloved wife or lady friend." Still reeling a bit from the blast of the full-flavored whiskey, I told him that, like nearly everything else I do in my life, I always have to learn things the hard way. George got a laugh out of that as well.

As we slowly consumed more of the golden liquid from our glasses, and beginning with the brand we now were drinking, George shared with me his seemingly endless knowledge of Scotland's most famous gift to the world. The single malt whiskies of Scotland's Western Isles, he said, are the most famous—some would say infamous (for they are an acquired taste)—for being exceptionally full-flavored.

First, there is the smell and taste of burning peat smoke that sets this region's scotches apart from their Highland and Lowland cousins. He told me you could smell some of these whiskies from across a living room. There is also a strong mineral component to their flavor, either from the mountain streams where the distillers get their water or from the salty sea breezes and fog that inundate this part of the world for a good part of the year. Finally, there is the sweet smell and taste of the ever-present Highland flower called 'heather'. He added that this taste can be found, however, to various degrees in all Scotch whiskies. How this ambrosia-like nectar gets into the very heart of the drink of Scotch he said is completely a mystery.

It was all an amazing lesson, and I think George could have spoken for hours, but as the night wore on, we both remembered we had to get up early the next morning. And he had to drive! Before finishing off the last mouthful of the Scotch remaining in his glass, one more time George held it up to the light and looked lovingly at the liquid as if he was saying good-bye to a dear old friend. As he did, George concluded his discussion of Scotch with the following declarative sentence: "I hold in my hand a Talisker, a native son of this grand and glorious Isle of Skye, and the only single malt distilled anywhere on the planet that manages perfectly to marry all of these tastes and smells and textures that makes the imbibing of Scotch whiskey one of the most delightful and resplendent experiences mortal man could ever have wished to partake in!" He then raised the glass to his lips and, with perhaps just a hint of melancholy, lovingly drained the glass.

Epilogue

You Can Never Go Home Again

> You can't go back home to your family, back home to your
> childhood … back home to a young man's dreams of glory
> and of fame … back home to places in the country, back
> home to the old forms and systems of things which once
> seemed everlasting but which are changing all the time
> – back home to the escapes of Time and Memory.
>
> –George Webber, lamenting in the Thomas
> Wolfe novel, *You Can't Go Home Again*

During the remainder of my navy enlistment, my old aircraft carrier would sail through the San Bernardino Straits two more times. The first of these additional passages was in 1974 as our carrier group, once again, headed her way westward back to the South China Sea and the Gulf of Tonkin; it would be my third tour with the old girl to the war zone. The ship was scheduled to enter the straits from its eastern approach sometime in the late morning. Unfortunately, and much to my great irritation, I'd gotten stuck below decks with having to give an "old salt" talk to the new guys in our division.

Every once in a while I reflect back on the irony of that particular assignment: there I was, just barely twenty-one, telling these men, several quite older than myself, what to expect during our upcoming liberty in Subic Bay, how not to get thrown in jail or have their throats cut by angry bar girls, and, ultimately, what to expect when we reached Yankee Station (code word for being anywhere off the coast of Vietnam and Cambodia.) They were all in high spirits and the new guys were all fired up and ready to "kick Charlie's ass!" Not wanting to seem too overly cynical, I went along with them; but I knew better. The biggest problem, however, was that by the time I'd finished with my talk and managed to get up to the flight deck, we'd already sailed past the narrowest part of the channel where a year before I'd experienced my first—for lack of a better term—vision.

My third and last trip through the straits was on the return voyage home from this same tour about eleven months later. The Vietnam War had been declared officially *over* a month before, and everybody on board was physically and mentally—mostly mentally—exhausted; we were burned-out, beaten down and tired! Our inner resources had been stretched to the limit during the evacuation of Phnom Penh, the chaos and inhumanities of the forced withdrawal from the then nation of South Vietnam, all of which was topped off by a long-forgotten, nasty little skirmish (the worst two days of my life as it would turn out) off the southern coast of Cambodia called The SS *Mayaguez* Incident.

Just prior to this last passage, our captain docked our ship at the huge naval base at Subic Bay (Philippines) to allow my shipmates to disembark the wounded and fallen Marines we had on board from the *Mayaguez* rescue. Afterward, as the ship was being provisioned and fitted out for our return trip across the Pacific, those of us who could went ashore for some much-needed, rowdy and rampageous R & R.

The following morning, we all began our journey homeward. Our course was to take us eastward through the San Bernardino Straits, but I have no conscious recollection of the event. That's because the majority of the crew—myself included—were so hung-over from our liberty the night before that we were well at sea for several days before any of us even had the faintest idea of where we were at.

> It is great to shake off the trammels of the world and public
> opinion and become the creature of the moment and to be known
> buy no other the title than "The Gentleman in the Parlour."

WILLIAM SOMERSET MAUGHAM, *THE GENTLEMAN IN THE PARLOUR*

Ten years after Theresa and I did our bus tour to Scotland, we returned to the country to attend the previously mentioned dermatology conference being held in Edinburgh. Recalling the conversation with our former bus driver, George, in reference to the one other place on the planet besides the Sligachan Hotel that had excellent smoked Scottish salmon, we decided to once again take his advice while attending the conference and stay at the Hotel George. We were not disappointed. She was a magnificent hotel in the grand old European style, and her service, from the doorman to the concierge was flawless.

When we got to our Edinburgh hotel it was mid afternoon. After a long overnight flight across the Atlantic, combined with an inhumanely packed commuter flight from London, we were both exhausted. Wanting to nap, Theresa elected to stay in the room; I went downstairs to the bar to down a pint—or two—of McEwen's lager to help me unwind a bit before turning in myself. Taking a seat at a table near the front of the room, I ordered a glass of beer and a bag of potato crisps. (In the British Isles, they call potato chips "crisps," so as not to be confused with the deep-fried potatoes that come with "fish and chips.")

The room was nearly empty with the exception of a couple of business-men standing at the bar and an elderly, very distinguished looking gentle-man sitting at a table near me. He was a short, pot-bellied man with jet-black hair and a well-groomed moustache, and he was impeccably dressed in a dark blue suit; the man had all the personal bearing of an a Italian count. I noticed as well, the waitresses seemed to fawn over him like he was a rock star. But what caught my attention the most was that one of the ladies had brought him a plate of smoked salmon. He said to her after she placed the plate of fish on his table (in the most gentlemanly of ways), "Luv, you know very well, my darling, that this most regal of fishes is not properly served until it has been dusted with a dash of freshly ground pepper!"

Although in those early days, even though I wasn't the most gregari-ous of persons, I couldn't stop myself from getting up, walking over to his table, and introducing myself. I said, "Sir, my name is Richard, and I am a veterinarian from upstate New York, and I am here in this magnificent city to attend a dermatology conference. Please excuse me, sir, I couldn't help but notice that you seem to be a man who enjoys his smoked salmon. I'm told that perhaps the finest example of this fish on the face of the earth is served in this very hotel."

Seemingly happy to have someone to talk to, he stood up, introduced himself as Antonio, and offered me to sit down. Asking him what he was doing in Scotland, all he said was that his home was near Sorrento, Italy, and that he was involved in the import/export business, and that this business occasionally brought him to this part of the world. When pressed by me as to exactly what it was he imported and exported, he always shifted the conversation back to the subject of smoked salmon. He said that every time he passed through this city he made it a point of stopping by the George before embarking on the sleeper train to London and then to the Continent.

By now, my traveling experiences had taught me that the fellow travelers I happen to meet on the highways, byways, and in the bars of this world all have a story to tell, and if they want to tell it, they will; if not, it's best not to push them to do so. Whether you're in a restroom in Bangkok or on a ship off the coast of Sicily or in a bar in Edinburgh, if people want you to know their reason for being in that particular place at that particular time, they will shout it from the mountaintop. If they don't, I've learned to just drop the question. Everybody is where they are at for a reason—sometimes good, and sometimes sinister—and this mysteriousness, this potential to be anonymous, is one of the thousands of things that make traveling the world so exciting! Once I realized that Antonio wasn't going to tell me what it was he traveled to Scotland for, then all I cared about was our shared love of smoked salmon.

Seeing that I didn't have anything to eat, he politely caught the attention of one of his favorite waitresses and asked her to please bring his new friend, me, a plate of the same salmon he now was about to eat. Insisting that I buy it myself, he said, "Nonsense young man, it would be my honor to share with you, a distinguished doctor, this humble bit of meal." I graciously accepted.

And just like George, our coach driver on our first trip to Scotland, this man was a connoisseur of all things smoked Scottish salmon. He favored the wild fish over farmed, although he predicted the two would someday be identical in quality. He liked better the taste of wood smoked fish found in the vast majority of Scotland than the peat-smoked varieties of the Western Isles. This would explain his failure to mention of the Sligachan Hotel's smoked salmon. He shared with George his total disdain for the herb-marinated varieties that he said I would find on the upper east coast. And the one thing that this Italian gentleman taught me that George did not was the absolute necessity of applying a few dashes of freshly ground pepper to the fish; good advice that I still follow to this very day

After the dermatology conference was over, we went on a fantastic road trip, driving from Edinburgh northward along the eastern coast, across the top of the country, and then southward down the west coast, with the ultimate intention of crossing over to the Isle of Skye. All along the way we stayed at small inns and hotels. And all along the way I sampled all of the single malt Scotches and local versions of smoked salmon I could find. I even had the opportunity at a hotel in Aberdeen to try the chef's own special variation of herb-marinated fish. With the first bite I knew why both George and the Italian count disliked the results; it was almost a sacrilege!

It is said that you can never go home again. I've found this to be the case in all of my life's journeys, almost without exception. Sensually, you're not the same person you were when you experienced a place for the first time when all was so very new and so exciting.

You see it all with different eyes, looking at the world now with a greater sense of humility and maturity—and hopefully, without the distortions of that greatest of all old-age curses, cynicism. You don't smell and taste with the same levels of awareness or keenness or vitality. And, as it has been since time immemorial, the world itself changes as well, and mostly (it seems) not for the best!

One of my first disappointments concerning my much anticipated return to Skye was that now you could cross over to the island on a bridge—a very expensive bridge! I was told by a waitress at a restaurant on the mainland that the ferry still made the crossing over the Kylerhea Narrows, but crossings were now limited to just a few times a day. With no other option available, we paid the exorbitant toll and drove across the bridge; in two minutes, from dry land to dry land, I was once again back home on the magical Isle of Skye. The experience of arriving just wasn't the same.

Nor was the first half mile of the highway. As happens with these sort of things, along with the bridge came commercial strip development: gas stations, roadhouses, souvenir stands. But surprisingly—and much to my delight—the development stopped quickly, and the same old Skye that I remembered returned in all of her glorious, mist-shrouded, majesty! Everything was how I remembered it (or how I wanted to remember it)! When we pulled into the parking lot of the old Sligachan Hotel, it, too,— with the exception of a small, tastefully-done, addition—seemed much the same ... not counting a very busy microbrewery building next door built upon the small knoll where years before I'd first took in the surrounding scenery.

But all this was of no real consequence to me: All I wanted was to get settled in, have a small snack for lunch, and hit the trail. With the exceptions of new locks on the doors and a much improved plumbing system (the dark, tea-colored bathwater was gone) the basics of the hotel were pretty much the same. After eating, we went back outside only to find that a thick-as-pea-soup fog had descended upon the glen, and you could not see your hand in front of your face. And even though supposedly I knew every nook and cranny of that valley from a previous incarnation, Theresa didn't want to test that theory by having us get lost and dying of exposure. Nor did I. And so we napped for a few hours, only to awaken to a torrential downpour that would not let up for that day and the next. And by that time, we had to leave for the last leg of our trip to Glasgow, where we would catch a flight back down to London. There we over-nighted and caught a mid-morning flight back to New York.

But I'm not giving up on my theory. I frequently check cruise line schedules to see if a San Bernardino Straits passage is planned for one of their sailings. Most tend to go around the northern side of the island of Luzon. The reason I was told was that these commercial ships prefer to avoid the straits because their waters are difficult to navigate and because of the danger of pirates.

And I've especially not given up on Skye. Who knows: maybe I will be able to go home again!

CHAPTER 15

Mother Ganges

❧

The wish to travel seems to me characteristically human: the
desire to move, to satisfy your curiosity or ease your fears, to
change the circumstances of your life, to be a stranger, to make a
friend, to experience an exotic landscape, to risk the unknown ...

–PAUL THEROUX, *THE TAO OF TRAVEL:*
ENLIGHTENMENTS FROM LIVES ON THE ROAD

IN INDIA, THE GANGES RIVER is affectionately referred to by all of her countrymen as Ganga Ma, "Mother Ganges." By length, she may only rank thirty-
sixth among the great waterways of the world, but her waters flow through
the most densely populated river basin on the planet. Also, for both the
Hindus of India and to their countrymen who live abroad, every inch of
the great river, from its origin in the lofty Himalayas to her distant estuary
in the Bay of Bengal, is considered sacred. The waters of Mother Ganges
provide life-giving sustenance, irrigation, transportation, and a source of
waste disposal for everyone who live within her immediate vicinity. Likewise,
her waters provide holy refuge for the absolution of sin and for the hope of
eternal salvation to those who die and are laid to rest within her watery bosom. Unfortunately, as a tragic consequence of the overwhelming demand
placed upon her by this unfathomable mass of humanity, who depends on
the waterway for both their lives and deaths, as both a sanctuary and a sewer,
the Ganges is also among the top five polluted rivers in the world.

It was along the northern reaches of the Ganges that we found ourselves as passengers in a rather beat-up but otherwise mechanically sound, air-conditioned Mercedes sedan on a hot and drippingly humid, late August day. In the front seats were our driver, Mr. Singh, and our certified mountain guide, Mr. Sharma. We'd all left early that morning from the Indian capital city of Delhi and were motoring our way northward across the vast, densely populated, flat-as-a-pancake Ganges River basin toward the Himalaya Mountains. Our combination road trip/mountain trekking destination for the next nine days would be a place that Hindus call Gomukh—the mouth of the cow.

> If travel has momentum and wants to stay in motion ... then
> adventure has the gravitational pull of a black hole. The
> more you do it, the more you find a way to keep doing it.

–JOSH GATES, *DESTINATION TRUTH: MEMOIRS OF A MONSTER HUNTER*

Friends and clients are always asking me how we come up with the unusual ideas for our trips. It's a fair question, but not always an easy one to answer. As frequent travelers, we receive many brochures and pamphlets in the mail, but the majority of these just go into the recycle bin. For my wife, her destinations of choice usually involves seeing a new critter or a certain breed of reef fish or shark, an unusual bird, or some rare orchid or tree. For me, I mostly have places in my mind that I've seen or read about or have watched on a television travel special. And, as the recurring theme that I've babbled on and on about throughout this whole book, I really do want to be "one" with everything and everywhere on this planet. Having said all that, both of us also find great joy and solace in visiting the sacred.

But our decision to make the trek into the high Himalayas to Gomukh—better known to westerners as the source of the Ganges River—was not all that mysterious. On a snowy January evening we were innocently watching a *National Geographic* special on the subject of the rare snow leopards of the Himalayan Mountains. In the film the producers showed a scene of a

Hindu holy man bathing in the freezing water that was gushing out from underneath a huge glacier. This was Gomukh, and the narrator said the spot is considered the holiest place for all of the Hindu religion. Fascinated by both the awesome beauty and monumental sanctity of the place, I casually mentioned to Theresa that I thought it would be a great place to visit, and she agreed.

And that was that!

As is the case with most nations or cultures, it's always difficult—at least for me—to precisely summarize the essences or the qualities of the places we've visited in just a few words. It's also quite unfair to the countries in question as well. Sure, I agree wholeheartedly that there are common aspects of the human condition that the great majority of people everywhere share to some degree: the belief in God or gods or some other form of higher power, their love of family, the endless struggle to gather the daily bread, and the universal knowledge of every man's mortality. It is the vast range of these multicultural behaviors and the profound differences of worldly outlooks that boggles, yet at the same time captivates, my mind. But I believe that it's the very uniqueness of these complex combinations of worldviews that serves to define a nation. I also believe that unless you are an intimate part of it all from birth, you can never truly know another country or her citizens.

All that travelers like me can do is simply share with others the most superficial of our impressions: whether a nation's citizens were friendly (Egypt and Aruba) or not (Martinique and U.S. Virgin Islands), if the cities and country sides were clean (Zurich and Yap) or garbage-strewn (Naples and Kathmandu), or if the scenery was phenomenal (England and Tibet) or tediously boring (Shanghai and Bora Bora.)

This inability to capture and put into words the spirit or character of a nation is nowhere more truer of any place that I've been to then that of the subcontinent nation of India. This behemoth of a country, with her over 1.2 billion people and twenty-two official languages, blatantly defies any description. And I'm not the only one who has had trouble. Some of the greatest western writers to have ever put pen to paper—Rudyard Kipling,

E. M. Forster, William Somerset Maugham—have also tried and, in my opinion, have failed. But I'm still going to try anyway!

> Initially you're overwhelmed [by India]. But gradually
> you realize it's like a wave. Resist, and you'll be knocked
> over. Dive into it and you'll swim out the other side.

-THE CHARACTER EVELYN, *THE BEST EXOTIC MARIGOLD HOTEL*

I truly *do* love India! I love the Indian people, I love her culture, I love her temples, her colonial architecture, and I especially love her Himalayan Mountains. But I'll warn readers that this vast and paradoxical country is not for the weak-of-heart! She is a land of humongous extremes: The physical beauty of the Indian people is extreme. The colors of their dress and their festivals are extreme; the smells and sensuous flavors of her foods are extreme; the Indian people's religious piety and the seemingly cruel way they treat their lower caste citizens are extreme; and the flagrant wealth of the upper classes and the abject, bone-crushing poverty of the urban poor are extreme in the extreme!

And so very often, like no place else on the planet, do these extremes coexist side by side with each other as they do in India. On the first morning of our journey to the mountains, while momentarily stuck in traffic on the outskirts of New Delhi, I saw up close along the highway a large group of beautiful, eight- to twelve-year-old girls (mostly) and boys—young children so strikingly beautiful they could have adorned the cover of a magazine—scavenging in one of the city's vast dumps. Being as our visit coincided with the tail-end of the monsoon season, these kids were now slogging along searching for anything they could find of value, up to their little knees along the muddy, indescribably filthy margins of that limitless sea of refuse. Our driver told us that the young children are relegated to searching the less lucrative margins of the mountains of debris by their older siblings or parents who themselves have to fight continuously for the choicer, higher and drier, more profitable pickings to be found on the upper reaches of the pile.

I witnessed another example of the side-by-side existence of two extremes at a the pilgrimage site in the Himalayan foothill town of Rishikesh.
The city is known as the Yoga Capital of the World. It was here in Rishikesh
that the Beatles spent time in 1968 studying Hindu philosophy and meditation at the ashram of the Maharishi Mahesh Yogi. Mr. Sharma told us
that the city takes its name from Hrishikesh, one of the thousand names
for Lord Vishnu; in ancient Sanskrit the word means "he who has con-
quered his senses."

Which turned out to be quite ironic, because if anyone from outside of
the Indian culture wanted to visit the "real" Rishikesh—and they wanted
to preserve their emotional sanity—they *really* needed to be able to control
their senses. For besides all of the usual sweet and sentimental travel book
scenes of her tranquil and pristine Ganges River (which has just broken
free of the Himalayas) flowing past the city's beautiful temples, all with the
stunning panorama of the towering mountains as a backdrop, there also
exists within her outer city limits unfathomable desperation and disease,
as well as outright cruelty. One of the guidebooks I'd read before the trip
said to bring along several rupee banknotes (worth about three cents each
at the time) to give as alms to the poor. But nothing else I could have done
in advance could have prepared me for the misery I was about to encounter.

It turned out that we were visiting Rishikesh during a festival of some
sort, and because the parking lots near the riverside temples and bathing
platforms (Ghats) were full to overflowing with pilgrims and tour buses,
our driver had to park us in a field about a quarter of a mile away. And, just
as we would have had to do at any famous place anywhere else in the world
on a festival day, we then had to walk through an ocean of humanity to get
back to the main event. In this case, the main attractions were the Ghats
located near the river. But the short walk through the crowd was different here in Rishikesh. The vision we beheld was something that probably
very few of the guilt-ridden business tycoons or the frustrated divorcees
who flock from all over the world to do their yoga in the upscale ashrams
across the river ever bothered to venture out into and see; for sure, it's not
anything the Beatles ever wrote a song about.

The sights and smell of death and dying, at least on the outer margins of the crowd, was unutterably horrendous. Lepers, their hands and legs and noses rotted off by the horrible bacillus, seemed to be everywhere. Closer to the river came the less abhorrent diseases such as cantaloupe-sized goiters, malformed, mutilated, or paralyzed limbs, and skin cancers of every description. As we got closer still, the wretchedness—for lack of a better term—became less heart wrenching, consisting now mostly of elderly blind men and women with their caretakers, emaciated people of every age, and a few just common bums. A few times our guide, either with a stern look or with a few gentle words, had to intervene to get one or several of them to give way to allow us to pass. As a general rule, the majority of the multitude was civil; but all were desperate: my fist-sized wad of five hundred one-Rupee notes were gone before I even got past the lepers!

Sadly, we never did get to the Ghats to see the pious bathers perform their ablutions in the sacred waters of Mother Ganges. It was simply too crowded. Although I was a bit disappointed, I found myself a little relieved to be heading back to the car. The misery was almost too much to endure! The sick and dying, knowing instinctively that we were tapped out financially, ignored us now as we passed. Being able to now concentrate on the sight and experience of it all, I manage to observe yet another example of those extremes in behavior that made my Indian experience so memorable.

Twice I saw what seemed to be devout upper-class (or at least healthy looking and well-dressed) women physically abuse several of the beggars. The first lady, as she made her way through the throng, had what I thought were two sons or servants accompanying her, and with canes these men were ruthlessly beating the sick people, shooing them away like dogs if they ventured anywhere near the woman. A second "pious" woman, festooned in a gorgeous lime green and orange sari and sporting several dozen golden bangles on her arms literally kicked at several of the more inattentive or bothersome beggars that blocked her path like as if they were a vermin of some sort.

I have striven not to laugh at human actions, not to weep
at them, nor to hate them, but to understand them.

-Baruch Spinoza

I found myself feeling actual anger and contempt toward these seemingly cruel people, but held my tongue. Later in the car, as we were
beginning the long climb up into the mountains, I mentioned what
I'd seen back at Rishikesh to our guide. He very patiently explained
to me a bit of the darker side of the Hindu caste system. Although it's
officially banned by the government and is supposed to no longer be
practiced, the religious and social divisions that historically have been
sanctioned by the Hindu faith are so deeply ingrained in his countrymen's DNA that no law or act of Parliament will ever erase the notion
completely from their behavior. With every ounce of their being the
higher castes believe that all of their fellow humans are in whatever
worldly condition they presently exist in as atonement of their "bad"
(or "good") behavior in their past lives.

I try my best to always leave my personal and cultural biases at the
doorway of a country's airport whenever I travel to a new destination.
I've learned that a people's socioeconomic system, religious traditions,
and all other forms of behavior associated with their view of the world
are often the result of many hundreds or thousands of years of trying
to survive at the game of life in the best way they know how; it's a matter of what works the best for them over time. And if you think about it,
those ladies mistreating the beggars is, in reality, no different from the
modern-day conscription of child-soldiers in the Congo, or the brutal
subjugation of women in all fundamentalist patriarchal societies, or—to
be fair—the treatment of slaves in our America's past. Again, I'm trying
my best not to judge this form of culturally dictated behavior, but there
is something about the remnants of the caste system that still rubs me
the wrong way.

We were now on our way to the city of Gangotri, 12,300 feet above sea level in the Himalayas, the seventh most sacred site in Hinduism, and, literally, the end of the road. From there, we would have to trek for another five days farther up the mountain to and from our ultimate goal: the source of the Ganges River. As a frontier town, Gangotri's very air seemed to be charged with the unquenchable sensation of great adventure and discovery. As a place of holy pilgrimage, she had as well the subdued and eternal presence of the divine. I remember thinking to myself that as I sat in that outdoor restaurant on the evening before our departure, breathing in that pure air under that big sky, and taking in the breathtaking majesty of the surrounding snow-covered peaks, that being in Gangotri was like being on the very threshold of heaven itself.

The only downside (and in retrospect, it was a small downside) was that like all pilgrim towns, the main streets were clogged with wall-to-wall hawkers of religious relics, fairly aggressive tourist shop owners, and coffee/tea houses. Conspicuously missing—much to my personal dismay— were the bars! Gangotri, it turns out, would be the first place I'd ever visited that was completely vegetarian (which I could live with) and alcohol free (which I didn't like, but had no choice than to live with!)

The three-day hike to the glacier at the base of Shivling Peak was a challenge. Even though on the map the walk technically amounted to only another three thousand feet of elevation, the countless small streams that emptied into the Ganges at the base of the valley we were trekking up required us to go up and down and up and down and up and down. More than once, in moments of breathless (literally) exhaustion, I'd almost consented to renting a horse (as a lot of the older Hindu pilgrims did) to carry my butt up the mountain. But I didn't.

However, as bad as I make it sound, it was a grand adventure to walk up that high mountain valley! Besides our mountaineer guide, we now had two personal porters to carry our backpacks, three other porters to carry the camping and food supplies, a cook, and a cook's assistant; all of these young men were from Nepal. To make sure we didn't fall prey to altitude sickness, Mr. Sharma made sure we took it all very slowly, which was good, because the walk up that rugged path was all so amazingly gorgeous. His forced rest stops gave us all a chance to really take in all of the grandness and magnificence that lie before us.

On the end of the second day of trekking we reached the riverside camp near the terminus of the Gangotri Glacier. The Ganges flowed past us now as nothing more than a gurgling mountain stream. Around us on three sides, rising into the infinite sky, were the 22,000-foot-high jagged snow-covered peaks of the Bhagirathi range. That night, in the early evening twilight, with their lofty heights still exposed to the setting sun, the mountains were bathed in all shades of dark to light purple at their bases and sides, to a fiery orange radiance blazing at their summits. Shivling peak, the largest of the group and considered by Hindus to be the earthly manifestation of the penis of the god Shiva, sat directly in front of us. Gomukh, the actual source of the Ganges, was still a quarter-of-a-mile hike away.

There is something about being in the mountains—any mountains—that magically amplifies the senses. There is a clarity and depth of vision, a sharpening and greater perceptiveness of all sounds and smells, and especially, at least for me, there is an amplification of the sense of taste. It's like having a sip from some mythical fountain of youth and being given back once again all of the acuity we all wasted away and took for granted as children and young adults. These rewards of restored sensual delights makes all the effort of chugging up those ruthlessly demanding slopes worth every strained muscle and breathless footstep.

We all feasted that evening on a meal of lentils and beans, white rice, and the most delicious French fried potatoes I've ever tasted. The mountain air was cool and clean, and at that high altitude, quite thin. But even though I had to breathe a bit harder and was excited about the adventures of the next day (and in spite of my not having my accustomed nightcap of a bottle or two of beer), I slept the sleep of a baby.

After a quick breakfast, we started back up the trail to our final destination, Gomukh, the "Mouth of the Cow," the source of the mighty Ganges River. The Gangotri Glacier, from under which the river begins its 1,500-mile flow to the Bay of Bengal, is one of the largest in the Himalaya range. The glacier itself is thought by many to originate up in the nearby Tibetan Plateau at the base of a mountain called Kailash.

The last several hundred feet of trail to Gomukh proved to be the most difficult and dangerous part of the trek. The path was strewn with boulders, some as large as a house, and rocky debris from the ever-present landslides. Mr. Sharma, with his mountain survival training, as well as our Nepalese porters, kept a very close eye on the situation. In no time, after having to hug the shore of the streambed in order to circle around a large chunk of mountain that looked as if just yesterday it had tumbled down from the surrounding peak, I finally got my first glimpse of our long-awaited destination.

I had trouble at first separating the Gangotri Glacier from the surrounding rock walls. After a millennium or more of scraping and gouging her way down from the distant origins way up in the mountains, she had consumed so much dirt and stone that it all looked like a giant dirty ice cube. But upon closer observation of her hundred-foot-high face, there were areas in which the deep, rich, iridescent blue of her frozen snow and ice matrix shone through like a giant turquoise gemstone. Just left of her center was a cave, and from this cave flowed the newborn Mother Ganges River.

It took several minutes for me to, first off, catch my breath. But once I did, the enormity of it all began to sink in. I was now standing at a place that was considered by Hindus everywhere to be their religion's most sacred site. And, as always is the case in these moments, when it all finally hits me, I found myself ecstatically overcome by the grandeur of it all! All I wanted to do was stop and take it in: the sanctity, the beauty, the transcendence, and the blessed peace of this holy ground.

Our tour's itinerary called for us to continue the trek up onto the floor of the glacier to a high alpine meadow some four miles away, and Mr. Singh wanted to get moving on so we could make it back to the nearby camp before dark. But I didn't care leave, not yet anyway. This is what I'd come to see, and I still needed to do what I'd been longing to do since my wife and I saw the *National Geographic* special on the snow leopards that inspired my trip: that is, I wanted to bathe in the waters. He and my wife decided to then press on. He left me in the care of one of the porters with very specific instructions to both of us to pay attention to rock slides.

I was now left alone to contemplate the wonder of it all and to ultimately become "one" with Mother Ganges. In a couple of minutes, I was standing as close as humanly possible to where the newly birthed Ganges flowed out from under the ice sheet. The Nepalese Sherpa, who was quite a pleasant and talkative fellow when his boss wasn't around to hound him, and who spoke perfect English, stood on the higher ground back up from the stream bank in order to better keep an eye out for any falling boulders. Also, at this time—and from seemingly out of nowhere—an ancient Hindu holy man appeared and quietly took up a sitting position on a large boulder next to where I, too, now sat. (Mr. Singh later told me the old sage had come to pray for me and to keep me safe from the avalanches.)

After several more moments—because everything takes longer to accomplish at high altitude—I removed my shoes and socks, rolled my pants up, and placed my feet into the milky gray-colored water. And Holy Cow! (no pun intended), was that water cold! Churning and roiling out from under that ice cap, its temperature had to be below freezing. I made the decision right then and there that for me to immerse my whole body into that frigid water would have probably caused my heart to stop. I settled instead on keeping my legs in the current until I could no longer stand it.

I also did something else. A thought occurred to me as I sat there on that boulder with my frozen feet, that unless someone else had crawled up there under that giant slab of ice for the sole purpose of going to the toilet, that I would be the first person at that moment in time to have imbibed her still pristine and sacred melt waters. And so I drank some water, several cups actually; it chilled my body to the core and gave me one of the worst brain freezes I've ever had, but I could now say that I would forever be "one" with Mother Ganges. Wow!

Unable to stand the freezing cold water any more, I stood up and moved to another rock up from the stream bed. The holy man, seeing me putting my shoes back on, climbed down from his rock and (very reverently) dabbed with his thumb a purple powdered dot onto both me and the Sherpa's foreheads, giving us both a blessing. I gave him a few rupees, and as mysteriously as he appeared, he was gone. Theresa, knowing from multiple past experiences that I tend to get myself into trouble when left alone for too long on these journeys, decided to cancel her push up to the glacier, and she and Mr. Singh joined me about a half hour later.

After filling a small quart-sized plastic jug with some of the Ganges water for a dear friend back in the US (and after one more cupful to drink for myself) we left that holy spot. With great sadness—and a vigilant eye for rock slides—we trekked our way back down to the base camp. After lunch, we started the long walk back to Gangotri. The Sherpas broke camp, and with almost extra-human ability, passed us an hour later. When we arrived at the midway point for our last evening of camping in the mountains, they were all set up for us. Later that night as we ate our lentils and beans and delicious French fried potatoes, Mr. Singh told us the following tale from the Hindu holy book, the Ramayana, of how—with a little bit of imagination—ancient Hindu myth and geological reality sort of came together back at Gomukh.

He told us that high up on the Tibetan Plateau, the mountain that the peoples of South Asia call Kailash is considered to be the traditional abode of Shiva, one of the major gods of the Hindu religion. He went on to say that in the days before time, there was a king who had 60,000 sons. (He must have been a really busy king!) These loud and boisterous sons made such an infernal noise all the time that they disturbed the intense meditations of a sage named Kapila. Angry beyond words at their unremitting antics, Kapila, with his powerful gaze, incinerated them all, forever abandoning their souls to the netherworld.

As the story goes, these poor men's only hope for salvation would be to have their ashes collected and then deposited into the Ganges. The trouble, however, was that at that moment in history, the river flowed only in heaven. In order for their souls to find peace, the river needed to be brought down to earth. The duty to rescue these men's souls fell to one of their sons, another king named Bhagiratha. This brave king traveled to Mount Kailash, and there he prostrated himself before Shiva, asking the god to allow the Ganges to fall to earth. After years of trials and rigorous penance Bhagiratha was ultimately granted his request.

One more problem still had to be overcome: if the Ganges were allowed to fall directly to earth, the mighty force of this deluge would devastate the planet and end up killing all of her inhabitants. To prevent this carnage from happening, Shiva then directed that the waters of the river be allowed to flow through his massive head of coiled hair. This in turn blunted the destructive force of the great river and allowed her to gently fall to terra firma.

Mr. Sharma ended the story by reminding us that the river's descent from heaven, falling first through the Shiva's dreadlocks, is a process that continues to this very day. "Think about it this way," he said. "The snow falls heavy high up in these mountains around the base of Mount Kailash. As the torrent of melt water zigs and zags and courses its way downward from that great mountainous height, the Gangotri Glacier could be thought of as the curled locks of Shiva's hair, holding back the great bulk of the waters and preventing the massive flow from inundating the people of the valley below.

> I am awfully greedy; I want everything from life. I want to
> be a woman [maybe not] and to be a man, to have many
> friends and to have loneliness, to work much and write good
> books, to travel and enjoy myself, to be selfish and to be un-
> selfish ... You see, it is difficult to get all which I want.
>
> —SIMONE DE BEAUVOIR

The next morning we awoke early and finished our walk back to Gangotri. As is always the case with me, it was with great sadness that I climbed into the car to begin our drive back to Delhi. I always hate good-byes and so I never looked back. Because there is so much I want to see and do and experience on this astounding planet, I didn't think it was likely I'd ever pass this way again. After many hours of navigating twisty-turning roads, elephant-sized potholes, endless switchbacks, and several near collisions by oncoming trucks, we stopped for the night at the riverside city of Haridwar. It was September 2, my fiftieth birthday.

The city of Haridwar is where the Ganges River breaks out of the Himalayan Mountains and begins her long, languid journey to the Indian Ocean. Mr. Sharma told us as we reached the hotel that the city is considered the fifth most sacred site in Hinduism (the first being the mouth of the cow where we had just been).

After settling in and eating our evening meal, I was surprised to find out that Mr. Sharma, the driver, and the rest of our team all got together and bought me a birthday cake. Apparently in India, next to the day of your birth, a person's fiftieth birthday is celebrated as one of life's major events. After sharing in this delightful little celebration, Mr. Sharma, himself a Brahman Hindu, insisted Theresa and I complete our celebration of this great milestone in my life alongside of Mother Ganges. I told him it would be my honor!

We then walked the couple of city blocks down to the ghats. Along the way we passed sidewalk dealers selling every strange and fantastical religious relic, statue, or souvenir you could imagine: paintings of thousand-breasted and thousand-armed goddesses, statues of elephant-headed gods, and endless portraits of Indian holy men and women. As we got nearer to the river, Mr. Sharma stopped at one of these markets and bought me a little shoe box-sized cardboard raft filled with bright orange and yellow marigolds and a single, pencil–sized candle sticking up through the center of it. He gave the little flower boat to me and said that I should release it into the flowing water as an offering. We arrived at the ghat just as the sun was going down over the nearby Himalayan peaks and we all sat down right next to the river on the ancient stone steps. Mr. Sharma suggested that we just sit quietly and watch the Ganges as she flowed gently past us. And so we did.

> God and Nature first made us what we are, and then out
> of our own created genius we make ourselves what we
> want to be. Follow always that great law. Let the sky and
> God be our limit and Eternity our measurement.
>
> −Marcus Garvey

It's at times like this that I wish I had the transcendental power of the poet to put it all into words. Because, there I was, like something out an exotic

Rudyard Kipling dream, among all of those thousands of devout worshipers: the heady aromatic smells of thousands of burning incense sticks and of the smoke arising from cooking fires and nearby smoldering funeral pyres, the chaotic colors of the dress of the pilgrims, the high-pitched, piercingly delirious sounds of the wind instruments and drums all blaring out and banging away in a frenzied disharmony, coalescing together in my mind as a blissful otherworldly vision, all taking place as peaceful, eternal, Mother Ganges flowed passed at my feet. I sometimes think that if God had chosen that moment to call me Home, I believed (at the time) that life could not have been better for me. I'd have left this world a happy and much fulfilled man.

Anyway, after several minutes of this state of near Nirvana, I became distracted by the sounds of the nearby worshipers around me all sort of oohing and aahing and giggling. I looked to my left and saw that both Theresa and Mr. Sharma were smiling as well. I then looked to my right and, although a bit startled at first, I saw that a young cow had quietly wandered herself up next to me and with great gusto, was now eating all of the marigolds from my flower boat.

Not knowing what else to do, I just calmly sat there and watched her as she contentedly consumed the entire bouquet. After a couple of minutes she finished her flowery snack and, seeing I had nothing else to offer her, casually ambled away. To my great surprise and delight, as soon as she was gone, everybody around me started patting me on the shoulders, shaking my hand, and hugging me. It turns out (so said Mr. Sharma afterward) that by choosing my basket—and by me not chasing her away—the little cow imparted upon me one of the highest forms of Indian blessings I could ever have hoped for. Wow!

When all had calmed down again, for just a few more minutes, we again returned to our silent contemplations. It all had been almost too much: Mother Ganges, her watery surface sparkling now under the brilliant bright spotlights like a sea of a million tiny stars into the infinite darkness beyond; that pretty little brown-eyed cow who ate my marigolds, a tangible earthly manifestation of the spirit of the great river flowing out from under the glacier way back up at Gomukh; ancient India—complicated, frantic, and overwhelmingly wondrous India; and finally, the whole world—this stunningly, stunningly beautiful world! Oh how I love her so very much, her warts and all!

My God . . . How I hated to let it all go!

When I looked back then at my now fifty-plus years on this planet, I knew with every ounce of my being that I was indeed a truly blessed man. And so in that moment of bliss by that holy river I once again thanked my own God for the chance He has given me to pass through this miraculous and astonishing gift called life. Yes, yes, yes, I know: There have been a thousand times I've had to share in the tears of this world—as we all have; but mostly it all has been good. Really good! And I wouldn't trade a second of it for anything.

And as we all got up to walk back to our hotel, I also changed my mind. Even though it will break one of my most important traveling rules, I've decided that if the Good Lord so chooses to grant me another fifty years, I think I'd like to return once again to this eternal place.

I can't wait!!!

Made in the USA
Middletown, DE
02 December 2015